# Big Boys' Rules

## The Secret Struggle against the IRA

# MARK URBAN

*faber and faber*

First published in 1992
by Faber and Faber Limited
3 Queen Square London WC1N 3AU
This paperback edition first published in 1993

Printed in England by
Mackays of Chatham plc, Chatham, Kent

A CIP record for this book
is available from the British Library

ISBN 978-0-571-16809-5
ISBN 0-571-16809-4

14 16 18 20 19 17 15

# BIG BOYS' RULES

Mark Urban was the Defence Correspondent of the *Independent* for more than three years, during which time he reported widely on the role of the Army in Northern Ireland. As Diplomatic Editor of the BBC's *Newsnight* since 1996, he has covered world crises from the Balkans to the Middle East.

*Big Boys' Rules* was followed by *UK Eyes Alpha: Inside British Intelligence*, which the *Sunday Times* found 'accurate, revelatory and fascinating'. *The Man Who Broke Napoleon's Codes* was described as 'a thrilling read' by the *Daily Telegraph*, and the bestselling *Rifles*, which was praised by the *Daily Express* as 'deeply researched, beautifully crafted and captivating'. Mark Urban's most recent book is *Generals*, described by General Lord Ramsbotham in the *Guardian* a 'a compelling read'. He lives in London with his wife and three children.

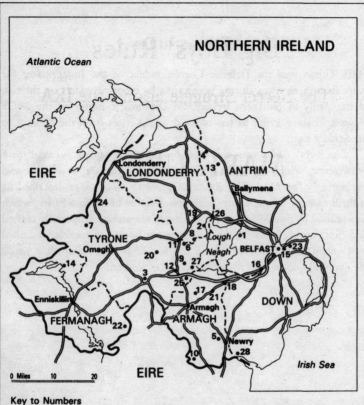

# NORTHERN IRELAND

*Atlantic Ocean*

EIRE

Londonderry
LONDONDERRY
ANTRIM
13
Ballymena
24
19 26
7
2
TYRONE
8 *Lough*
1
Omagh
20 11 6
Neagh
BELFAST 23
9 27
15
12
16
3
25
17 18
21
Enniskillin
DOWN
Armagh
FERMANAGH 22
ARMAGH
14
5
Newry
10
28

*Irish Sea*

0 Miles 10 20

EIRE

## Key to Numbers

| | | |
|---|---|---|
| 1 Aldergrove | 10 Crossmaglen | 19 Magherafelt |
| 2 Ardboe | 11 Cookstown | 20 Pomeroy |
| 3 Balleygawley | 12 Dungannon | 21 Portadown |
| 4 Ballymoney | 13 Dunloy | 22 Rosslea |
| 5 Bessbrook | 14 Kesh | 23 Stormont |
| 6 Cappegh | 15 Knock (RUC HQ) | 24 Strabane |
| 7 Castlederg | 16 Lisburn (HQ NI) | 25 Tammamore |
| 8 Coagh | 17 Loughgall | 26 Toomebridge |
| 9 Coalisland | 18 Lurgan | 27 Washing Bay |
| | | 28 Warrenpoint |

For
Dana, Leah and David

Contents

# Contents

PART FOUR: 1984-1987

# List of Illustrations

# Chronology

**1969**

August        British Army is sent to Northern Ireland by Harold Wilson's government after RUC lose control of nationalist rioting and loyalist backlash.

**1970**

October       Hunt Report criticizes RUC handling of previous year's riots.

**1971**

August        Disastrous policy of 'internment' of terrorist suspects starts.

**1972**

January       Thirteen civil rights demonstrators are shot dead by members of Parachute Regiment in 'Bloody Sunday'.

June          Partly to atone for internment, special category status is granted to paramilitary prisoners.

**1974**

14 April      First member of 14 Intelligence Company, Captain Anthony Pollen, is killed on active service.

**1975**

February      Labour Secretary of State Merlyn Rees engineers short-lived ceasefire with IRA.

August        Three members of Miami Showband are killed by UVF loyalist terrorists.

| | |
|---|---|
| **1976** | Under Chief Constable Kenneth Newman, and the new policy of 'Police Primacy', the RUC begins to take overall responsibility for security in Northern Ireland. |
| January | First SAS troop of twelve men is deployed in Ulster. |
| March | Special category status for paramilitary prisoners ends. |
| | IRA member Sean McKenna is arrested after alleged abduction by SAS from Republic of Ireland. |
| April | Peter Cleary is killed by SAS near Forkill. |
| May | First republican protest in the H-Blocks of the Maze prison begins. |
| | Eight armed SAS men are arrested by Gardai after 'accidentally' entering the Republic. |

| | |
|---|---|
| **1977** | Major General Dick Trant is appointed CLF. |
| May | Captain Robert Nairac is captured and killed by IRA. |
| July | IRA man Seamus Harvey is shot dead by SAS in Culderry. |
| December | INLA member Colm McNutt is killed by 14 Company lance-corporal in Londonderry. |
| | Corporal Paul Harman of 14 Company is killed by IRA in Belfast. |

| | |
|---|---|
| **1978** | |
| January | Bessbrook SAS Squadron's area of deployment is extended from south Armagh to the whole of Northern Ireland. |
| February | Two IRA men are ambushed by SAS near Ardboe; one, Paul Duffy, is shot dead. |
| April | Republican 'dirty protest' begins at the Maze prison. |
| 20 June | Three IRA men and one Protestant bystander are killed by SAS and RUC special forces in Ballysillan postal depot incident. |
| September | Protestant James Taylor is mistakenly shot by SAS soldiers. |
| 24 November | IRA member Patrick Duffy is shot dead by SAS at arms cache in Londonderry. |

| | |
|---|---|
| **1979** | |
| February | Major General James Glover is appointed as Commander Land Forces. |

| | |
|---|---|
| March | IRA starts terrorist campaign on the Continent with the killing of the British ambassador to the Netherlands. |
| 30 March | Airey Neave is killed in Westminster by an INLA car bomb. |
| 27 August | Eighteen soldiers are killed by IRA bombs at Warrenpoint. On the same day Lord Mountbatten and three others are blown up by a bomb on board their boat near Mullaghmore. |
| October | Maurice Oldfield, former chief of SIS (MI6), is appointed Security Co-ordinator in Northern Ireland. |

**1980**

| | |
|---|---|
| Summer | Maurice Oldfield is removed from post (dies in March 1981). |
| September | SAS apprehend two IRA members from Dungannon at an arms cache in Tyrone. |
| 27 October | H-Block republican prisoners begin their hunger strike (suspended on 18 December). |
| Autumn | James Glover is succeeded as CLF by Major General Charles Huxtable. |

**1981**

| | |
|---|---|
| January | Jim Lynagh's IRA gang murder Sir Norman Stronge and his son at Tynan Abbey. |
| 14 March | Seamus McElwaine and three other IRA members are captured by SAS near Rosslea. |
| 5 May | Bobby Sands, MP for Fermanagh and S. Tyrone, dies of starvation in the Maze. |
| 28 May | 14 Company officer shoots two armed IRA men dead and wounds another in Londonderry. |
| 3 October | Hunger strike is called off, after eight IRA and three INLA members have died. |
| November | Christopher Black, to become most celebrated of the 'supergrasses', is arrested. |

**1982**

| | |
|---|---|
| August | IRA member Raymond Gilmour turns supergrass, severely compromising IRA organization in Londonderry. |

| 27 October | Three IRA men are killed by police firearms squad near Lurgan, in the first of three incidents leading to the Stalker inquiry. |
| 24 November | Michael Tighe shot dead by police undercover unit near Lurgan. |
| 12 December | Unarmed INLA members Roddy Carroll and Seamus Robinson are shot dead by HMSU member Constable Robinson. |

## 1983

| February | One INLA member Liam McMonagle is shot dead, and another (Liam Duffy) wounded, by plain-clothes soldier in Londonderry. |
| August | Thirty-five of thirty-nine charged are found guilty on Black's evidence. |
| 25 September | H-Block prisoners stage an escape from the Maze; sixteen are recaptured, but twenty-two remain at large. |
| October | Republican 'informer' Robert Lean holds press conference causing severe embarrassment to RUC about their handling of supergrasses. |
| 4 December | SAS shoot dead two IRA members in ambush near Coalisland, the first such fatalities for five years. |

## 1984

| 14 March | Assassination attempt in Belfast by UFF gunmen seriously injures Sinn Fein leader Gerry Adams. |
| 24 May | John Stalker, Deputy Chief Constable of Manchester, is appointed to the 'shoot-to-kill' inquiry. |
| September | Douglas Hurd succeeds as Secretary of State for Northern Ireland. |
| 19 October | SAS ambush IRA team at Tamnamore as they prepare to kill a UDR officer: IRA gang escape, and bystander Frederick Jackson is accidentally killed by SAS. |
| 1 December | SAS soldiers are involved in gunbattle with IRA at Drumrush Lodge, near Kesh, resulting in the deaths of an SAS soldier and IRA man. |

| 6 December | Two IRA men are killed by SAS in ambush at Gransha hospital, Londonderry. |

**1985**

| 23 February | Three IRA members are shot dead by SAS soldiers at Strabane. |
| 28 February | IRA mortar attack on Newry police station kills nine RUC officers. |
| November | Anglo-Irish Agreement between Westminster and Dublin is signed. |
| December | IRA's Tyrone Brigade continues its campaign against isolated police stations at Ballygawley, Castlederg and Carrickmore. |

**1986**

| 18 February | Francis Bradley is shot dead by SAS while recovering weapon from arms cache in Toomebridge. |
| May | Stalker is removed from 'shoot-to-kill' inquiry, pending investigations into his contact with Manchester businessman Kevin Taylor. |
| 2 July | Three RUC officers are shot dead by Provisionals in central Newry. |

**1987**

| March | John Stalker resigns from the police force. Second IRA campaign on the Continent begins. |
| 8 May | Eight IRA members, including Jim Lynagh, are shot dead in SAS and RUC special forces ambush at Loughgall. |

**1988**

| February | Pat Finucane, a Belfast solicitor known for representing republicans, is murdered by loyalist terrorists. |
| March | Three IRA members, unarmed but on a bombing mission, are shot dead by SAS soldiers in Gibraltar. |
| June | Northern Ireland Police Authority narrowly rejects further investigation of the behaviour of RUC Chief Constable John Hermon and his deputies during the Stalker and Sampson inquiries. |

**1989**

21 May         Collette O'Neill, suspected IRA 'Loughgall informer', is picked up by police in car with two alleged IRA men.

# Preface

On the morning of Sunday 9 May 1987 I awoke to hear the news that British soldiers had killed eight members of the Irish Republican Army in the village of Loughgall in Armagh the day before. I assumed at first that the IRA men had simply been unlucky. I regretted their deaths but, like many other people who had become tired of the long saga of IRA killings, I assumed that the Army operation was necessary. It was only when I learnt more about the incident – in particular, that a motorist passing through Loughgall had also been shot dead by soldiers – that I became curious about this kind of action against the IRA. I realized that my own background and the contacts I had built up over many years could direct me towards avenues of investigation not open to other journalists. The story which I pieced together is one of a hidden contest between a covert élite within the security forces and the republican movement, its mortal enemy. Loughgall was the most spectacular manifestation of this contest.

For most of us the conflict in Northern Ireland is represented by a few strong visual images – running soldiers, marching bands, sectarian graffiti, hooded figures at gravesides – but these are the symbolic, outward signs of the conflict. The real struggle, which accounts for so much loss of life, takes place in an unseen arena. In recent years most of the IRA members who have been shot were not killed by uniformed soldiers or policemen, but either by one of the special units of the security forces which act on intelligence (most famously the SAS), or by the IRA itself, in an attempt to flush out informers from within its own ranks. Many of the arrests of active terrorists are also the result of undercover work.

This is the first published account of the Northern Ireland conflict in which SAS men, intelligence officers and senior decision-makers frankly describe their attitudes – to the risks of their work in Ulster; to the death of IRA members; to the use of deception to protect intelligence sources; and to the moral dilemmas surrounding the exploitation of that information.

The readiness of the security establishment to deceive journalists, and more importantly the courts, is one reason why I feel this story should be investigated. What justifies the deception of the institutions which these forces aim to defend? How far can the end be said to justify the means? Perhaps the attitude of soldiers and police officers does no more than reflect society generally, for many people seem to applaud the elimination of republican terrorists and are less than curious about the moral tightrope that must be walked to make such actions possible. Yet I came to believe that it is the very inability of security chiefs, politicians and the media to acknowledge and question the less savoury aspects of such operations that makes Ulster's undercover conflict a vital area for journalistic inquiry.

There is a view that such a book should not be written, for security reasons, until peace comes to Ireland. I reject this. The British government has been fighting the IRA for many years – between twenty-three and eighty, depending on your definition of events – and the end of the Troubles is nowhere in sight. Meanwhile, many Catholics' perception of the British state as unjust and murderous is an important factor in the IRA's continued support. If a democracy is to be able to check terrorism, the forces engaged in that struggle must parade their adherence to the law at all times. In the eyes of organizations such as Amnesty International and of the courts in other countries which have refused to extradite to the UK suspected Northern Ireland terrorists, the British authorities have clearly not succeeded in this aim. That failure results almost entirely from the desire to protect intelligence sources and to retain the ability to exploit information in covert operations. Yet such activities prevent the government from gaining greater support in the Catholic estates of Northern Ireland and tarnish Britain's reputation abroad. In this context, the potential trade-off between the long-term benefits of openness and the short-term, operational advantages of secrecy justifies investigations like mine and warrants wider public debate.

This book covers the period 1976–87, but I am not suggesting that covert operations were unknown before 1976 or that they have ceased since 1987. I chose this period because in 1976 whole units of SAS men were committed to Northern Ireland. The substantial transfer of resources to undercover operations which followed has received little attention until now (no doubt because undercover units are excluded from the published order of battle of the Army and RUC, and because in some cases their parent organizations do not admit to their existence).

There were also significant changes in the way security chiefs used the intelligence at their disposal during this period. In 1976 the RUC was being transformed into a more militarized force and was about to take over the direction of all security operations from the Army. During the transition individual personalities came to dominate strategy and tactics, and the use of intelligence and covert action was not subject to systematic control. However, by 1987 the role of particular units and organizations had become more clearly established, often as a result of incidents involving the deaths of terrorists or members of the security forces. Both in terms of shifts in overall security forces policy and changes in the structure and strategy of the undercover units themselves, the period from 1976 to 1987 was a critical phase in the development of covert operations.

Much of the information was obtained in some sixty interviews conducted specifically for this book. I guaranteed anonymity to all those I interviewed and therefore cannot thank them by name. About eight were ex-members of special forces (the SAS and Army surveillance unit 14 Intelligence Company); twelve had been in senior positions in the security forces and at Stormont; and a further ten or so had been involved in specialist intelligence work in Ulster. Where I attribute information to 'an intelligence officer' that is a person who has worked on the collection, collation, analysis or dissemination of intelligence. It could be a member of the Army, RUC Special Branch or the Security Service (MI5). I also conducted interviews with a wide range of people including solicitors, republican activists, constables and soldiers on the streets, and members of the public who had witnessed gunbattles.

Almost all of the interviewees who agreed to meet me unofficially were approached on an informal basis. Some people approached in this way did not agree to take part. As defence correspondent of the *Independent*, between 1986 and 1990, I was entitled to seek non-attributable briefings from the Ministry of Defence – official information given on the basis that it is not sourced to any individual or section within the Ministry of Defence. I did make two visits to the Army in Northern Ireland while in that post, and these provided important background knowledge, but I decided not to request such a briefing for this book. I have also received briefing and guidance from the Army and the RUC in my subsequent work for BBC TV's *Newsnight*. In some places I have made use of such information, although I have tried to make it clear in the text where information was gleaned during briefings arranged as part of those visits.

The decision not to seek the co-operation of the Ministry of Defence was a difficult one. In my dealings with members of the department, they have never volunteered a potentially damaging story, but they have very rarely avoided confirming something I have discovered. None the less, my research for this book has uncovered many instances of the Army and police deliberately giving the press false information about covert operations in Ulster. In 1990, Tom King, the Secretary of State for Defence, told the House of Commons that the authorities used disinformation to protect lives and for 'absolutely honorable security reasons'. In several of the incidents related in this book journalists have been used to relay these untruths. In view of this, I decided to seek the opinions of senior Army and police officers in private, without the presence of Whitehall or Stormont officials and their tape recorders. This did not provide absolute insurance against deception, but I am convinced that it did lead to greater candour and often resulted in interviewees giving accounts of incidents which differed significantly from the official version.

It may be that some of those interviewed were willing to talk to me because I had been a member of the regular Army for nine months in 1979. I served in the Royal Tank Regiment, but I did not do so in Northern Ireland, and this book is not based in any way on my own reflections and experiences while in uniform. It is a journalist's appraisal of the dilemmas facing both police officers and soldiers, and of the government policies they are expected to carry out.

I am aware, of course, that certain categories of information are useful to terrorists, and consequently I have not used the names of living people unless their views have already been published. This rule has been applied to protect the potential victims of loyalist as well as republican terrorism. I have not given the location of barracks housing Army and police special units, to avoid them being chosen as targets. And I have concentrated on tactics and technology used by undercover units already known to have been compromised.

Some members of undercover units whom I interviewed argued that an emphasis on incidents in which people had been killed would provide a false impression of their duties in Ulster. I have tried to give examples of operations where nobody was killed, but the fatal incidents are, by their very nature, the most documented and the most open to question.

I do not examine the shooting of three IRA members in Gibraltar in 1988 in any great detail, as I wanted to concentrate on events that have been less subject to media interest and scrutiny. It is in any case these events which provide the context crucial to an understanding of the soldiers' behaviour and of the authorities' attitude during the inquest procedures in Gibraltar.

Shortly before this book was published, I was contacted by the Secretary to the D Notice Committee, a semi-official body which liaises between journalists and government departments. His intervention followed expressions of concern from the Army and the Security Service about the possible contents of my book. I agreed to allow them sight of proof copies, which were by that stage circulating among certain journalists. The Secretary asked that changes be made to the book on fifteen separate topics. In only four cases was I satisfied that alterations were required. The Secretary presented new and compelling arguments that these points constituted a real threat to life. I was satisfied that removing them did not diminish in any way the investigation of key issues contained in the book.

Finally, I would like to thank the various people who helped me with the project, including Susanne McDadd, my editor at Faber and Faber; Walter Macauley and Kathleen Higgins, librarians of the *Belfast Telegraph* and *Irish News* respectively; Vincent Dowd and Beth Holgate for their helpful comments on the manuscript; and all those who agreed to be interviewed – without whom this book would not have been possible.

Mark Urban
April 1992

PART ONE: 1976–1979

# I

# First Blood

It was just after five on a dark February evening in 1978. Two young men, members of the Irish Republican Army, were speeding in a white Volkswagen along a road near Ardboe in the county of Tyrone. The area to the south west of Lough Neagh is a bastion of the republican community in Ulster. The men were on their way to recover several small home-made mortar bombs which had been hidden in a farmyard; one of them was about to be killed by the SAS.

The car pulled up, the men got out and walked into the farmyard. As twenty-year-old Paul Duffy picked up one of the mortar bombs he was hit by a burst of rifle fire, which killed him almost instantly. The other man turned and ran back towards the Volkswagen. As he started the car the windows were hit by bullets, and he was showered with glass. He got away, but later surrendered himself for medical attention. He had three bullets in him, but survived.

This type of incident was to be repeated many times by the SAS in Northern Ireland. Several suspected IRA men had been arrested in the area two days before the Duffy operation. An informer had told the security forces about the mortar bombs and their imminent collection. The soldiers had been in hiding for two days and nights, waiting for someone to appear.

Duffy was not the first IRA man to be killed by soldiers of the SAS, but the operation marked an important step in the struggle against republican terrorism. Until the beginning of 1978 the SAS had been under orders to remain in south Armagh, close to the border with the Irish Republic, the area the popular press calls 'bandit country'. Now they were to be employed throughout Northern Ireland – a development which followed a period of uncertainty about how the security forces should exploit their most sensitive intelligence and their most highly trained soldiers.

The British Army is normally unwilling to confirm or deny either the presence of SAS soldiers in an area or their participation in a particular incident. This policy stems from a desire to increase the mystique surrounding the Regiment, and from the need to protect its members and the sources of intelligence on which it acts. But on this occasion Army commanders were keen to spread the word that things had changed. The Army's Headquarters Northern Ireland (HQNI) press office at Lisburn confirmed 'that the patrol which killed a terrorist . . . and wounded another came from the Special Air Service'. Reporters were also told of the change in policy allowing the soldiers to operate outside south Armagh. The Army was sending a clear signal to the Provisionals.

It was in January 1976 that the first twelve members of the SAS, Britain's most highly trained military unit, arrived at Bessbrook in south Armagh. The strongly Protestant community in the village was living through a grim period of sectarian killings. Both Protestant and Catholic death squads had been stalking the countryside of south Armagh, and had killed twenty-four civilians in the six months before the SAS was committed to the region.

For the small community of Bessbrook those first weeks of 1976 were a time of crisis. Following a killing by Protestant terrorists of five local Catholics, a group calling itself the 'South Armagh Republican Action Force' had stopped a bus and gunned down eleven men who were on their way home from work. Only one survived. The bus driver, a Catholic, was released. Most of the dead were from Bessbrook. It was this incident – and the loyalist response to it – which prompted the then prime minister, Harold Wilson, to send the SAS to south Armagh to supplement the regular Army, which had been in Northern Ireland since 1969.

SAS squadrons had previously been deployed in Northern Ireland in 1969 and 1974, and several SAS men had served there in other units, but there has always been an air of secrecy surrounding the Regiment's role in the region, so it is worth examining the structure and practice of the unit to separate some of the myth from the reality. The 22nd Special Air Service Regiment, or 22 SAS as the special forces unit is correctly known, is based in Hereford. It only recruits from other Army units and usually takes officers for three-year tours. They tend to be in their mid to late twenties when they first attempt selection. Most are not graduates, although many have been to public schools. These young officers have a limited effect on the Regiment's ethos, since they are attached to it for a finite period, even if some do go on to a second or third three-year tour later in their career; for other ranks there is no fixed leaving date – 'Once you're in, you've cracked it,' as one SAS man describes it. The ordinary soldiers almost invariably epitomize the working-class culture of the sergeant's mess. Many become indispensable and long-serving regimental characters. The only officers who stay in the Regiment are normally raised from the ranks after a career as a non-commissioned officer (NCO).

The novice SAS soldier is given the rank of trooper – equivalent to private – regardless of his rank in his parent regiment. However, the soldiers do not suffer financially: they usually receive the pay of a rank above their pre-SAS status and a special forces bonus of several pounds a day. If they leave Hereford they are restored to their pre-SAS rank.

SAS soldiers tend to be more mature and fitter than their counterparts in the Army, but the idea that they are particularly intellectually gifted is, by and large, incorrect. One SAS officer says, 'The ordinary bloke is just thinking about his next team task. He's just wondering whether it'll be abroad and whether to buy a new hi-fi when he gets back.'

The most experienced soldiers are concentrated in the SAS Training Wing, which is responsible for the twice-yearly selection of new recruits. Some other NCOs can be found running training in the two Territorial Army SAS Regiments. Some of the older SAS soldiers have become psychological casualties, referred to Army hospitals after years on operations, or have been given a training posting as a reward for their service. Two of the SAS veterans who have recently published memoirs admit to having spent time under psychiatric observation. Not surprisingly, the Ministry of Defence is unwilling to discuss whether the number of SAS soldiers who succumb to mental disorders is higher than that in the Army as a whole.

Most of those who serve in 22 SAS retain the cap badge of their parent regiment, and may return to their old unit, even after years at Hereford. Any soldier can be 'returned to unit' (RTU'd) if he falls foul of the Hereford hierarchy. Attitudes to service in the SAS vary in different parts of the Army. In the Parachute Regiment, which supplies much of Hereford's raw material, failure to pass selection or being RTU'd can carry a considerable stigma. The natural desire to avoid being RTU'd prevents many soldiers from voicing misgivings about orders or challenging the Training Wing NCOs who have such a strong influence on the ethos of the Regiment. In other regiments, where members rarely become members of the SAS, a soldier who tries for selection will be respected whatever the outcome of his attempt.

Officers and soldiers usually spend about five months after selection undergoing SAS training, which ranges from practising ambushes to learning medical skills and the Regiment's special signals system. They serve in one of the four sabre squadrons – A, B, D and G (Guards) – usually for at least two years. Then they may move to the Training Wing, which undertakes many of the SAS's more sensitive tasks outside Britain, or to other specialized parts of the Regiment.

SAS selection requires enormous physical stamina. The four weeks of evaluation culminate in a 45-mile endurance march to be completed in twenty hours while carrying a 50lb bergen rucksack. To meet this challenge many candidates will train for up to a year in their spare time, pushing themselves for months over difficult terrain in all weathers and enduring pain from injuries.

Officers are selected largely by the Regiment's veteran NCOs, and many tend to feel they are still being judged after they have passed. As one says, 'In general they have contempt for what they call "Ruperts". They do not listen to reason. The only way to earn their respect is through physical achievement – which makes it rather difficult to discuss the finer arguments about our role.'

Many hours of an SAS soldier's training are spent on the range, acquiring a high degree of proficiency with different weapons. Specialized courses include sessions in the 'Killing House', where soldiers are confronted with various situations in which they must make split-second judgements about whether to fire, with live rounds, at targets. Training emphasizes the need to open fire, with the minimum of hesitation, if the target is recognized as hostile. In some exercises fellow soldiers stand among dummies, placing their lives quite literally in the hands of their comrades who burst into the room and have to disable the 'terrorists'.

SAS soldiers are scornful of civilians who believe that it is possible, western-style, to shoot a weapon out of a person's hand or to disable someone with shots to the legs. In the terror of close-range combat a soldier cannot waste time aiming at a fast-moving limb; he is trained to shoot at the trunk – putting as many bullets into a person as is necessary to ensure they will be unable to use their weapon.

The skills which the SAS was meant to bring to Ireland were those fostered by the Hereford regime. A soldier who has the self-discipline to push himself across the Brecon Beacons with a huge bergen on his back in sub-zero temperatures will have the stamina to lie in wait for days in a hole in the ground, defecating into a plastic bag and sleeping in soaking wet clothes while waiting for a terrorist to arrive.

But the new arena of Northern Ireland was to reveal some vital defects of the Hereford system. Judgements between friend and foe were rarely as simple as in the Killing House. In Northern Ireland soldiers faced the threat that the enemy might shoot them first. Classroom doctrines about controlled 'double taps' – bursts of two rounds – were often forgotten in the terrorist battleground when SAS soldiers would let fly dozens of bullets, sometimes at people who were no more than bystanders.

The introduction of the SAS in Ulster was a political act. The symbolic value of sending an élite squadron to Bessbrook, the village from which most of the eleven victims of the 1976 bus shooting came, was clear. Although a London newspaper derided the despatch of twelve soldiers in January 1976 as a 'token' presence, in fact they were merely an advance party: several weeks later the SAS sent its D Squadron, numbering seventy-five, to Bessbrook.

From the outset, the SAS's presence was publicized for political ends. Even though secrecy was vital to the type of operation the SAS wanted to conduct, various political figures and members of the security forces were keen to exploit the propaganda value of the Regiment. The republicans also understood, even before the SAS arrived, that fear of these anonymous British Army bogeymen, highly skilled in killing, could be exploited for their own purposes. The Regiment's acronym became associated with every mysterious happening. It acquired a mystique akin to that of the hated and feared Black and Tans, the local troops levied by British governments in Ireland in the 1900s who had a reputation for brutality. Thus the SAS were to become leading players in the propaganda contest to win the hearts and minds of the people of Ulster.

Merlyn Rees, the Northern Ireland Secretary at the time, later reflected that the commitment of the Regiment, which had gained a fearsome reputation in the counter-insurgency campaigns that accompanied the dissolution of the British Empire, had not been clearly thought out: 'It was more presentational and mystique-making than anything else.'

But by sending the SAS to south Armagh Harold Wilson also provided the Army with a valuable resource for covert warfare. Army chiefs wanted to use the SAS not to separate feuding communities but to prosecute their struggle against the highly effective armed republican movement. One IRA unit in south Armagh seemed able to kill soldiers with impunity – forty-nine had been shot or blown up there since the commitment of the Army to Northern Ireland in August 1969.

However, the arrival of the SAS further complicated the struggle between the police and the Army for control in Ulster – a struggle dominated by the personalities of the security chiefs. The SAS's mission in Northern

Ireland was to be governed by the interaction of key figures in these establishments and by their differing interpretations of how the troops under their command could use lethal force yet remain, or appear to remain, within the law. Confusion about the exact role of the SAS even extended to some Army officers. One, writing anonymously in *The Times*, stated that the SAS would be 'told to do what the Army has so far failed to do, *kill terrorists*'. However, he went on to explain that 'to anyone who knows [the SAS] well, the IRA claim that they have been used as undercover assassins in Northern Ireland is absurd'. Such a confident distinction between an assassin and a soldier carrying out an order to kill terrorists is less than clear, given that a simple order to eliminate terrorists whenever possible would be against the law in Britain.

There was even uncertainty as to who should command the troops. On paper the Army's chain of command was clear. Initially, the SAS Squadron was under the control of the head of the local regular Army unit, a lieutenant colonel commanding the battalion based in south Armagh on a four-month tour. But those in authority higher up the security forces hierarchy tried to exert their own influence. As the sensitivity of the Squadron's operations became apparent, the local battalion commander would increasingly refer them to his superior for approval – to the commander of 3 Brigade in Portadown, or even to the Commander Land Forces, the officer responsible for all Army operations in Ulster.

Although the Squadron was under the Army's jurisdiction, it soon became clear that the initiative for using it often came from the police, especially as the RUC's informer network provided the SAS with the best intelligence for its operations. A system of liaison officers was set up to make the Army the executive arm of police Special Branch intelligence, but the lack of clear lines of authority and continuing personality clashes hampered matters. Two years later, in 1978, special regional centres were created to control SAS activities; their evolution will be described in Chapter 10.

During the early months of the SAS presence in Northern Ireland, there was a scarcity of intelligence good enough to use for covert operations. The Bessbrook Squadron undertook duties much like those of the more conventional Army units posted to the area. SAS troops went out on patrols lasting several days, mounting observation posts, checking cars and moving across country with the intention of countering terrorists in action. But in time the Squadron came to specialize in surveillance and ambushes based on the highest quality intelligence available to the security forces.

A series of SAS operations in 1976 and 1977 led to the killing of two

IRA men, Peter Cleary and Seamus Harvey, and to the arrest of several more. Army chiefs regarded these operations as successes and officers were keen to point to the alarming rate of sectarian murders before 22 SAS's D Squadron arrived and the absence of such crimes in south Armagh during the remainder of 1976.

Although Army commanders were under strict orders not to cross the Irish border, some apparently chose to do so. In March 1976 Sean McKenna, identified by the Army as a key local IRA commander, was taken from his home in the Republic of Ireland and deposited in Northern Ireland, where an Army patrol promptly arrested him. The IRA said he had been abducted by the SAS, a charge denied at the time by Army headquarters at Lisburn. However, a British officer involved in undercover operations in south Armagh at the time confirms that McKenna was indeed 'lifted' by the SAS.

In April Peter Cleary was killed by soldiers in D Squadron. Army intelligence said he was an important Provisional who had been living in the Republic, crossing the border for operations as well as social engagements. On the night in question he had been visiting his fiancée near Forkill, 50 metres north of the border. A four-man SAS team had been observing the house for some days, in two observation posts. The four soldiers had had little sleep and were exposed to the elements. When Cleary arrived they arrested him and radioed for a helicopter to pick them up. According to the Army, three of the soldiers went to light a landing zone for the helicopter while one stood guard over the prisoner. It was then, the soldiers said, that Cleary tried to overpower his guard and was shot during the struggle.

The IRA alleged that the man had been murdered. As is normal after a shooting, an investigation was started and the SAS men subjected to prolonged questioning from the RUC. The Special Investigations Branch of the Royal Military Police, in effect the Army's in-house CID, also questioned the soldiers.

Another incident occurred one month later. At 10.50 p.m. on 5 May 1976 four SAS men in an unmarked car were apprehended by a member of the Gardai, the Republic of Ireland police force, at Cornamucklagh. The Army later claimed they were on a reconnaissance mission and had made a map-reading error. Two more cars were sent out when the soldiers were missed. They too followed the road down to the border and misread their position, only to be detained by the same zealous Garda. By the end of the night the Irish police had arrested eight SAS men and held three cars, four sub-machine guns, three pistols and a pump-action shotgun.

One year later the men were tried in Dublin on charges of possessing arms with intent to endanger life. They were acquitted because, the judge said, the prosecution had not proved that the soldiers had crossed the border intentionally. The same officer who maintains the SAS abducted Sean McKenna insists that the later border incident did indeed arise out of map-reading errors. But given that courts in the Republic are unlikely to have sympathy for the SAS, the significance of the acquittal lies in the fact that prosecutors failed to provide solid enough evidence to obtain convictions.

All the same, despite the pleas of innocence and the verdict of an Irish court, the incident provided the IRA with an opportunity to propagandize what they saw as incontrovertible proof of the Army's operations in the Republic. In the bars along the border speculation about the SAS's cross-border abduction and assassination activities could be fleshed out with details of the soldiers' parent unit, of unmarked cars and of sub-machine guns and pistols.

It is important to see the SAS men's error in the light of the other accidental border violations which were taking place at the time – because it is unmarked in many places, the frontier could easily fool soldiers. One incident, which could have been even more serious than that involving the SAS, is related by a member of the Parachute Regiment. A patrol commanded by a colourful NCO nicknamed 'Banzai' was landed in a field by an RAF helicopter. The pilot had made a map-reading error, putting the soldiers down too far south, well inside the Irish Republic. When Banzai and his patrol sighted Irish Army armoured cars and troops moving to the north of them, they concluded that they were witnessing an invasion of Northern Ireland. Alarmed, British Army officers were readying their own armoured cars to fight the Irish Army before it was realized that Banzai's patrol was inside the Republic.

There was further controversy in July 1976 when two men were arrested by British soldiers as they worked in a field inside the Republic. It was subsequently established that they were unconnected with terrorism and they were released. But, again, the incident was used by Sinn Fein to cast doubt on the legality of SAS operations and so rally support for republican terrorism.

In April 1977 the Bessbrook Squadron was involved in a second fatal shooting. Seamus Harvey, an IRA man, was killed as he approached a parked car in the village of Culderry. SAS soldiers had been lying in wait following a tip-off that the car was to be used by terrorists. It had already been used in an incident in which a soldier had been killed. Harvey, carrying a shot-gun, was killed in a gun battle after other IRA members, in concealed positions, apparently opened fire on the soldiers. The Army said that at least two other IRA members were just behind Harvey, claiming that one had been injured though neither was captured.

Events like these in south Armagh and over the border in the Republic represented the first signs that a new policy of stepping up undercover operations had been adopted by the security chiefs in Army and police headquarters (at Lisburn and Knock respectively). The commitment of a whole SAS squadron in early 1976 gave them an essential new tool in their covert war against the IRA which was then rapidly evolving into a more professional fighting organization than it had been in the early 1970s.

Two years after the deployment of D Squadron, this aggressive new strategy for combatting terrorism, which involved an extension of SAS activity outside its initial area of responsibility in south Armagh, bore its first fruit. The shooting of Paul Duffy in February 1978 in county Tyrone was just one incident in a pronounced shift in policy on the part of the police and Army. Beginning in 1977, intelligence resources in Northern Ireland were switched away from the publicly visible 'Green Army' to small, highly trained units of specialists, whose operations were cloaked in secrecy.

There had been many undercover operations before then, certainly, but the number and scale of them increased significantly. Whereas in 1975 the Army had fewer than 100 soldiers in Ulster whose main task was clandestine surveillance, by 1980 this number had trebled. Similarly, the Royal Ulster Constabulary (RUC), which began to assume overall responsibility for the campaign against terrorism in 1976, also developed a variety of specialist surveillance and firearms units of its own.

One important factor in the move towards a new consensus on security policy was the effect of new personalities in positions of political and military leadership. In 1976 Roy Mason took over as secretary of state for Northern Ireland: the one-time coalminer took a less cerebral approach than his predecessor Merlyn Rees. A key security adviser recalls that Mason seemed uninterested in political initiatives, believing simply that Ulster needed substantial economic help and that the pressure on the IRA should be stepped up. He had no hesitation about escalating operations against them, and said publicly that he intended to squeeze the IRA 'like a tube of toothpaste'.

Then, in 1977, two new senior military officers who shared Mason's convictions were appointed to Northern Ireland. Both Lieutenant General Timothy Creasey, the General Officer Commanding (GOC), and Major General Dick Trant, Commander Land Forces (CLF), believed that increasing undercover operations offered the chance to cut Army casualties. Further, they would – they believed – intimidate the IRA, increase the success rate of court prosecutions by obtaining more detailed intelligence about suspects, and restore the morale of the uniformed soldiers and police officers who were relatively vulnerable as targets for bombers and snipers. The two senior officers signalled their intention to intensify undercover operations in a series of press leaks during 1977.

Enthusiasm for the new strategy seemed a little more muted on the police side. Kenneth Newman, appointed Chief Constable of the RUC in 1976, had a critical attitude towards some SAS operations. Steeped in the principles of minimum force during his long and varied police career, Newman let it be known that, while he admired the professionalism of the SAS, he believed it was best reserved for operations that allowed ample preparation and rehearsal, preferably also in rural areas. Operations which involved the deployment of SAS soldiers, often at night, in strongly republican areas following vague tip-offs from informers, precluded the opportunity for either.

Nevertheless, Newman was prepared to agree to the new policy – despite his misgivings – because he understood the critical importance of improving surveillance and intelligence-gathering if his force was to combat the paramilitaries effectively. Besides, the overt presence of the Army on the streets and in the estates was a source of resentment among the nationalist community; the reduction in visible Army activity which covert operations would bring also served his purposes.

John (Jack) Hermon, Newman's senior deputy and later successor as chief constable, was also perturbed about extending SAS operations, according to a senior officer who worked with him at the time. Particularly in Hermon's case, however, these reservations may have had more to do with jealously preserving the principle of Police Primacy established in 1976 – which gave the RUC ultimate control of security forces activity in Northern Ireland – than with a squeamishness about undercover operations as such. Under Hermon's leadership the RUC was to develop an expanded array of specialist units with covert surveillance and firearms capabilities.

These, then, were the key figures around the table at weekly meetings of the Northern Ireland Security Policy Committee. Mason, Creasey, Trant, Newman and Hermon all favoured a more aggressive role for undercover forces in the administration of security policy in Ulster. But while there was a consensus about the benefits of countering the IRA in a more effective but less visible way, there were deep differences over other areas of policy. The most significant disagreements involved the questions of who should take overall control of the security effort, and how an integrated structure for the sharing of intelligence could be created. The failure of the security establishment to resolve these issues, stemming from distrust and rivalry between the Army and the RUC, was to plague the whole anti-terrorist campaign.

# The Security Establishment

By the late 1970s the social and political landscape of Northern Ireland had been transformed by a decade of sectarian violence. A large standing military and police establishment had developed, charged with keeping order in a region with a population of 1.5 million people.

The Army had been deployed in Ulster in August 1969 after the police, the Royal Ulster Constabulary, had proved unable to control local rioting. As a medium-size provincial police force the Royal Ulster Constabulary had lacked the means to deal with an increasingly violent nationalist insurrection and loyalist counter-violence. The RUC lost responsibility for maintaining public order to the Army; and the need to contain the unrest led politicians to violate many of the principles on which the rule of law is based in Britain.

In August 1971, the policy of internment without trial was implemented, which led to large-scale round-ups of people suspected of terrorist connections. Internment proved highly controversial because the intelligence on which it was based was so poor – a great many people with no connection with terrorism were held, whereas many senior members of the IRA escaped – and because it constituted an admission that the security forces were short of any evidence which could be presented in court against the suspects. Holding people in this manner further alienated the nationalist community. The introduction of Special Category status in June 1972 for convicted terrorists was meant to soothe local feelings by allowing paramilitary groups extra privileges in jail. In fact, by allowing the terrorists to claim they were prisoners of war, Special Category status marked yet another violation of normal law in the rest of Britain.

Northern Ireland's devolved Parliament at Stormont, which had considerable autonomy before the Troubles, was dissolved early in 1972 to be replaced by direct rule from London with all executive powers invested in the newly appointed Secretary of State for Northern Ireland. The politicians believed the embattled people in Ulster would consider this system fairer.

The RUC had emerged deeply shaken from the early years of the Troubles. The Hunt Report, an official government inquiry, published in October 1970, had blamed the force for mishandling the republican disturbances in August 1969 in Londonderry (Derry to nationalists). Decision-makers in Whitehall believed nationalist passions would be soothed if the RUC was reduced virtually to a force of unarmed warrant-servers.

Army numbers peaked at around 22,000 in 1972, at the height of the Troubles, when soldiers went into the republican heartlands of London-derry and Belfast to break up the paramilitaries' 'No Go Areas'. The virtual collapse of the police and the desire of Army commanders not to inflame matters had allowed sectarian extremists on both sides to claim control of large areas of Belfast and Londonderry. But 1972 also saw a growing awareness in Whitehall that the Army's role would have to be reduced in the long term. The shooting by soldiers from the Parachute Regiment of thirteen demonstrators in Londonderry on 'Bloody Sunday' in January of that year led to an inquiry into the Army's behaviour. Army casualties peaked during that year too, causing some senior officers to agree with politicians who were looking for ways to reduce the military commitment to Ulster.

By 1977 the Army had fourteen battalions, units of about 650 soldiers each, and various supporting elements in Northern Ireland. They were deployed in fixed areas, known to the troops as their 'patch' and in Army jargon as Tactical Areas of Responsibility or TAORs. In some areas locally raised troops of the Ulster Defence Regiment (UDR), a reserve unit formed in 1970 and manned largely by part-timers, had taken over responsibility for order from the RUC's B Special reserve. The idea was that, as part of an Army controlled by disinterested British generals, the UDR would be perceived as fairer than the B Specials who were regarded by many Cath-olics as the strongest bastion of hardline loyalism. The RUC, successor to the Royal Irish Constabulary – the police force of Ireland prior to partition – was left without the B Specials and with most of its officers disarmed. The force endured several demoralising years when it could carry out few tasks independently of the Army.

Despite these intentions, the UDR too soon became deeply unpopular among Catholics. In the early days of the Troubles many politicians had great hopes for the UDR. It had been set up with a reasonably large

Catholic contingent: one in five of the people in its ranks. Most had left by the late 1970s. Many regular Army commanders had little respect for the military capabilities of the UDR, believing it was dangerous to let part-timers into hard republican areas. In 1978 the force was reorganized in an attempt to make it more professional. Several companies were disbanded so that their members could be concentrated more effectively in certain areas. Measures were also taken to boost the number of full-time UDR soldiers. It was apparent that the strains of holding down a job and carrying out dangerous patrols in their spare time were too much for many people. There were only 844 full-timers in 1972 but more than 2500 by the mid 1980s. Some distrust remained between the regular Army and the UDR, however, because of connections between some of the local soldiers and loyalist paramilitary groups.

From 1969 Ulster was divided by Army commanders into battalion patches, the more dangerous of which were occupied by regulars and the remainder by UDR units. Regular and UDR battalions were divided between three brigade headquarters: 39 Brigade in the Belfast area, 8 Brigade in Londonderry and 3 Brigade in Portadown covering the border. The brigade commanders stood between the units conducting operations at a local level and the two senior commanders – both generals – with wider responsibilities.

Each of the brigade commanders reports to the Commander Land Forces (CLF) at Lisburn, who is a major general and the top Army commander in Ulster. Above him is the General Officer Commanding (GOC), who, although an Army officer, is also in charge of the Royal Air Force and Royal Navy detachments in Ulster and for high-level co-ordination with the police and ministers. The barracks at Lisburn, a largely Protestant town near Belfast, extend over a large area and include Victorian buildings occupied by the headquarters of 39 Brigade and a new set of buildings – featureless 1960s municipal architecture at the base of a concrete communications tower, which is home to Headquarters Northern Ireland (HQNI).

The Army complex is named Thiepval barracks, after a First World War battlefield. Thiepval has a deeper meaning to many in Ulster not immediately obvious to an outsider. It was the area where the 36th Ulster Division was decimated by German artillery and machine guns. It is remembered as a place where a blood sacrifice was made by those loyal to the British crown, after republicans took advantage of the war to plot their Easter Rising in Ireland against Westminster's rule. The loyalist members of the 36th Division are reported to have shouted 'Fuck the Pope' as they went over the top of their trenches.

The Northern Ireland Office (NIO) was Whitehall's instrument for the direct rule of Ulster. From early 1974 it studied various ways of restoring the status and credibility of the RUC. In 1975 a committee of senior Army, RUC and intelligence officers chaired by John Bourn, an NIO civil servant, produced a document called 'The Way Ahead'. It was to become the most important security initiative of the late 1970s, leading to a policy known as Police Primacy. Under this plan, the role of the regular Army was to be reduced and overall direction of the security effort given to the RUC in 1976, thus requiring an expansion of locally recruited forces.

Most Army officers believed the RUC was more professional than the UDR, although in 1976 many still considered the police incapable of taking charge of security on the ground, as opposed to in the committee rooms. The RUC had grown in numbers from 3500 in 1970 to 6500 in the mid 1970s.

Like the Army, its forces were organized on a hierarchical system. Police stations were grouped into sixteen 'divisions' corresponding roughly to Army battalions. Several divisions were grouped into each of three 'regions' – Belfast, South and North – each with an assistant chief constable in charge who had the same degree of authority as the Army's three brigadiers. The three assistant chief constables reported to the chief constable at RUC Headquarters at Knock in east Belfast.

Army and RUC activities had been integrated from the top down. The chief constable and GOC saw one another at least once a week at meetings of the Security Policy Committee. The deputy chief constable and CLF usually had daily discussions to co-ordinate operations. Lower down there would be similar conferences, for example between a police division commander and his local Army battalion commanding officer. But there were often problems at the local level. Members of the police considered Army commanders to have too short-term a view; while RUC officers frequently refused to accompany the Army on missions, either because they thought it too risky or felt they would antagonize local people.

The police faced the unenviable task of having to carry out ordinary duties such as regulating traffic, investigating petty crime or serving court summonses while under lethal threat from the IRA. Despite the plan for Police Primacy, the reality in the mid 1970s, a senior RUC officer concedes, was that 'In the more difficult places you found the police staying in their stations and going out occasionally to accompany the Army.'

In the early days of the Troubles the police force had aroused the hatred of the nationalist community by driving into their neighbourhoods firing machine guns and appearing to represent the repressive arm of the Protestant establishment. Following the riots of 1969 and the Hunt Report the following year the RUC's chief constable had declared that the force would be restructured along what he had called non-aggressive, non-retaliatory lines. As a result, in republican areas the RUC had effectively ceded responsibility for policing to the Army. In these areas soldiers had been left to face riots and exercise law and order. Police Primacy required the restoration of the RUC's anti-riot units and the emergence of a police force with the protection and arms needed to go out on the streets.

Kenneth Newman, a diminutive Englishman who had started his career in the Palestine police, was given the job of implementing Police Primacy in 1976. Most constables' work kept them in their stations. Yet in order to make the new policy effective the Chief Constable required squads trained in the use of firearms and riot control which needed to be mobile in order to respond effectively to trouble. In some senses Newman needed to militarize the police. The Special Patrol Group (SPG) was the nearest he had to such a thing in 1976. The SPG was founded in the early 1970s replacing the Reserve Force, a skeleton unit of fulltimers, fleshed out by reservists during crises, as the RUC's mobile anti-terrorist squad. There were SPG squads in Belfast, Londonderry, Armagh, Omagh and Magherafelt. With the advent of Police Primacy came an expansion from about 100 full-time police officers assigned to such duties to about three times this number. Under Newman they were given riot control training and improved firearms. Police appeared on the streets with flak jackets and Ruger rifles. The Chief Constable also started a public relations campaign designed to create a more favourable image of the police, particularly among young people.

Although they expressed admiration for one another in public, it was inevitable that soldiers and police officers would feel a degree of mutual disdain. It was important for the self-esteem of many Army officers to feel that the RUC was in some sense tainted by sectarianism, because this view helped to justify their own presence. One officer says, 'I don't know what the RUC would do if the Troubles ended. It is so important to the Protestants' view of themselves as a community under siege. They are rather like the Boers in South Africa.'

And many police officers regarded the Army as outsiders, often on short tours of duty, who alienated the population with needless shows of force. As one RUC chief inspector puts it, 'We will never make permanent progress until we have no military support. It is far better for the IRA for the British war machine to be seen bearing down on them.' The adoption of Police Primacy as official policy would do little to resolve this rivalry.

The primary effort of the security forces, both police and Army, was directed against the republican groups, the Provisional IRA and the smaller Irish National Liberation Army (INLA), although during sectarian fighting in the mid 1970s loyalist terrorist groups had killed more people. But the loyalists did not attack the security forces and the number of incidents attributed to them declined in the late 1970s. Many Army officers see combating the better-organized republican terrorist groups as the real challenge. As one officer puts it, 'Among some people there is a kind of admiration of the IRA, of its professionalism. Nobody has any respect for the loyalists.'

By 1977 the level of republican and loyalist terrorist incidents had reduced considerably. In 1972 there had been more than 10,000 shootings – the only year of the Troubles in which more than 100 soldiers had died; in 1977 there was one-tenth the number of shootings. The terrorists realized that allowing their members to roam the streets with arms was a sure route to large numbers of casualties and arrests. Instead, they put more preparation into their attacks and refined their methods. Soldiers posted to Ireland from the mid 1970s no longer expected on their patrols to walk into what one referred to as the 'Wild West-style gun battles' which erupted during the early days; now they were faced with sophisticated terrorist operations. Better intelligence was needed to combat this threat.

From 1977 to 1979 rivalry between the police and the Army was to become acute. It was often focused on intelligence matters, the lifeblood of the anti-terrorist effort. The Army's manual *Land Operations Volume III – Counter-Revolutionary Operations* (Northern Ireland is defined as a counter-revolutionary conflict) was issued in August 1977 and became the bible for Army operations in Ulster. It states that intelligence is the 'key to success'. Events had already demonstrated this to the security hierarchy.

The internment policy had proved counter-productive largely because the intelligence had been so poor. The IRA, too, had learned from its early mistakes and was more careful about how and when it engaged the security forces and about leaving evidence which could convict a member. The need for a competent, centrally directed intelligence apparatus to replace the existing web of feuding agencies was clear.

Before the reorganization, anti-terrorist intelligence activities were handled by departments in both the Army and the RUC. There were, moreover, two departments within the RUC: C Department, the Criminal Investigations Department (CID), was in charge of interrogating suspects and gathering evidence following incidents; E Department, the Special Branch (SB), ran the informer networks vital to successful anti-terrorist measures. SB had been relieved of the task of interrogation after the end of internment. Putting the CID in charge of interrogation, or as the Army liked to call it, 'screening', was partly a gesture. It matched the official policy of treating terrorism as crime rather than subversive activity following the ending in March 1976 of political status for all paramilitary prisoners. However, the CID's assumption of responsibility for interrogation also followed a series of damaging public allegations and government inquiries into inhumane treatment of suspects by the SB.

It was crucial for the success of anti-terrorist operations for these two departments to work together. A CID interrogator, for example, might believe a suspected member of the IRA was ready to work as an informer for the SB. In practice there were frequent problems with the relationship. A senior RUC officer recalls, 'There had been a slavish adherence to the need-to-know principle. The Special Branch was passing minimal information to the CID.'

Following an internal reorganization by Kenneth Newman, the two police departments presented a united front, though their relationship with Army intelligence remained poor. The Army ran its own informers or 'touts' in Ulster's slang. Ordinary officers who had no experience of Northern Ireland could find themselves running an agent while on a four-month tour. The life of that agent sometimes depended on the competence of those ordinary officers.

In addition to the intelligence activities of ordinary units, the Army had some specialist units. Lisburn was also headquarters for 12 Intelligence and Security Company, a part of the Intelligence Corps formed in Ulster in 1972, which grew to number more than 200. The Company was divided into sections servicing Lisburn and the brigade headquarters. Although initially it engaged in some agent-running, its members were involved largely in paper-pushing: preparing reports for senior officers and keeping card indexes of suspects.

From 1972 the Army also had the Special Military Intelligence Unit

(Northern Ireland) – (SMIU NI) – an organization of about fifty officers and NCOs who were meant to act as go-betweens for Army chiefs and the RUC Special Branch at various levels of command. They were involved in most of the exchanges of sensitive intelligence between the Army and the RUC and were to be particularly affected by the growing competition between the two organizations.

Among the officers to have served at SMIU in the mid 1970s was Captain Fred Holroyd, an officer in the Royal Corps of Transport who sought an attachment to Army Intelligence in Northern Ireland. In a series of press interviews and in his book, *War Without Honour*, he was subsequently to detail the rivalry between various intelligence organizations and the incompetence of some of his fellow operators. Others who served in similar posts confirm Captain Holroyd's allegations about battles between the different intelligence-gathering organizations. Investigations by Duncan Campbell, a journalist working for the *New Statesman* magazine and the *Irish Independent* newspaper, corroborated other aspects of Holroyd's story. However, controversy surrounds some of Holroyd's more serious allegations, which will be examined in chapter five.

In addition to Army and police information-gathering organizations, the Secret Intelligence Service (SIS or MI6) and Security Service (MI5) were also active. Both organizations attempted to recruit agents and were more concerned with the political dimension of the unrest than were the Army or police. Although SIS had played a prominent role during the early days of the Troubles, its influence had been shaken by allegations in 1972 that it had encouraged two agents, Kenneth and Keith Littlejohn, to rob banks in the Republic of Ireland. The Irish Government asked for the two men to be extradited from Britain following the discovery of their fingerprints after a bank robbery in Dublin in 1972. Kenneth Littlejohn, a former member of the Parachute Regiment who had turned to robbery, subsequently alleged that SIS had intended to use his gang to discredit the IRA through robberies and to assassinate its members. Maurice Oldfield, at that time the second highest ranking officer in MI6, is reported to have called staff to a meeting at the organization's headquarters in London to deny the allegations. Although the Service may have dismissed some of the Littlejohn allegations, it was clear that the brothers had been agents of the British government – the Attorney General having insisted that the hearing on their extradition to Ireland be held in secret for reasons of national security. The Littlejohns were subsequently sent to the Republic where they received heavy sentences for the Dublin bank robbery.

At the same time as the Littlejohns' extradition was happening, John Wyman, a man believed to have been an SIS officer, was arrested in Dublin. He was detained, along with a sergeant in the Gardai Special Branch who had provided him with sensitive intelligence documents. Wyman was released early in 1973 after serving a three-month sentence on remand. The Littlejohn and Wyman cases were said to have convinced Oldfield, who became chief of SIS in 1973, that his organization should not sully its hands with the business of fighting the IRA in the United Kingdom, and to have prompted him to begin scaling down its activities.

The succession of MI5 from MI6 as the leading agency in the anti-republican secret intelligence effort was accompanied by much rivalry and ill-feeling. Both organizations maintained liaison offices at Lisburn and Knock. By the late 1970s SIS had lost most of its agent network in Ireland and, although SIS maintained its liaison office at Stormont and its station in the British embassy in Dublin, MI5 had assumed a greater role.

The Army was well aware of the principles which should have governed the running of the intelligence establishment. Its manual, *Counter-Revolutionary Operations*, states: 'Intelligence and security must be centrally controlled to ensure the efficient and economic exploitation of resources. Thus there should be a single, integrated intelligence organization under either a director of intelligence or the senior intelligence officer in the area of operations.'

But in practice, the generals were violating such principles by building up the Army's own rival intelligence operation. In his memoirs (published in 1989), Lord Carver, Chief of the General Staff in the mid 1970s, stressed that the RUC's Special Branch had lost the will to carry out rigorous interrogation, and highlighted the problem of gaining convictions. He wrote:

> The Army's frustration in both these fields led to gradual and increasing pressure that it should rely less on Special Branch and do more to obtain its own intelligence, a tendency which I was initially reluctant to accept, all experience in colonial fields having been against this and in favour of total integration of police and military intelligence. However, the inefficiency of the RUC Special Branch, its reluctance to burn its fingers again, and the suspicion, more than once proved, that some of its members had close links with Protestant extremists, led me finally to the conclusion that there was no alternative.

As a result of this decision, the Army set up a new élite surveillance unit, which would become known as 14 Intelligence Company, and increased the resources committed to intelligence-gathering. But the new policy exacerbated rivalries with the RUC. Although many constables and soldiers on the ground continued to co-operate, by 1977 the situation in the corridors of Lisburn and Knock had grown more difficult.

A senior officer who was party to the rivalries remembers that the most difficult area was the sharing of informer intelligence: 'There was an element of "if you tell them everything we haven't got a position have we?" In the intelligence business knowledge is power.' Another officer who served at Lisburn says, 'Fighting the Provisional IRA was about number nine on my list of problems every morning.'

The consequences of compulsive secrecy and non-co-operation could be seen at all levels of the security effort. Peter Morton, the Commanding Officer of the 3rd Battalion of the Parachute Regiment, recalled in his later book, *Emergency Tour*, a typical incident during a tour of south Armagh in 1976 when soldiers received information from a member of the public:

> I should have known better, but I agreed to let them search seven occupied houses which they did at 06.35. In terms of organization it was a miracle. But the result was to find two shotguns and to incur the wrath of HSB [the local Head of Special Branch], because we had not cleared the searches with him. One will never know, but in all probability at least one of the houses searched belonged to one of his contacts.

Accidental arrests of informers, the failure to inform other security organizations of movements of key IRA figures, and the compromising of one another's sources became routine. A senior officer who served at HQNI concedes, 'I have no doubt that the Special Branch regarded the Army, and its attempts to gather information, as cowboy.'

A member of a Whitehall team subsequently sent to Ulster to conduct a review of intelligence-gathering activities is blunt about the situation in the late 1970s: 'I was surprised and shocked at what we found. We came across some phenomenal cock-ups. Many of the problems surrounded the use of highly sensitive human source material. There was over-confidentiality and secretiveness in the management of the work.' People died as a result of these errors, he says, but declines to give specific examples. However, he does reveal, 'Information had been available, there had been foreknowledge of bombs, for example, which people had never been told about.'

In the mid 1970s an intelligence official had been sent to Stormont to act as Director and Co-ordinator of Intelligence (DCI). But the holder of the post could not compel recalcitrant Special Branch or Army intelligence operators to work more closely. Caught between feuding organizations the DCI was effectively impotent. An intelligence officer recalls, 'The situation deteriorated and it became obvious that the DCI couldn't perform the tasks which were set him.'

The mismanagement of intelligence and improved expertise of the IRA combined to blunt the activities of the security forces. The seizure of weapons caches are a good indicator of the quality of intelligence management since they most often result from tip-offs. Statistics show how things were going wrong for the security forces. In 1974, 465 rifles were found; in 1976, 275 and in 1978, 188. The amount of explosives seized dropped from 53,214lb in 1974 to 7966lb in 1978. It was not that there were fewer informers, but rather that the information being given by them was not being shared properly and the IRA was becoming more expert at hiding its munitions.

At the Ministry of Defence in London events were being viewed with increasing alarm by Brigadier James Glover, a wiry, ambitious infantry officer who headed the intelligence section of the General Staff. Some time after taking up the post in 1977, Glover prepared a highly classified paper, *Future Organisation of Military Intelligence in Northern Ireland*, setting out the way ahead. It stressed the need for more effective central control of intelligence, with the DCI wielding greater authority, and for setting up an effective system for sharing intelligence lower down the chain of command. His suggestions, combined with changes which were taking place in the RUC under Kenneth Newman, were to do much to reduce friction and improve the effectiveness of intelligence-gathering and dissemination.

Brigadier Glover had grasped the crucial fact that the IRA itself had developed into a highly sophisticated organization and had adopted a new strategy. It was clear, too, that the old anti-terrorist tactics would have to change. Senior officers in the Army, RUC and MI5 would come to the conclusion that improved co-operation among the information-gatherers and stepped-up covert operations were vital in order to counter the evolving IRA.

# 3

# PIRA

The late 1970s were not only a time of flux for the security forces. Their opponents in the Provisional Irish Republican Army – or PIRA, to use its British Army acronym – were also experiencing profound changes.

The organization was trying to regain the initiative after the collapse of the 1975 ceasefire engineered by Merlyn Rees. This began in February but broke down later in the year, as a result of the IRA leadership's feeling that the government was not serious about concessions, and its increasing difficulty in containing the frustrations of its members in the face of a large-scale campaign of killing by loyalist terrorists. Many British and loyalist politicians had questioned the wisdom of a ceasefire, fearing it would confer legitimacy on the republicans. In fact it had caused profound problems for the IRA. The Provisionals had found themselves unable to attack the Army and police. Instead they carried out attacks on Protestants, often in retaliation for killings by loyalist paramilitaries in the bloody spasm of sectarian violence which occurred during the ceasefire.

Many of the IRA's members drifted away during the ceasefire. Martin McGuinness, the IRA leader from Londonderry, alluded to the negative effects of the ceasefire when he commented, 'Good operations are the best recruiting sergeant.' The strains which arose from the deal also caused a shift in power, from the South to the North, from older to younger men. The Army Council, the IRA's ruling body normally composed of seven senior figures, had hitherto been dominated by southerners, older men who were veterans of skirmishes against the British in the 1950s. But the people now in the forefront of the movement, in the North, became disillusioned with the southern leadership during the ceasefire and in November 1976 held the first meeting of the newly formed Northern Command. This body, while still stressing its loyalty to the IRA Army Council and 'GHQ' in the South was to be a vehicle for the ambitions of emerging northerners like McGuinness and Gerry Adams.

Adams, a native of west Belfast whose father had been imprisoned for his republican activities in the 1940s, was released from the Maze prison in 1976 after serving three years for an attempted escape from internment. Although even Adams' adversaries now respect him as an astute politician, he spent many years at the sharp end of the 'armed struggle'. According to the Special Branch, Adams had been commander of the Ballymurphy unit of the Provisionals before he was interned in 1971. He was released the following year, taking part in secret talks in London with the British government, and becoming commander of the Belfast Brigade. During his second period of incarceration, Adams and Ivor Bell, another leading Belfast Provo, are believed to have drawn up the plans for a fundamental transformation of the IRA.

The changes in the IRA were a culmination of a process which had begun in December 1969, when the IRA had split into the Provisional and Official factions. The leaders of the Provisional wing left because they believed the IRA should maintain a policy of abstentionism – of remaining outside the political process and boycotting elections.

The Officials stopped being a worry to the security forces in 1972 when they began an indefinite ceasefire. However, the committed left of the republican movement produced another breakaway faction three years later when Seamus Costello founded the Irish Republican Socialist Party. The Trotskyite IRSP had a military wing, the Irish National Liberation Army, which was to gain a reputation for ruthlessness though failing to match the IRA in competence or even rudimentary standards of discipline.

PIRA was interested less in the Marxist, utopian ideology of the Officials and IRSP, which envisaged the proletariat replacing British rule with a workers' state, and more in the simple but potent egalitarian tradition of Irish nationalism which burned in the Catholic estates. The triumph of the northerners was marked in 1977 by the appointment of McGuinness as Chief of Staff of the Army Council, and therefore head of the IRA.

McGuinness had originally joined the Officials, but they had appeared more concerned with interminable debates on Marxist ideology than with carrying out attacks on the British state. The Officials believed in a form of republicanism which involved the entire working class, whatever its religious origin: it had even recruited a company in Shankhill, bastion of Belfast Protestantism. The Provisionals did contain a handful of Protestants, but greater efforts were made to recruit them by the Official IRA and by the INLA. The Officials' Shankhill Company was a short-lived affair –

most of its members drifted away as soon as the sectarian battle lines were drawn after the Troubles began. Only a few individuals continued to be involved with republican groups, the most important of whom was probably Ronnie Bunting, son of a scion of Ulster loyalism, who became commander of the INLA in Belfast during the late 1970s. The Provisionals, while anxious in their public pronouncements not to come over as a sectarian force, were privately more ready to accept that they did fight for a community which was, almost to the last family, Catholic.

Northerners like Adams and McGuinness had for some time realized that the tone of much republican propaganda, which implied that another week of struggle would be enough to kick the Brits out, was unrealistic. Since the breaking of the 'No Go areas' in 1972 and the peak of violence which followed, the conflict had changed. The willingness of both Conservative and Labour governments to hold ceasefire talks had been at the root of the republican leadership's conviction in the early 1970s that one more 'big push' could bring victory. But the leadership was coming to the conclusion that Rees had never intended to make a permanent deal, rather he had used the ceasefire to buy time. And during the ceasefire the struggle had subtly changed in character. It was no longer a mass rising but instead had begun to take on the characteristics of a protracted guerrilla struggle.

A new doctrine, known as the 'long war', was conceived. It was first floated in June 1977 at the annual republican commemoration at the grave of Wolfe Tone in a speech by Jimmy Drumm, a member of an influential republican clan. The idea gained approval and republican propaganda changed accordingly. The significance of the change, and the reaction of volunteers – as the IRA calls its frontline members – was described years later in an interview with an IRA man:

> During the early 1970s everyone had this belief that freedom would come the following year. It's now been accepted by the IRA, particularly by ordinary volunteers, that this is going to be a long, long war. We're not prepared to set a time on it. At the same time we're not prepared to take an all-out offensive in such a way that it would jeopardize our chances of chipping away at the British Army and therefore the British government.

But admitting to its supporters that the struggle was going to be a long one meant that the IRA needed to step up its political work. Republicanism would have to be carried forward not just by arms, but by agitation and participation in elections. The activists of Sinn Fein, the political wing of the republican movement, found a new campaigning issue in the conditions in which republican prisoners had been held.

By early 1976 the government was introducing 'criminalization', abandoning the special category status for those convicted of terrorist offences which had allowed them rights not enjoyed by prisoners anywhere else in the United Kingdom. Under the new rules loyalist and republican terrorists would be treated as ordinary felons. The drill parades and other paramilitary trappings which had been permitted in internment camps were no longer allowed. From May 1976 this was to become a major issue in the nationalist community as the first inmate in the newly built H-Blocks at the Maze prison refused to wear regulation clothing.

The shift of power in the IRA from South to North created uncertainty in Army intelligence. It was evident that the northerners were becoming more powerful, but intelligence chiefs were confused about the extent of the shift and about the role of Southern Command. In 1978 James Glover, the Brigadier General Staff (Intelligence) who was trying to consolidate information-gathering activities, wrote another report, *Northern Ireland: Future Terrorist Trends*. A copy of the secret document was subsequently obtained by the IRA, much to the embarrassment of Whitehall. In it Glover confessed:

> 'We know little of the detailed working of the hierarchy in Dublin. In particular we have scant knowledge of how the logistic system works, nor do we know the extent to which the older, apparently retired, republican leaders influence the movement.'

The use of military terminology by the IRA infuriates many in the British Army and the loyalist community, and the association of the IRA's bombing and assassination activities in the 1970s with its struggle decades before is also offensive to many in the Republic. However, sympathy for the Catholics of the North in their struggle against social disadvantage runs deep within mainstream politics in Ireland. Many politicians who were critical of the Provisionals' methods were therefore reluctant to take concrete action against them. The issue of cross-border security – or rather why the Irish government was not doing more to improve it – remained a major irritant with the chiefs at Lisburn and Knock. Despite this, there was a gradual shift in attitude in Dublin. Slowly Irish governments were beginning to recognize that the IRA represented a threat within their own state. The advent of Police Primacy in 1976 was a positive step for Dublin, since it removed the Army, with whom the Gardai would not deal, from control of operations.

Apart from the ignorance of the security forces about the command structure of the IRA, the generally lacklustre performance of the intelligence community had been reflected in the dramatic drop in seizures of weapons during the period 1974 to 1978. But by early 1977 a combination of factors was leading to a greatly improved performance. The Army had been systematically expanding its undercover surveillance since the beginning of 1976 – the same year that the RUC had also set up special surveillance units.

Besides these exceptional measures Kenneth Newman, first as senior deputy chief constable and later as chief constable, had attempted to improve the basic standard of police work. He had, for example, organized the shipment of more than 20,000 fingerprints to England for analysis. As a result there had been several hundred arrests. Newman tried to instil better practices in the force, with greater effort made to protect forensic and other evidence which might offer the only chance of gaining convictions.

The RUC's CID officers took over interrogation of suspects, mainly at Castlereagh, from the Army. The reorganization of police work meant that interrogators were more often able to confront suspects with a full dossier on their associations and activities. This panicked many into confessions. At the same time changes in the law allowed people suspected of terrorist crimes to be held for three or seven days, allowing interrogators to work for longer on hard cases. However, subsequent investigations were to show that the CID's improved results – there was a steep rise in confessions during 1974 to 1976 – was in some cases being achieved by recourse to beatings. The Commanding Officer of an infantry battalion returning from a tour in Belfast's Andersonstown told his superiors in a classified report: 'The CID are not emasculated by the same restrictions on the methods of questioning terrorist suspects as those imposed on the [Special] Branch at Castlereagh, all of which work to the advantage of the terrorist. The results CID have achieved during our tour have been impressive.'

Newman also set up a Regional Crime and Intelligence Unit at each of the RUC's three regional headquarters. The units were jointly staffed by CID and Special Branch officers so that the activities of the two departments became interwoven.

IRA chiefs became increasingly concerned at the effectiveness of the interrogation process coupled with the introduction of longer terms of detention under the Prevention of Terrorism Act. At a trial in Dublin in 1978 the court heard extracts from an internal IRA paper which had been found in the possession of Seamus Twomey, a leading Provisional, when he was arrested. It stated that, 'The three- and seven-day detention orders are breaking volunteers and it is the Republican Army's fault for not indoctrinating volunteers with the psychological strength to resist interrogation.'

Twomey's paper also discussed the inefficiency of the IRA's command structure and the need for reorganization. It was precisely this restructuring which Ivor Bell and Gerry Adams had already been addressing themselves to in the Maze.

Volunteers had, until then, been grouped into companies. These usually contained ten to thirty people rather than the ninety or a hundred which is normal in armies. The companies were grouped into battalions, containing volunteers (the active terrorists) and auxiliaries. The auxiliaries were a sort of 'Dad's Army' combination of older men and younger ones who lacked the experience for incorporation into active units. It was intended that auxiliaries should be available for protection of the nationalist community in the event of a major sectarian conflict and to carry out less sensitive tasks in the meantime. In Belfast and Derry battalions were grouped into brigades.

Using military terminology to describe its units was part of the Provisionals' attempt to root themselves in the tradition of insurrectionary republicanism which had won independence for the South, the Republic of Ireland, nearly sixty years before. Then, the IRA had deployed an extensive military force, organized in a conventional way. Sinn Fein propaganda always attempted to paint the Provisionals as soldiers fighting a struggle akin to that of the French resistance in the war, and following in the tradition of the armed republicanism which made possible the formation of the Republic of Ireland. Perhaps because of this, the organization has maintained a higher degree of control over its members and been capable of more ambitious operations than other paramilitary groups.

However, this organization led to several problems. The most important was that far too many people knew who was who in their local IRA infrastructure, exposing the organization to informers. In addition, maintaining the administrative structure of companies required the recruitment of too many unreliable people and kept a large number of those who could be trusted tied up with organizational work rather than operations.

Under the reorganization the people who actually carried out acts of violence were to be regrouped into cells. The IRA drew on the example of urban guerrilla movements in Latin American countries, which had used cells to great effect in the 1960s. Instead of a gunman knowing the identity of his superior commanders, explosives experts, quartermasters and members of other units, he would in future have contact only with the three or four other members of his own cell. The IRA called its new groups Active Service Units (ASUs). Only the ASU commander would have contact with the next level of authority.

The IRA cut away the company level of command and eliminated many battalions too. It was left with brigades in Belfast and Derry, although the term continued to be used by groups elsewhere. There were smaller units in south Armagh, Newry, east Tyrone, mid Tyrone, west Tyrone, north Down, north Antrim and north Armagh, as well as across the border in Donegal and Monaghan in the Republic. It was intended that only the commander and possibly his adjutant or assistant should know the full details of a forthcoming operation. They would order ASUs to complete various tasks with different groups observing the target, hijacking vehicles and actually carrying out the attack.

Brigadier Glover, in his report *Future Terrorist Trends*, noted that, 'By reorganizing on cellular lines PIRA has become less dependent on public support than in the past and is less vulnerable to penetration by informers'. It was not that the intelligence services could not find informers, but rather that the knowledge available to any one volunteer was dropping significantly. The identity of many IRA men and women was still widely known in the tightly-knit communities of west Belfast's Turf Lodge or the Creggan, but the reorganization meant that people were less aware of what they were actually up to.

Transition from 'one more push' to 'long war', and from companies to cells, together with the stepping-up of convictions based on confessions, meant that IRA membership shrank. Patrick Bishop and Eamonn Mallie, in their authoritative book *The Provisional IRA*, estimated the number of active members to have gone down from about 1000 in the mid 1970s to around 250 ten years later. The drop happened despite the release of many men being held on short prison sentences which had been predicted by Brigadier Glover in his report. He had believed that the expected release of 761 republican and loyalist paramilitaries in the three years after his report was completed in 1978 would fuel the terrorist campaign.

The Brigadier's own estimate of the Provisionals' strength was a high one. He believed them to have 1200 active members. This contrasted with public pronouncements by the Army which usually stressed the small size of the organization but also shows that Army intelligence was slightly behind in understanding the slimming down which reorganization would bring. By the mid 1980s some Army officers were suggesting there were as few as fifty active IRA members, which appears to have been a deliberate underestimate. I estimate that the Provisionals' strength remained between 250 and 350 active members – meaning those with the means and prepared to kill – during the decade after the reorganization.

What is beyond doubt is that the Army Council of the IRA used the reorganization to remove many members whom they considered to be hot-headed, disloyal or prone to break under interrogation. The ones who remained were a mixture of types. There were those like Mary Farrell, later killed in Gibraltar, who had benefitted from a middle-class upbringing and convent school education. On the other hand, there were brutalized sons of the estates who could live with the screams of people whose kneecaps they had crushed under concrete blocks. The intellectuals not only gravitated towards positions of command: people with special skills were drawn into bomb-making and the IRA's own intelligence work.

Most people who joined the Provisionals were deeply influenced by their environment. Mark Lennaghan entered the IRA in the late 1970s after his family was bombed out of its house by loyalists. He was subsequently convicted of an attempt to ambush an Army patrol in 1982 and while in the Maze prison renounced violence. In an interview for the BBC's *Newsnight*, Lennaghan told me: 'At that time [the IRA] was very popular, everyone was in it, it was a peer thing . . . there was a lot of identity, status, prestige, ego-tripping – all that sort of stuff . . . the whole sub-culture of west Belfast is very political, it gives a great sense of "1916" [the republican Easter rising against British rule], of your identity'.

Although many volunteers shared his sense of being heir to a long history of violent republicanism, few were as intellectually accomplished as Lennaghan, who passed his Queen's University finals exams while on remand in the Crumlin Road jail. According to one lawyer who has spent much of his career dealing with republicans in police custody, 'The ordinary volunteer is pretty stupid, he's not terribly political'. But the Provisionals became adept at providing recruits with what they were seeking: there was a coherent ideology for those who might otherwise have pondered the morality of killing, and there was plenty of action for those who were ready to use violence without question.

The standard of bomb-making in the early years had been low. From 1972 to 1973, dozens of IRA men and women were blown up by bombs which had gone off prematurely. But competent explosives experts had survived this gruesome form of 'natural selection'. They began to incorporate safety devices in their weapons, as well as introducing other modifications to catch out those sent to defuse them.

Shipments of weapons had improved the standard of firearms available too. In the early days they had relied on a handful of ancient Thompson machine guns and other weapons. IRA members had stepped into streets and engaged patrols with wildly inaccurate fire. The incidents were often poorly planned and prepared, leading to the apprehension or death of those involved.

In 1970 sympathisers in the United States sent several hundred Armalite rifles. In many ways it was a weapon superior to the Self-Loading Rifle (SLR) issued to British Army troops. The Armalite could fire fully automatic like a machine-gun, which the SLR could not. Its smaller, lighter bullet – 5.56mm compared to the SLR's 7.62mm – was less likely to go right through its target and injure the innocent. The weapon became an important propaganda symbol. It manifested itself in painted murals and in the argot of republicanism.

In 1976 more supporters in America raided a US Army National Guard armoury, stealing seven M-60 machine-guns. The weapons, which fire belts of 7.62mm rounds, were too big to be easily concealed and using them carried a high risk of civilian casualties. But the display of M-60s, like the appearance of Armalites before, had propaganda value in showing nationalists that the IRA could obtain the most up-to-date military firearms.

With the reorganization, the IRA set itself new targets. Attacks on businesses in city centres, common in the early 1970s, were reduced, the leadership realizing rather late in the day how unpopular they had become. In the early days of the Troubles there had been qualms about attacking soldiers and policemen off duty. These attacks, some members believed, ran counter to the principles which the IRA as an army should uphold. But the increasing difficulty of carrying out successful attacks on patrols and the desire to intimidate members of the locally raised security forces led them to put aside such considerations.

Increasingly, members of the RUC and UDR were shot or blown apart at home, often in front of their families. Such attacks were often accompanied by statements in republican newspapers which sought to justify such actions, often by vague references to alleged crimes against the nationalist community or suggestions that the victim had been associated with a loyalist paramilitary group.

Attacks against armed troops and police were more often carried out in rural areas where surveillance was less intense and government forces more dispersed. South Armagh and Tyrone, the biggest county stretching across the south west of Ulster, became more important to the Provisionals as security improved in the cities.

Reorganization, new strategy and improved weapons compounded the problems faced by the security forces. Although some steps had been taken to unify intelligence-gathering activities, by 1977 it had become apparent to senior Army and police officers that there was a real danger that it would not be possible to make further progress against the IRA. This growing realization of the seriousness of the situation prompted moves to make further improvements in intelligence co-operation.

# 4

# Watchers

The growing professionalism of the IRA and the security chiefs' desire to intensify information-gathering activities were to spawn several 'undercover' units – groups whose activities and even names were shrouded in secrecy. At the time of the IRA's adoption of a cellular structure only one specially selected and trained observation unit existed. The Army's élite undercover surveillance unit is without doubt its most secret body of soldiers.

In 1987 its members gained the same privileges as those belonging to the SAS and the Special Boat Service, the Royal Marines Special Forces. The members of all three groups qualify for extra pay and are under the administrative control of one brigadier known as Director Special Forces (DSF). Prior to that there had been a brigadier who ran the Army's special forces known as Director SAS, but it was decided that the different elements should be more closely woven together.

Although members of the surveillance unit are, therefore, the professional peers of the SAS they have received a small fraction of the press and political interest. This is largely due to the fact that the unit was from the outset hidden beneath an extraordinary web of cover names and secrecy. In the Army it became known during the 1970s as the Reconnaissance Force, RF, and during the 1980s as 14 Intelligence Company, the latter having originated as a cover name and become customary.

It was set up between late 1973 and early 1974 following the Army's realization, in Lord Carver's words, 'That it should rely less on Special Branch and do more to obtain its own intelligence'. He added, 'For some time various surveillance operations by soldiers in plain clothes had been in train, initiated by Frank Kitson when he commanded the [39] Brigade in Belfast, some of them exploiting ex-members or supporters of the IRA.'

Brigadier Kitson's special unit was called the Mobile Reconnaissance Force (MRF). Kitson himself was a veteran of the counter-insurgency campaigns in Kenya, Malaya, Oman and Cyprus. In Kenya he had been involved with 'counter-gangs', British-led groups of former Mau Mau rebels who confronted their former comrades when they found them in the bush.

On his appointment in 1970 to command 39 Brigade in Belfast, Kitson had received the approval of his superiors to set up the MRF. He recruited 'turned' IRA members, nicknamed the 'Freds', who were sent to live in a British Army married quarters at Palace Barracks in Holywood, east Belfast. The undercover unit started out as a handful of soldiers under the command of a captain who operated only in Brigadier Kitson's area of responsibility and were known by the nickname of the 'Bomb Squad'. The name Mobile Reconnaissance Force was only given several weeks after the soldiers had begun to operate.

MRF operations were, to start with at least, basic. Soldiers in plain clothes and unmarked cars would sit in places where they expected the IRA to plant bombs. Sometimes they were there on intelligence tips; at others it was no more than somebody's hunch that the bombers might turn up. The unit recruited many soldiers of Irish origin who would be able to pass for locals. MRF soldiers would cruise Belfast's Falls or Whiterock Roads accompanied by 'Freds', who would point out characters or places of interest.

Within months of its establishment, the MRF's operations became more unusual. The unit became involved in several operations involving highly complex cover activities, the aim of which was to allow the Army to penetrate the republican heartlands, where the presence of strangers on intelligence-gathering missions is usually noticed quickly. In one operation the Army started its own massage parlour; in another women soldiers posed as door-to-door sellers of cosmetics. But the MRF's most celebrated operation involved setting up the Four Square Laundry.

Four Square was intended not just to allow disguised MRF members to carry out reconnaissance trips in laundry vans but also, it was hoped, to allow them to inspect the dirty linen of suspected terrorists for traces of explosive. However, the operation was compromised when one of the Freds was turned by the IRA and told the Provos all about various MRF operations, including this one. A van carrying two MRF soldiers, one of them a woman, was ambushed by the IRA as it made its way through the Twinbrooks estate. The male soldier was killed but the female soldier escaped. The Fred who provided the information was said by a later account to have been killed by the IRA.

In another incident Sergeant Clive Williams, who was serving with the MRF, was charged with attempted murder after he had opened fire from an unmarked car on two men at a bus station in Belfast – a third man was also wounded by a stray shot. He claimed the men had been armed and was subsequently acquitted by the court. But during the court case Sergeant Williams revealed many details about the MRF including that it comprised about forty men, how they were trained and how patrols were carried out. By late 1973, a little more than two years after it had been set up, the operation had been thoroughly compromised, with the Irish newspaper *Hibernia* running a lengthy exposé headlined 'Belfast's Dept. of Dirty Tricks'. Much of the reporting about the unit was unclear, and most accounts were mistaken about what 'MRF' actually stood for, but the exposure both of the Force and its activities, and of the founding role of the commander of 39 Brigade, with his pedigree of colonial wars, were important propaganda gifts to the Army's foes.

The republican movement fixed on Brigadier Kitson, elevating him to one of its central hate figures. The Brigadier was unusual among the officers known to republicans in that in 1970 he had published a book, *Low Intensity Operations*, which had declared publicly what he believed the lessons of Britain's counter-insurgency campaigns had been. The Brigadier seemed to have provided a blueprint for the security state which nationalists saw emerging around them. That many other officers were trying to apply experiences gained elsewhere to the unique environment of Northern Ireland was something largely ignored because their writings took the form of classified internal army papers.

Even today, in the view of some officers, Sinn Fein continues to over-estimate the importance of Kitson in its propaganda. But Kitson's name, and the existence of the MRF unit, were among the few facts which journalists and republican propagandists could latch on to in seeking to explain the strange events which they saw around them.

One intelligence officer describes the MRF's operations as 'a series of cock-ups'. The idea of using the Freds, Belfast's 'counter-gangs', may in hindsight have been foolish. It ignored the nature of the nationalist community – notably its ability to win back the loyalty of IRA men who had changed sides. An officer who was involved with the MRF justifies its use of the Freds on the grounds that there was a dearth of intelligence available to the Army at the time and that there was value in what the turned IRA members had to say before they left the unit.

Lisburn drew two important lessons from the compromise of the MRF. First, the trial of Sergeant Williams had shown the danger that sensitive intelligence-gathering operations might be revealed in court: the Army knew it would have to show greater ingenuity in preventing similar mistakes happening again. Officers of the Army Legal Service were told to be on hand to prepare the soldiers' statements and senior officers sometimes tried to use their influence with the RUC to prevent prosecutions. Second, the MRF had told the RUC and commanders of normal Army patrols on the streets virtually nothing about its operations. This presented several dangers, not least that the security forces might open fire on one of these undercover units. It also denied the plain-clothes soldiers the possible back-up of uniformed units in a critical situation like the attack on the laundry van and thereby created bad feeling in the RUC because of the lack of co-ordination.

The MRF was disbanded early in 1973. Within a year the new surveillance unit had emerged – later known as 14 Intelligence Company – a group which was to set far higher standards, and to maintain its cover for many years. This unit, like the SAS, was formed from soldiers who had volunteered from other units and passed a rigorous selection course.

The surveillance unit did not consist predominantly of SAS members, although some soldiers with SAS experience were part of it. Neither was the unit part of the SAS in an organizational sense. A few SAS soldiers did help to set up the surveillance unit, but the flow of expertise was frequently in the opposite direction – some of the 14 Intelligence Company's operators then went on to serve in SAS squadrons bound for Ulster, where their experience was valued. Selection for the surveillance unit, which takes place twice a year at a training area normally used by 22 SAS, emphasizes the need for resourcefulness and psychological strength, rather than the physical stamina needed for the Special Air Service. It is designed to find people, usually bright officers and NCOs in their mid to late twenties, who are able to bear the strain of long-term surveillance, sometimes only a few feet from people whom they know to be dangerous terrorists. An unusual physical characteristic, for example a scar or prominent tattoo, can be enough for a candidate to be rejected since its members must be as unobtrusive as possible. 14 Intelligence Company recruits from the Royal Marines as well as the Army.

By 1975 the unit's structure had solidified, remaining the same to this day. The unit has one detachment with each of the three brigades in Ulster. Each detachment or 'det', in Army parlance, is normally commanded by a captain and consists of about twenty soldiers. Like the SAS it is often short of soldiers, a consequence of the high standards set during the selection course. When they are available, a second officer is appointed to each det, usually a lieutenant or another captain who is known either as the liaison officer (LO) or the operations (Ops) officer.

The surveillance unit has used a variety of cover names. Each is chosen to sound like another army unit which carries out work of a more mundane kind. The screen of secrecy was erected in part to prevent it being compromised as quickly as the MRF was and perhaps, given Lord Carver's insight into its origins, to prevent the RUC intelligence-gathering agencies from fully understanding its activities. It is also undoubtedly true that the shady identity of the force has prevented the republican movement from demonizing it in the way that it did with the SAS.

In its early days, people posted to the Company were often listed as going to NITAT or NITAT (NI). NITAT stands for Northern Ireland Training Advisory Team. The real NITAT sends soldiers with recent experience of Ulster to train other regiments in Germany or Britain, which are about to go there, in the arts of normal soldiering: for example, how to mount patrols or how not to be caught out by the latest design of booby trap. In fact the people going to 'NITAT' in Northern Ireland itself were involved in very different work.

Suspicions at HQNI that the name NITAT was becoming too widely known prompted a change to another cover name by 1978 to 1979 – Intelligence and Security Group (NI) or Int and Sy Group. There is an Int and Sy Group in England and another in Germany, comprising large bodies of Intelligence Corps soldiers grouped into companies and commanded by a lieutenant colonel. Their daily business in the 1970s and 1980s consisted mainly of disseminating to fighting units the latest information about the Soviet Army and watching out for attempts by Warsaw Pact spies to suborn British soldiers. But Int and Sy Group, like NITAT, meant something very different in Northern Ireland.

In the early 1980s another name was introduced – 14 Intelligence and Security Company. This name, usually contracted in speech to 14 Intelligence Company, 14 Company or simply 14 Int, became widely used within the Army. Indeed most people who have worked with the Army in Northern Ireland know it as such and that is why I will use this name, even to describe activities in the mid 1970s before the Army adopted it. This cover name suggested an analogy with 12 Intelligence and Security Company, a unit of report writers, index keepers and computer programmers rather than an organized force of undercover surveillance specialists.

Research in Army regimental magazines has allowed me to trace the postings of many individuals who have been identified by contacts as members of the unit and through this to chart the development of its cover names. Picking one's way through this labyrinth requires patience, but is necessary because the unit became involved in several fatal shooting incidents and was to become the subject of 'dirty tricks' allegations by Captain Fred Holroyd, the one-time intelligence officer.

One of the unit's first recruits was Captain Julian Ball. He had served in the ranks of the Parachute Regiment and had done a tour with the SAS. Promoted to officer, he got a commission in the King's Own Scottish Borderers (KOSBs). Captain Ball passed selection for 14 Intelligence Company and commanded the 3 Brigade detachment of the unit, which used the cover name 4 Field Survey Troop. His number two, or liaison officer, was Lieutenant Robert Nairac, later promoted to captain.

Fred Holroyd alleges 4 Field Survey Troop was an SAS unit operating in Ulster before the government admitted the Regiment had been sent there. He also alleges that the unit was involved in 'dirty tricks', something which will be discussed in the next chapter. My research indicates that Captain Ball and Lieutenant Nairac were not in the SAS during their 1974 tour with the surveillance unit, the time when Holroyd met them.

Captain Ball went on to join the SAS in mid 1975, when he was listed as '22 SAS' in his regimental journal. Lieutenant Nairac was never in the SAS; although he died later in Northern Ireland, his name was not inscribed on the clock tower at the Regiment's camp in Hereford where all SAS men who fall in action are listed. During the 1970s there was no great sensitivity about listing a soldier's assignment in a regimental journal as being to the SAS. It may strike the reader as odd that while the Army would lie to the press and even to the courts about its undercover activities in Northern Ireland, it would not do so in a regimental journal. The reasons lie partly in the fact that such journals are not intended to be seen by people outside the regimental community and partly in the carelessness of those who put such journals together. They often transposed a regiment's classified list of where its officers and NCOs were serving into their journal without realizing the sensitivity of some of the information. Lastly, many of the officers who put such magazines together consider that inserting false information about someone's posting in their regimental journal would be tantamount to deception of regimental brothers. While people assigned to the surveillance unit are sometimes not listed in their journals – or more often one of the unit's cover names given here is used – I have never discovered, in many hours of research, one instance where the soldier's posting was listed falsely.

One soldier from the unit who served with Captain Ball, who had won the Military Cross during his time with the KOSBs, remembers him as a highly unusual, instinctive soldier. He was a hard man physically – the soldier says, 'Our joke about him was that his idea of a good time was to wrap himself in barbed wire and run about a minefield in the pouring rain.' After two tours as an officer in the SAS he went to run the Sultan of Oman's special forces. He was killed in a car accident in Oman in 1981.

Another example of a soldier who served in the special unit at the time was William Hatton. As a young NCO he was posted from the Parachute Regiment to the surveillance unit, where he became involved in many observation operations. Hatton subsequently went on to join G Squadron 22 SAS, reaching the rank of corporal. He was one of sixteen members of the Regiment killed in the Falklands War in 1982 when their helicopter crashed into the sea. Corporal Hatton's official obituary reads: 'He was present with his squadron on four operational tours in Northern Ireland when his vast depth of experience in the theatre was of quite inestimable value.'

Most missions carried out by 14 Intelligence Company involved either setting up static observations posts (OPs), or watching people from unmarked cars (Q cars). An OP in an urban area might be a derelict house or, in the countryside, a roadside ditch – neither offered much protection. Q cars were fitted with 'covert radios', invisible to the casual observer. But the presence of a strange car was in many areas noticed quickly – particularly as there was a tendency to use relatively new British-made saloons. Outsiders could become prey to the gun law of the republican estates where youths, often armed, hijacked cars for use by the IRA or INLA, or simply for the thrill of joy riding. Soldiers assigned to the unit usually carried a standard 9mm Browning automatic pistol for self-defence. Sometimes they also used small sub-machine guns – in the early days the American-designed Ingram and later the German Heckler and Koch MP-5K. They were not normally equipped with assault rifles, as the SAS often are in Northern Ireland, for unlike them 14 Company's mission was not to confront paramilitaries but to watch them. Their weapons therefore had to be small enough to be easily concealed.

The IRA soon became aware of the stepping-up of surveillance. Overt OPs on the top of blocks of flats, like the Divis tower on Belfast's Falls Road, announced their presence to everybody. Covert OPs allowed members of regular units and 14 Intelligence Company to observe suspects, seeing who their associates were. This in turn allowed the collators of intelligence at

Lisburn and brigade headquarters to investigate links between meetings of particular individuals and patterns of terrorist activity.

Operators in the surveillance unit usually abandoned Army regulation appearance. One of its men remembers, 'The long hair and beards were the result of typical soldier's thinking. If there is something you are not allowed to do and then the rule is waived, then everybody does it.' As a result they were in danger of creating another uniformity, albeit different to and hairier than that of the uniformed soldier on the street.

The difficulty of unobtrusive penetration of the tightly knit nationalist community meant that the presence of OP teams and Q cars in republican areas carried risks. Brigadier Glover, in his 1978 report on terrorist trends, had warned, 'The terrorists are already aware of their own vulnerability to Security Force intelligence operators and will increasingly seek to eliminate those involved.' His warning followed an IRA ambush on an OP in south Armagh in which three soldiers had been killed in 1975. According to a member of the élite surveillance unit, three of its members were killed in incidents between 1974 and 1978. The first member of 14 Intelligence Company to die was Captain Anthony Pollen, a member of the Coldstream Guards attached to its Londonderry Detachment. On 14 April 1974 he and another member of the unit were in plain clothes when they were cornered by republicans at a demonstration in the Bogside, where they were attempting to take photographs. The other soldier escaped but Captain Pollen was shot dead.

Following the south Armagh ambush procedures were tightened. An OP consisting of two to four soldiers would be sited nearby in such a way that its members could be supported by arms fire from at least one more OP of a similar size. They would be backed up by a Quick Reaction Force (QRF) of soldiers and/or police at the nearest convenient security forces base. The QRF would be only a few minutes away from the OP team, able to respond to a call for help over the radio. Despite these new precautions, the scene was set for a sequence of lethal confrontations between 14 Intelligence Company and the republican paramilitaries. At midday on 12 December 1977 the Officer Commanding (OC) Londonderry Detachment of 14 Intelligence Company briefed his soldiers on a forthcoming surveillance operation in the republican Bogside and Brandywell areas of the city. The team was to use five unmarked cars. Each of them, the OC later said in a statement to the RUC, 'was equipped with covert radio and in addition each member of my staff was in possession of various items of very sensitive military equipment. Such equipment is kept in each car and is concealed from view.' The OC was referring to advanced photographic and eavesdropping equipment carried on operations.

At 1.30 p.m. the Q cars moved into position. One of them, a red Hillman Hunter saloon driven by a young lance-corporal, was noticed by two young members of the INLA. Colm McNutt, a low-level INLA commander known by the nickname 'Rooster', who was carrying an unloaded Webley revolver, and Patrick Phelan noticed the car parked with one person sitting in it. In a later interview with the police, Phelan said: 'We went over to the car and we told the boy to put down his window. He screwed down the window a bit. Rooster told him he wanted the car. The driver said he wasn't giving it. Rooster then pulled the gun out of the waistband of his trousers.'

The Lance-Corporal, who witnesses said had long hair and was wearing jeans, got out of the car and Phelan climbed into the driver's seat. As McNutt walked around to the passenger seat, the Lance-Corporal drew his 9mm Browning and fired at him. McNutt stumbled with the impact of the shots and then tried to run away. The soldier fired again, killing him. Phelan threw himself out of the car and escaped. He was later arrested and charged. Republican activists used what was to become a familiar ploy, saying the SAS were responsible for the incident. They were not and the Army denied it. Although, as we will see, the IRA had discovered a great deal about the activities of 14 Company, it would appear that its propagandists preferred to play on the potent emotional response in republican bars and housing estates which attaching the three letters 'SAS' to an incident would trigger.

To the layperson, the use of lethal force by the Lance-Corporal to protect himself and the equipment in the car might seem excessive. Just two days later, however, there was to be another confrontation with quite different results.

Corporal Paul Harman, of Belfast Detachment 14 Intelligence Company, was on duty in the city's Turf Lodge estate. The soldier had served in the 16/5th The Queen's Royal Lancers before transferring to the Intelligence Corps and being selected for 'special duty' in Northern Ireland. As he stopped his red Morris Marina at the junction of Monagh Road and Monagh Avenue, he was approached by an unknown number of assailants.

It may be that Corporal Harman tried to talk his way out of the situation rather than using force; certainly no republican terrorists were killed during the incident. Later the Corporal was found shot dead with bullets in the head and back. The car had been set on fire and police found no trace of his Browning pistol. The IRA announced that it had captured intelligence files from the car. According to an Army intelligence officer, radio code books and surveillance equipment were also missing from the car.

The officer says Corporal Harman's death was a major setback for 14 Intelligence Company which then found itself under IRA counter-surveillance. Operations were halted, with the Detachment's Q cars taken off the streets for several weeks while officers tried to assess what the Provisionals had learned from the incident. Procedures were tightened afterwards, with more efforts made to find different types of car and restrictions imposed on soldiers operating alone.

Six months later there was another incident in Londonderry. Two IRA members approached a Q car with two members of the surveillance unit in it. The soldier in the passenger seat opened fire, hitting Denis Heaney in the chest with three rounds. He was killed instantly. The RUC said they recovered a weapon from the scene. Sinn Fein said Heaney had been shot by the SAS and that night there was rioting in the republican estates.

Heaney's death was probably a failed element of a deliberate IRA operation to target members of 14 Company. A few weeks later the Derry Brigade were to mount a successful attack against one of Londonderry Detachment's Q cars. It appears that they had spotted Lance-Corporal Alan Swift driving alone in an unmarked car in a republican district of the city.

At 1.30 p.m. on 11 August 1978 IRA terrorists hijacked a Toyota van. Several automatic weapons were recovered from a cache and an operation set in train. Lance-Corporal Swift had been spotted in his parked car on a layby off the Letterkenny Road in the Brandywell area of Londonderry. At about 3.30 p.m. the Toyota pulled up in front of his car and at least two terrorists opened fire from the rear of the van. The Lance-Corporal was killed. The Army Press Office said he had been 'in plain clothes and on duty' when he died.

Whatever the dangers of such work, there was a consensus among security chiefs that plain-clothes surveillance could yield still better results. So, from 1976 to 1978 there was a proliferation of special units besides 14 Intelligence Company's detachments which were intended to do similar work, albeit in less demanding situations. The Army and the RUC did not agree a master plan, rather there was general agreement that many more soldiers and policemen could be used for such duties without crowding the existing Army surveillance unit. An entire detachment of 14 Company could be tied down on mobile and static observation of a single suspect and there were, after all, a great many more suspects whom the intelligence experts wanted watching. The need for these teams was such that the RUC would have found it hard to oppose the Army's commitment of many more men for observation duties because, despite the advent of Police Primacy, people at Knock understood that the Army had a great many more operatives to call upon than the RUC could muster.

Major General Dick Trant, appointed Commander Land Forces at Lisburn in 1977, was the driving force behind a large expansion of Army surveillance resources. Trant, a tall man with the genial manner of a country vicar, wanted to restore to each unit the capability for intelligence-gathering which had been lost when infantry battalions were relieved of their reconnaissance platoons during an Army reorganization. Complementing 14 Company, the CLF had at his disposal a force, formed little more than a year before, of a few dozen soldiers from various units serving in Ulster called the Northern Ireland Patrol Group. He decided that this arrangement was not satisfactory, partly because the soldiers stayed for a few months only and partly because they were not properly trained.

Major General Trant decided to introduce Close Observation Platoons, units of thirty in each of the battalions serving longer 'residential' tours of up to two years and in one of the four-month tour battalions, the one based in south Armagh. The COPs, as they became known, would take the best soldiers from the battalion and give them expert training in observation techniques. The CLF and brigade commanders would be able to use the new platoons anywhere in Ulster, not just inside the area of responsibility of the particular battalion to which they belonged. COPs were to become important in establishing the regular patterns of activity among ASUs and movements of key republicans. Although 14 Intelligence Company or SAS operators were usually brought in when there was good intelligence of a forthcoming operation, the COPs often provided the basic data about an area and IRA activities in it.

Lisburn leaked details of the new groups, which in press briefings were described as 'SAS-type units', in the hope that proliferation of such groups would intimidate the IRA. In June 1977 *The Times* announced 'First of 300 Arrive for Army's New Undercover Drive'. The number was something of an exaggeration, there being about 200. The journalist noted that they were going to gather information designed to bring suspects to trial but added, 'The Government is also expecting publicity about secret Army activities to increase their deterrent value.'

The Parachute Regiment, battalions of which had retained their own reconnaissance unit, known as Patrol Company, was to take an important role in training the COPs and the new surveillance units of the RUC. Chief Constable Kenneth Newman was naturally interested in expanding the surveillance activities of his force. Under Police Primacy the RUC were meant to be taking over the direction of security matters and he did not want them to be left out of what he felt was an important area of operations.

The Special Patrol Group (SPG), the RUC's mobile anti-terrorist unit, had in 1976 set up a firearms and observation unit called Bronze Section. Its members were selected for special training in undercover activities and initially operated mainly in the Belfast area. Michael Asher, a former soldier in the Parachute Regiment who joined the SPG as an ordinary police constable, describes various Bronze Section activities in his book *Shoot to Kill*. Asher's account suggests that most Bronze operations, many of which were based on informer intelligence, were failures. The RUC surveillance operators, like their Army counterparts, adopted beards and long hair en masse. They appeared, he wrote, 'exactly like policemen trying to look like ordinary citizens'. In some respects, the RUC's occasionally farcical early experiments with Bronze Section were reminiscent of the Army's experience with the Mobile Reconnaissance Force.

Asher says that on one occasion the SPG was deployed by Bronze Section following intelligence that a loyalist assassination squad was going to kill a Catholic lawyer. The police lay in wait all day outside the lawyer's flat, until 'it occurred to one of the Bronze Section's bearded men to check if he was in'. It was only then that they discovered the target of the loyalist death squad had emigrated to Canada.

Partly as a result of such episodes, partly in recognition that Bronze Section performed too broad a function, in that it dealt with firearms as well as observation, senior RUC officers decided to establish a new surveillance unit. They were impressed by the results obtained by 14 Intelligence Company and wanted to create a similar unit within the police force. In 1977 Special Branch formed a surveillance squad which was part of E4, its Operations Division. The unit, E4A, was later to become the subject of many allegations of wrong-doing by republican activists. But pre-meditated confrontations with terrorists were not part of E4A's brief, just as they were not part of the Army surveillance unit's duties. The RUC later set up special firearms units which were meant to give the force its own 'SAS' capability. E4A concentrated on mobile and static covert OPs while other sections of E4 were to specialize in technical surveillance, being equipped with advanced monitoring apparatus – for example video cameras with fibre optic lens attachments, which could be used to observe a room through a tiny hole, and state-of-the-art listening devices. The SB surveillance unit evolved close contacts with MI5 which has its own research laboratories developing bugging devices and other equipment.

E4A set higher standards than Bronze Section. It allowed the SB to conduct many more surveillance operations than before. A senior security forces officer says, 'E4A were much more professional than Bronze, who got something of a cowboy reputation.' In its early years E4A tended to be used more in inner-city areas and 14 Intelligence Company in the country-side, although by the 1980s the units were apparently regarded as largely interchangeable.

Chief Constable Newman used the creation of another undercover squad to try and bypass a long-running source of tension with the Army. The Chief Constable was keen for the police to have a presence in border areas, particularly in south Armagh. He proposed that the Special Patrol Group should send uniformed units into the area. The Army, however, still main-tained that it was too dangerous, and urged that soldiers deployed by helicopter should undertake the patrols instead. But they had other reasons for sticking to this position – as one Army officer puts it, 'They were well-meaning but amateur. They were to a man Protestants, and the place they wanted to go and sort out was [Catholic] south Armagh.'

Eventually, in 1979, Chief Constable Newman set up the Bessbrook Support Unit (BSU), an undercover outfit numbering twenty-eight. Details of the BSU's operations were later published by the *Irish Times*. The unit was commanded by an inspector and had three squads each led by a sergeant. The BSU operated very much on military lines. Members wore camouflage outfits and set up long-term covert observation posts. Several, apparently all ex-members of the British Army, were deployed as an OP team with one of the other squads waiting nearby as a QRF.

As the number of RUC special units grew to match the Army's expanding undercover operation, training in observation and surveillance techniques was given to an increasing number of men. Between 1975 and 1980 the number of Army soldiers available for specialist surveillance duties trebled to about 300. At the same time the RUC developed its own units, adding perhaps another 100 to the total. The result, according to a senior officer who served at Lisburn was that, 'We began to pick up an immense amount of information through visual sightings.'

By mid 1978 an IRA suspect might have been under observation by men or women from one of 14 Company's three detachments, one of the four

SAS troops in Northern Ireland, or the seven Army Close Observation Platoons, the Special Patrol Group's Bronze Section, or one of several squads from E4A. Although each of these units had its place in formal police and Army command structures, their use often depended on a complex market driven by the personalities of various security chiefs. There were dozens of people who could request the use of specialist surveillance units, ranging from an Army brigade commander, to the Commander Land Forces, to a police division commander or a local head of Special Branch. The attitude of these people differed for quite arbitrary and individual reasons: one SB member might be a great believer in 14 Company but another might veto its use because of an unhappy experience on a previous operation.

Although the Army helped train Bronze Section and E4A, during their early years there were few joint operations. The command arrangements were complex. The Special Branch initiated most surveillance operations because it had the most informers – people whose tip-offs were most likely to lead to close observation of a particular individual. Having E4A helped the SB a great deal, but the unit was clearly too small to allow all leads to be followed. So the SB often asked for help from Army units. They were most often used at the discretion of the CLF and his three subordinate brigade commanders and, despite the fact that the Army understood the quality of SB's sources, could not always be spared. The Army had no desire to compromise the activities of its special units since Lieutenant General Creasey, the General Officer Commanding, believed the police were not ready to undertake many of the more 'muscular' aspects of counter-terrorism. The RUC contained very few officers with experience of covert operations, and the familiar fears remained that the organization harboured loyalist extremists.

While some security chiefs insisted there was no problem, others understood that the confused arrangements over the use of surveillance units, while explicable because of the speed with which such squads had proliferated, could not be allowed to continue. Help was on its way from two of the key protagonists. Kenneth Newman was overcoming rivalry and poor co-ordination between the RUC's CID and SB by the creation of Regional Crime and Intelligence Units – a system with obvious potential for involving Army operations as well. At the same time, Brigadier James Glover, the General Staff intelligence officer in London who had proposed improved intelligence-sharing procedures, understood that the Army's interest in maintaining control over its surveillance units would have to be sacrificed in the cause of improved co-ordination. But while these two men struggled to make new systems for undercover operations work, they remained constrained – as security chiefs had been before and have continued to be since – by persistent allegations of collusion between locally recruited members of the security forces and Protestant paramilitaries.

# 5

# A Question of Allegiances

Uncertainty about the ultimate loyalties of many members of the RUC and UDR has produced a rich vein of speculation about their involvement in terrorist groups and the exploitation of these groups by intelligence agencies in Ulster. These allegations are based on an extension of the simple fact that the forces of law and order are drawn largely from a Protestant community which considers itself under siege, to the suspicion on the part of nationalists and some of the Labour left in Britain that the link between the lawkeepers and loyalist terrorists has been exploited by security chiefs to terrorize the republican movement through a policy of assassination.

Some soldiers from Northern Ireland regarded their Regiment as a legitimized form of loyalist 'doomsday force', able to defend the Protestant enclaves if Westminster ever abandoned them. These UDR members were also sometimes members of the largest loyalist paramilitary group, the Ulster Defence Association (UDA). The UDA grew out of the inner-city violence at the outset of the Troubles as an umbrella for loyalist vigilante groups. Even in the late 1970s its membership was estimated to be as high as 10,000. Most, however, were people who were available to defend their estates in the event of trouble but did not belong to the Ulster Freedom Fighters (UFF), the UDA's military wing, outlawed in 1974, which carried out a campaign of sectarian killing.

The idea of Protestants banding together to fight the prospect of rule from Dublin, as they had in 1912 when thousands of armed men had paraded, was a potent one among loyalists. Another branch of the UDA revived the name given to those early loyalist formations, the Ulster Volunteer Force (UVF). Sir Edward Carson, architect of the original UVF, had become a key figure in loyalist legend by organizing the appearance of thousands of armed men on a hillside, demonstrating to Whitehall the dangers of abandoning the Protestants to rule by the Catholic majority of Ireland. Carson's powerplay still influenced people sixty years later: the

British government feared the possibility of a large-scale loyalist insurrection if it pushed them into a closer bond with the Republic of Ireland; and the Protestants themselves longed for the unity and decisiveness of which Carson had been capable but their contemporary leaders were not.

The modern UVF was not, however, the armed wing of a united loyalist movement but a sectarian terrorist group, which by 1972 was believed to have around 1500 members. Its attacks on Catholics in the mid 1960s were an important stimulus first in the development of the Catholic civil rights movement and later for contemporary armed republicanism. The UVF and UDA were riven by deep factional rivalries which undermined their operations against the republican groups. Much of the daily energy of these groups was devoted to fund-raising through racketeering. They did not attack the Army, although there were often street confrontations with it, but relations with the RUC were often tense – particularly in the days following the signing of the Anglo-Irish Agreement in November 1985.

The notion that the UDR and RUC contain men and women whose loyalty is to the principle of Protestant hegemony in Ulster rather than to the rule of law finds currency at many levels within the Army. During the early 1970s soldiers often found that loyalist paramilitaries had been tipped off prior to raids. Lord Carver, the former Chief of General Staff, casts doubts in his memoirs about the loyalties even of some Special Branch men. However, most of the disquiet both within the Army and among Catholics surrounds the locally recruited soldiers of the UDR. The Army's classified training manual for intelligence specialists bound for Ulster in the late 1970s noted with a candour absent from its public pronouncements: 'Units must be aware of the fact that, in some instances, the UDR has been penetrated by extremist loyalist organizations, and this will affect the permissible limit of intelligence dissemination, particularly in relation to Protestant extremist activities'.

At its foundation almost one-fifth of the UDR were Catholics. But the IRA's policy of assassinating Catholic UDR men and the difficulty facing the soldiers in upholding policies like internment which were deeply unpopular in the nationalist community led to the steady erosion of this figure. By the 1980s only about three per cent of UDR members were Catholic, the RUC doing rather better with about one in ten. There is a general consensus in Ulster that the RUC has maintained higher standards of professionalism and has had more success keeping Protestant extremists out of its ranks.

The UDR pays its members considerably less than the RUC (who also give generous overtime rates). Relative poverty is at the root of many of the UDR's problems. While the RUC is considerably oversubscribed – there being more than ten applicants for each vacancy – the UDR is less able to be choosy. UDR members are often unable to afford housing away from the working-class estates where extreme loyalism is entrenched. One senior figure who had served at Stormont referred in private conversation to a particular UDR battalion as being recruited from 'the cesspits of east Belfast'. RUC applicants are also vetted by the SB, and community ties are sufficiently close for one person from Ulster usually to be able to establish whether another has connections with loyalist extremism. In contrast, UDR vetting remained largely in the hands of Intelligence Corps members from other parts of Britain.

Outsiders who have become involved with the police in Northern Ireland are usually deeply impressed by the commitment of its officers. Kenneth Newman has described the RUC as containing the finest police members he has encountered in a long and varied police career. Michael Asher, however, the former paratrooper who served as a constable in the Special Patrol Group in the late 1970s, did detect prejudices against Catholics and the English, the latter being considered outsiders. He sums up the complex motivation of police on the beat: 'Most RUC men were scrupulously honest. They were the bravest men I ever met. But most of them had been reared in the strong loyalist culture which had also bred the paramilitaries like the UDA and the UVF. Sometimes they were required to go against "their own people", but they could never forget where they had come from.'

Interviews with police and soldiers reveal a widespread perception that only a minority of UDR soldiers are actively involved with extreme loyalism, although many sympathize. There is also broad agreement that the figures are still smaller in the RUC. Although many Catholics say they find the theory of a few 'bad apples' in the security forces unconvincing, recognition that the RUC has maintained higher standards of professionalism can be seen in various demands made by the non-violent nationalist parties. Their request that UDR patrols should be accompanied by police officers, to reduce the possibility of threats and other misbehaviour by the troops, is evidence of a measure of trust in the police as well as a concern about the UDR.

As the targets for republican terrorism, but with few opportunities to confront it directly, the rank and file of the police and UDR sometimes vent their feelings on Catholics whom they encounter at roadblocks or in holding cells. Republicans frequently complain that their lives have been threatened or that they have been beaten. Intelligence officers confirm that taunts of the 'we're going to get you' variety do occur, giving them as the reason for the increasingly restricted dissemination of intelligence during the late 1970s and early 1980s. Ordinary police officers and soldiers are told virtually nothing about forthcoming undercover operations because of the risk that they may taunt suspects with this knowledge.

Events like the murder of three members of a Catholic pop group, the Miami Showband, in 1975 implanted deep mistrust of the UDR among nationalists. The killers, members of the UVF, had been dressed as soldiers. Two UVF terrorists killed at the scene were UDR part timers and two of those later convicted for the murders were also UDR soldiers.

It is sometimes claimed that intelligence agencies have exploited loyalist sympathies to eliminate republicans of whom they cannot openly dispose, providing the information, weapons or freedom from arrest for loyalist paramilitaries to kill them. On this question a profound gulf opens between the views of those in the republican community and what those who have been involved in intelligence work say even in private – and even if they are being sufficiently candid to admit to other misdemeanours by the security forces. During the mid 1980s serious allegations of collusion between the intelligence services and loyalist paramilitary groups were made by Fred Holroyd, the former intelligence liaison officer who had worked in the border area during the mid 1970s. Colin Wallace, a former Army information officer who made allegations about 'black propaganda' campaigns directed at politicians against whom the security forces held a grudge (see chapter seven), also said that there were links between the intelligence apparatus and killings by loyalist terrorists.

Some of Holroyd's allegations concern Robert Nairac, the young Grenadier Guards officer who had served as liaison officer for the 3 Brigade Detachment of 14 Intelligence Company, known by the cover name 4 Field Survey Troop. Holroyd says that Nairac told him he was involved in the killing in January 1975 of John Francis Green, a prominent republican, inside the Irish Republic. Holroyd says that Nairac gave him a photograph of the dead man, with fresh blood on the ground around him – evidence that the young Guards officer had been at the scene around the time of the shooting. Holroyd says that 'the evidence suggests' that Nairac was also involved in the Miami Showband killings. A pistol used in this attack was later matched ballistically with one used to murder Green. He believes that the Army and SB 'worked closely' with loyalist terrorists. He says that

4 Field Survey Troop had a stockpile of untraceable non-Army issue weapons which it could hand out for such crimes.

Captain Nairac returned to Northern Ireland in May 1976. He was apparently requested by Julian Ball who, promoted to major, was then serving with 22 SAS. Someone who knew the two men says that Ball wanted Nairac to fill a newly-created post, liaising with the RUC for the SAS squadron committed to south Armagh that year – similar to his previous role for the surveillance unit detachment. In May 1977 he was kidnapped from a pub where he may have been on an information-gathering mission, tortured and shot. He was later awarded the George Cross and lionized by the popular press. Captain Nairac was not a member of the SAS, even if he worked closely with it – his George Cross citation indicating that he was a member of the 3 Brigade staff.

Colin Wallace has also made allegations about connections of this kind. In 1986 he wrote to Peter Archer, a Labour MP, saying: 'During the first six months of 1975 thirty-five Roman Catholics were assassinated in Ulster. The majority of these were killed by members of the security forces or loyalist paramilitary groups such as the UVF, UFF, PAF, UDA etc., working as agents of the security services and supplied with weapons by the security services.'

Albert Baker, a loyalist terrorist sentenced to twenty-five years in jail for involvement in a series of attacks in 1972 and 1973, has claimed that UDA killing squads were given weapons and told their targets by the RUC. His allegations are seen by many nationalists as supporting the claims of Holroyd and Wallace, although they do not specifically refer to the Green and Miami Showband incidents or the killings of early 1975 mentioned above.

Those who believe the Holroyd, Wallace and Baker allegations point out that the three men stood to gain little from making these claims but had much to lose by antagonizing the security apparatus in the ways which they undoubtedly have. Others point out that each of them did in fact have something to gain: Holroyd wanted to erase the stain on his record left by the way he was removed from duties in Northern Ireland and referred for psychiatric observation; Wallace also wanted to clear his name having been dismissed from his civil service job at Lisburn and subsequently sent to prison for killing a Sussex antiques dealer – a crime which he has consistently denied; Baker, facing a life jail sentence, could have been trying to get his case reopened. However, more importantly, in many interviews with people involved with undercover warfare, none has endorsed these allegations of widespread collaboration between intelligence officers and loyalist paramilitaries; on the contrary, they deny such claims vigorously.

One former senior officer says that the security forces did sometimes have foreknowledge of attacks by one IRA faction on another, during the feuds in the organization in the early 1970s, which they made no attempt to stop. Another indicates that the intelligence agencies deliberately stirred up the rivalry between the Officials and Provisionals by planting stories in the press. Although admitting these activities against the IRA, the senior officer adds, 'Never, ever, was there any suggestion of us playing the loyalists off against the Provisional IRA. If you light that fire, it's like putting a match to petrol.'

I have interviewed two people who worked with Robert Nairac. Both deny Fred Holroyd's claims of involvement in assassinations. One, a member of 14 Intelligence Company, says that he remembers the killing of John Francis Green and that both Captain Ball and Lieutenant Nairac were involved in a surveillance operation in a different part of Ulster at the time. He denies that the unit kept non-standard weapons and says, 'There's no way we'd go out and murder people. You have to fight wars within the law.' The idea that the surveillance operators carried non-standard weapons is further undermined by the evidence of the McNutt and Heaney shootings and that of Corporal Harman in 1977 and 1978: in all cases the undercover men were carrying standard issue 9mm pistols.

Those who believe the Holroyd allegations may argue that it is hardly surprising that those who worked with Captain Nairac deny them. Holroyd's most serious allegations involved people who are dead. Cynics in the Army say that, of all the people whom Holroyd could have chosen to link to such crimes, he has courted controversy by choosing an officer regarded by many as a hero, and who is hardly in a position to sue him.

Martin Dillon, a Belfast-born writer, used contacts in loyalist terrorist groups to investigate the Holroyd claims in his book *The Dirty War*. He says he has interviewed people close to the groups which carried out the Green and Miami Showband killings and that there is no substance to the claim that Nairac was involved in either. Both acts were carried out by loyalist gangs, without state support, he contends. Dillon finds Holroyd an unreliable witness and believes 'he was obliged to construct a conspiracy' to rationalize his own removal from SMIU and referral to a psychiatric hospital at the time of his marriage break-up in 1975.

In September 1987 the *Independent* published a lengthy article critical of the more sensational Holroyd and Wallace allegations by its Belfast-based correspondent David McKittrick. Colin Wallace subsequently appealed to the Press Council that the articles had contained inaccuracies about him, a complaint which was upheld. Among many liberal-minded commentators there was both surprise that the newspaper should have devoted so much space to a 'knocking' story, and a feeling that McKittrick may have been fed disinformation by the RUC. Many felt that the subsequent government inquiry into the dismissal of Wallace, which judged that he had been unfairly dismissed and recommended the payment of compensation, vindicated his allegations. But matters were hardly this straightforward.

McKittrick reproducd a page from what was said to be Holroyd's scrapbook. It showed a photograph of Green taken many hours after his death by Irish police photographers, according to the *Independent*, and was accompanied by notes saying that Green was killed by loyalist paramilitaries. Holroyd maintains that the picture shown was not the one given him by Nairac which he says was taken some hours before the Gardai photographers got there.

Albert Baker, the prisoner who claimed the security forces had used him to kill republicans, has not been backed in his allegations by others among the 200 or more loyalist terrorists serving life sentences for murder. None of the ninety or so convicted of murders in early 1975 have endorsed Wallace's claim that the security services put them up to it. It may be argued that they would not do so out of fear of reprisal, either against themselves in jail or against their families. However, it may equally be said that a man facing a minimum thirty-five-year stretch in jail, as the killers of the Miami Showband were, might say anything if he thought such allegations would lessen his sentence. The willingness of loyalist paramilitary groups to embarrass the government has been apparent on other occasions; for example, in 1989 there was a wave of leaks of security forces documents on republican terrorist suspects, prompting an inquiry into possible links between loyalist terrorists and the security forces.

McKittrick did not contest in his article Wallace's own claims that he had been involved in disinformation in his role as Army intelligence officer, smearing politicians in Ulster. But some other journalists believed there was more to it than just that: investigations by the *This Week* television programme and by Barrie Penrose of the *Sunday Times* provided a measure of confirmation for some of Wallace's other claims. Penrose tape-recorded a telephone conversation with Peter Leng, Commander Land Forces in the mid 1970s, which indicated that, as Wallace had claimed and contrary to the position of the government in various inquiries on the matter, the Army had had knowledge of homosexual abuse of youths at the Kincora boys' home. The revelation is a serious one because it shows that successive ministers have misled Parliament about just how much the authorities knew about abuse at this home. The suggestion is that the Security Service (MI5) blocked moves to stop the abuse because it provided them with valuable blackmail material to be used against a member of a loyalist terrorist group who worked there and was one of the alleged abusers.

Neither McKittrick nor the soldiers who speak in Nairac's defence can prove that the Captain was definitely not involved in illegal killings. On the other hand, the government inquiry in 1990 which found that Wallace had been unjustly dismissed, and confirming that Wallace had indeed been involved in disinformation, do not invalidate the main point of McKittrick's article – the questioning of allegations by Holroyd and Wallace that the intelligence services colluded with loyalist hit squads. And such allegations have not been confirmed by the government or substantiated by other journalists.

Much of what the two men have said is undoubtedly true: there was a deep rivalry between SIS and MI5 of a kind described by Holroyd in his book and articles, and politicians were smeared, as Wallace claims. The fact that many of their allegations are rooted in fact has given them a wider credibility. There is a community of journalists and people active in politics which believes all of their allegations are true. Another group believes the two men have failed to prove their most disturbing suggestions: that the security forces colluded with loyalist death squads to dispose of dozens of republicans and (in Holroyd's case) that serving British soldiers were directly involved in a number of killings.

The schism between the believers and those who are sceptical has become acrimonious – journalists have labelled one another as gullible or as instruments of state disinformation. My own research has not produced any evidence to support the claim that the security forces colluded with loyalist death squads in any planned or deliberate way. Soldiers who served with Captain Nairac have, on the contrary, denied Holroyd's allegations. In the absence of conclusive evidence one can say only that the most serious charges levelled by Wallace and Holroyd remain unproven.

Republican activists and some journalists also allege a link between the intelligence services and the killing of several people connected with the Irish Republican Socialist Party and its military wing the INLA. In June 1980 Miriam Daly, a senior IRSP figure, was shot dead in her home in

Belfast. The killing was reported as the action of an unspecified loyalist group. In October another senior IRSP figure, Noel Lyttle, and an important INLA commander, Ronnie Bunting, were also killed. They too, it was assumed, had been killed by an unspecified loyalist group. Robert McConnel, a UDA man later convicted for his part in the killing of a moderate nationalist politician soon after the murder of Daly, alleged later that he had been in contact with Army intelligence, who had asked him for information on leading IRSP figures.

Some people have connected the killings to the death of Airey Neave, arguing that the intelligence services killed them in revenge. On 30 March 1979 Airey Neave, the senior Conservative who had orchestrated Mrs Thatcher's campaign for the Party leadership, was killed by a car bomb outside the Houses of Parliament, and the INLA had claimed responsibility for the blast. Neave had enjoyed close contacts with the intelligence establishment and had called for a stepping-up of SAS operations in Northern Ireland.

The writer Martin Dillon has also investigated the INLA killings. He says claims that they were carried out by the SAS are 'nonsense' and, through his own paramilitary contacts, concludes that they were the work of a UDA hit team. However, he suggests that the actions of the killers, deep in republican territory, may indicate that local UDR members had colluded in the murders.

Like many other rumours surrounding the intelligence services in Ulster the 'Neave revenge' thesis cannot be comprehensively disproved, but it must be said that the evidence to support it is feeble and circumstantial. Loyalists had also killed an INLA man in Armagh in 1978, before Neave's assassination; that they did so afterwards as well proves nothing.

Any operation which appears to be the work of loyalists, but which shows a level of sophistication higher than simply shooting the nearest available Catholic, tends to attract the suspicion of republicans. The killing of John Francis Green in 1975 was an example. The more interesting, and perhaps more plausible, charge against the intelligence specialists is not that they have run loyalist groups but that in cases where they have learned of an imminent loyalist attack against a republican target, they have made only half-hearted attempts to stop it. Allegations of this kind have been made to me about the attempt in 1984 on the life of Sinn Fein leader Gerry Adams. He was seriously injured as he was being driven away from a court house. Republicans said the loyalists had been put up to the attack; Army and police officers retorted that Adams would have found it rather hard to thank the soldiers who intercepted the attackers for saving his life. The assassination attempt will be examined more closely in chapter eighteen. Despite the Adams incident, it must be noted that if ever anybody in the intelligence world did commission loyalist terrorists to kill senior IRA figures, they failed to do so during the late 1970s and early 1980s.

During 1989 many official documents identifying republican suspects came to light. These were said to have been used to target people for assassination and were later leaked to journalists by loyalist paramilitary groups. The loyalists did prove more effective in targeting leading republicans during the late 1980s, although many put this down to them learning the IRA's lesson and putting more preparation into their attacks. Once again, however, there is a great difference between obtaining such documents and proving that the intelligence services, or elements within them, were conspiring with the loyalists.

After the high tide of loyalist sectarian murder in the mid 1970s the rate of killings dropped considerably. During the late 1970s and 1980s the rate of killing by loyalists of active republicans was low compared to the number killed by the IRA itself for informing. Two active IRA and two INLA men were killed during 1977 to 1987 by loyalists, compared to more than twenty-four Catholics killed by the IRA itself as informers. Of course the loyalists killed many other Catholics who were not in the IRA, including people involved in republican politics during this period, but their attacks were, by and large, poorly targeted. This is not what one would have expected if intelligence agencies, frustrated by their inability to put senior IRA members behind bars, were behind the killings.

# 6

## Lethal Confusion

At about 9 p.m. on 20 June 1978 four men arrived at the Shamrock club in the republican Ardoyne area of west Belfast. They found the owner of a car and asked him to hand over the keys. Afraid, he allowed the men, IRA members of the 3rd Battalion of the Belfast Brigade, to take his car, a blue Mazda.

The IRA men – William Mailey, thirty-one, believed to be the leader of the Active Service Unit; Denis Brown, twenty-eight; James Mulvenna, twenty-eight, and another who was at the wheel of the car – went to collect several explosive incendiary bombs.

Each bomb consisted of a plastic container full of petrol, an explosive charge and a timing device. When the explosive detonated it caused a fireball. Three months before an explosive incendiary device had incinerated twelve people at the La Mon House hotel in County Down. The incident caused widespread revulsion, drawing an admission from the Provisionals that the nine minutes of warning given had been 'totally inadequate' and calls from loyalist leaders for tougher measures against the IRA.

On that night in June the bombers had a different objective. As they drove north into the strongly loyalist area of Ballysillan they came in sight of their target, a Post Office depot. A little after midnight they parked the car in Wheatfield Drive and Mailey, Brown and Mulvenna began taking the bombs from it. None of the three was carrying a gun. The IRA's aim was to destroy the depot and vehicles parked behind it.

But the security forces had been tipped off. A joint SAS and RUC force, including members of the SPG Bronze Section and Special Branch, was lying in wait. As the men walked towards their target they were intercepted by the soldiers. The Army said later that warnings had been shouted. The soldiers opened fire, killing the three IRA men.

They knew from their surveillance that there was a fourth member of the bombing team. SAS men found a man standing in the playing field next to the depot and shot him. They had killed William Hanna, a twenty-eight-year-old local Protestant who was walking home from the pub with a friend. Hanna's companion hid beneath a hedge. The fourth IRA man fled across the nearby housing estate, banging on doors, pleading for help. He had chosen the wrong part of Belfast's tribal patchwork to look for mercy, although he managed to escape on foot. Another bystander was injured after shots were fired into a car at a roadblock near the scene. Five SAS soldiers and one policeman had fired a total of 111 shots.

Experience from previous incidents involving undercover forces had left security chiefs with the belief that they had to get their version of events to the media before the IRA did. But following the incident the Army press office at Lisburn distributed versions of what had happened which some people at headquarters knew to be inaccurate, suggesting deliberate deception rather than mistakes made in haste.

Newspapers were told that the IRA had opened fire first and that Hanna had been killed in a 'crossfire'. Hours later it was admitted that no guns had been found. Two days later a Belfast newspaper carried a police claim that the fourth IRA man had been armed and it was he who had opened fire. When the SAS men came to account for their actions at an inquest two years later, no evidence was offered that the fourth man had opened fire. Instead the soldiers said they had seen 'flashes' and heard what they believed to be gunshots.

While inaccurate information on whether the terrorists were armed might have been released accidentally, other elements of the version given to the press were deliberately misleading according to an Army officer then serving at Lisburn who was fully briefed on the operation. Journalists were told that the soldiers who took part were not SAS but one of the 'SAS-type units', which had been set up the previous summer. The *Belfast Telegraph* reported, 'Security chiefs – pleased with the success of the SAS-type stake-out at the depot – are considering stepping up "undercover" operations in Belfast and Londonderry.' The officer confirms that the claim that an 'SAS-type unit' or Close Observation Platoon, as they are properly known, was used was untrue and designed to 'deter' the IRA.

Press officers also claimed that security at the depot had been stepped up following a statement in *An Phoblacht/Republican News*, the Sinn Fein paper, that the IRA was going to target communications centres. In fact the SAS had been there as a result of information from an informer. Admitting to foreknowledge of an IRA operation can cause the Army problems, since it could prompt questions about whether it was necessary to use force at all or whether other measures could have been used to protect life and property.

Some Army officers told the press that William Hanna was a member of a loyalist paramilitary gang. Whether or not this was true should have had no bearing on the case; and it appears that this was an attempt to deflect any sympathy which might have attached to the accidental killing of a passer-by.

The Provisionals issued a statement saying that the men had been captured but were 'summarily shot in an orgy of British Army and RUC concentrated fire'. The IRA, apparently in reference to the stated desire of Army commanders to frighten it through increased undercover activities, added, 'Death is no stranger or deterrent to the volunteers of the Irish Republican Army.' An estimated 2000 people joined the funeral procession for the three bombers. The mainly Catholic Social Democratic and Labour Party (SDLP) said the killings were part of a 'shooting-without-question' policy by the Army and asked for an inquiry into the incident – a request which was turned down by Roy Mason, the then Northern Ireland Secretary.

At HQNI, Lisburn, there was jubilation following the shooting. It was felt a great success had been scored against the Provisionals. The view at RUC headquarters, Knock, was different. Jack Hermon, Deputy Chief Constable, is said to have told Major General Trant forcefully at one of their regular meetings that he did not want shoot-outs on the streets of Belfast. Senior officers at Knock appear to have succeeded in checking the Army's desire for more undercover operations of the Ballysillan kind in Belfast. It was to be ten years before another person died in an SAS operation in Belfast, and that was a passer-by who was not a member of a paramilitary gang.

Despite the desire at Lisburn to step up covert SAS operations and the increase in intelligence information available, it remained difficult for intelligence specialists to gain reliable foreknowledge of a terrorist attack. Most informer or 'tout' intelligence was extremely vague. A certain person was going to be killed, for example, but the tout didn't know where or when. As a result many operations by the SAS, COPs and 14 Company produced no information, no arrests and no dead terrorists.

Unsuccessful operations of this kind led to Army impatience with informers and the Intelligence Corps briefers or 'green slime' as they are known in special forces slang – a reference to the Int Corps' bright green beret – who liaise with them. 'Soldier I', an SAS sergeant who subsequently wrote his memoirs, remembered an operation which produced no results:

'Bastard, I thought, all this pissing about for nothing! The sharp acid of frustration started to well up and corrode my insides. My skull seemed to grow tighter and press in on my brain. The fucking tout had got it wrong. How much was the green slime paying him anyway?'

By late 1978 it had become clear that the use of the SAS carried political risks. Killing the wrong person, particularly if they are unarmed or not members of a paramilitary group, can carry a heavy political penalty. It confirms a belief among many Catholics that the SAS are a force of state executioners. The death of William Hanna marked the beginning of a string of mishaps for the SAS.

The month after Ballysillan a group of four SAS men travelled to Dunloy in County Antrim. The village is set in close, rolling country. Its Catholic population reside in a predominantly Protestant area. Outside the village, on the side of a hill overlooking the road from Ballymena to Ballymoney is a small, disused graveyard. It is connected to a small road which runs up the hill by a track with hedges on both sides.

Quite close to where the path enters the graveyard and fairly central to the small, square, burial area which is surrounded by a hedge is a fallen headstone. It was underneath this slab that John Boyle, the sixteen-year-old son of a local farmer, made what he must have thought an exciting discovery. Secreted beneath the slab was an Armalite rifle, a pistol and other terrorist paraphernalia. John rushed home to his father, Con Boyle, who immediately phoned the police.

A train of events had begun which were to claim a life and see SAS men brought to trial. Senior police and Army officers decided that the SAS should stake out the graveyard, in case terrorists returned to the cache.

Four SAS men were sent to cover the graveyard. They had split into two groups of two, each in what the Army calls an 'Aggressive OP'. The mission in such an observation post is to wait and see what happens but to open fire if the circumstances justify it. Corporal Alan Bohan and Trooper Ron Temperley occupied the OP closest to the gravestone.

Early the next morning, 11 July 1978, Con and his two sons, John and Harry, set out to work the fields. A couple of hours later John Boyle left his father and brother working in the fields and curiosity took him back to the graveyard.

At about 10 a.m. Con Boyle heard shots from the graveyard. He went across, joined by his son Harry. As they approached two soldiers with blackened faces and camouflage clothing appeared and threw them to the ground. Con remembers one of the soldiers saying, 'The other bastard's lying dead.' Initially the soldiers were in high spirits, but their mood 'soon changed.

John Boyle the teenager who'd found the cache, had been shot, felled by SAS bullets. A few minutes too late a detective from Ballymoney police station rang the farmhouse, telling Mrs Boyle that under no circumstances should anyone return to the graveyard. Shortly after the soldiers realized what had happened they were taken away by helicopter. Other troops came to secure the area.

The incident grew into a public relations disaster for the Army. Matters were compounded by the Lisburn press office's release of inaccurate statements about what had happened in an attempt to make the soldiers' actions seem justifiable.

At first journalists were told that an Army patrol had stopped three terrorists. In fact the Boyles had no connection with any paramilitary group and it would be difficult to imagine how any Catholics finding an IRA arms cache could have behaved more responsibly. It was then suggested that John Boyle had pointed a loaded rifle at the soldiers. The Army press statement said, 'The Armalite was subsequently found with its magazine fitted and a round in the breech ready to fire.' In fact there were no bullets in the gun. There were claims that the soldiers had shouted a warning, but later admissions that it was impractical to do so.

The RUC was furious with the Army, which it considered to have behaved in an irresponsible manner, and RUC press officers hinted to journalists that the Army's initial version of events was not true. The police backed a move to put the SAS men on trial for murder. So began a remarkable prosecution – the only one in Ulster so far to have involved soldiers from the SAS.

Corporal Bohan and Trooper Temperley, the men who had fired the shots, found themselves standing in the dock in front of Lord Lowry, Ulster's Chief Justice. The Army was anxious to protect secrets of the SAS operation. Its attempts to prevent the court learning the soldiers' identities verged on the farcical. At first it would provide only the soldiers' initials. Then, on their first court appearance, the Army put five other men into the box with them with the idea of confusing people. The judge, finding the idea of seven men standing in the dock throughout the case to be unacceptable, insisted that only the two accused should stay there.

The twenty-eight-year-old Corporal answered for both men's actions. He said the RUC had told them the weapons had been found by a ten-year-old boy. The soldiers had been sent there to apprehend whoever attempted to recover the weapons but the suspected terrorist had turned and pointed the weapon directly at them, he added.

There was a great deal of discussion during the case about whether the three bullets which had killed John Boyle had been fired from behind, as he stooped to pick up the weapon, or whether the fatal shot had entered the front of his head. If it could be proven that they had come from behind, the SAS Corporal's version about Boyle turning to face him would have been shown to be untrue. In the end, Lord Lowry accepted evidence that the bullet had entered the front of John Boyle's head, meaning that he had indeed been looking towards the soldiers when the shot was fired.

But in many other respects the judge cast doubt on the soldier's statements. Corporal Bohan's suggestion that the gun had been pointed at him was 'self-justificatory and, in the context of the Boyle family's reputation, untrue'. Although the Corporal said the plan was to capture the terrorist he was vague and unsatisfactory when questioned as to the details of the plan.

Lord Lowry pointed out that if the soldiers had inspected the weapon they would have seen that, unloaded, it could pose no threat to them. If Corporal Bohan had thought the deceased was a terrorist, 'One wonders why he let him get the rifle into his hands, if the rifle might have been loaded.'

The judge said Corporal Bohan was 'an untrustworthy witness, eager to make unmeritorious points'. He said in his summing-up, 'Nothing would have been easier with better planning than to capture the deceased alive, always assuming that to be the primary object.' But the judge, although he said quite plainly that Corporal Bohan had told lies, could not find them guilty of murder. The prosecution was not able to prove beyond reasonable doubt that the soldiers had gone there with the intention of killing whoever came into the field.

The case provided an enormous opportunity for Sinn Fein because it appeared to confirm the view of many Irish people that the SAS were trigger-happy thugs who flouted the law which stipulated that soldiers could use only such force as was reasonable and necessary to prevent a crime. And it wasn't just committed Provisionals who came away with this impression. The attitude of John Boyle's father, reflecting on the incident years later in an interview with the *Belfast Telegraph*, is revealing. He said he did not feel bitterness towards the SAS men because: 'They were doing their job, which was to kill whoever entered the graveyard. That is what the SAS are employed to do.'

The acquittal of Corporal Bohan and Trooper Temperley, like the case of the SAS men released after crossing the border into the Irish Republic, had a deeply harmful effect on the perception of the Regiment among a broad band of political opinion in Northern Ireland, not just committed republicans. Although the Army had grudgingly accepted that the men should stand trial in the first place, the cases convinced many in the legal establishment that it would be very hard ever to get a conviction against the undercover soldiers since vital facts could be withheld from the court. One barrister, commenting on the judge's summing-up in the Boyle case, told me: 'The language he used about Bohan was so derogatory that in any case not involving the Army, I would have thought it virtually impossible not to have had a conviction in that court.'

Bohan and Temperley returned to regimental duty after the trial. Colleagues say the men were changed by the experience and felt deep regret at the teenager's death. The Army did not regard the Boyle incident as a blemish on the SAS mens' records. In fact, I was able to establish while researching this book that in 1990 – thirteen years after the death of John Boyle – both Bohan and Temperley were still serving in frontline squadrons of 22 SAS.

In September 1978 the mistakes continued when the SAS shot dead James Taylor, a Protestant. He had entered a field near Lough Neagh carrying a shotgun, while looking for game. He had no connection with any paramilitary group.

There was a further confrontation between SAS soldiers and a member of the IRA on 24 November 1978. Patrick Duffy, a fifty-year-old auxiliary in the IRA had gone into an unoccupied house in Maureen Avenue, Londonderry. It is likely that Duffy was a member of the Derry Brigade quartermaster's staff. A variety of weapons, including several rifles and bomb-making equipment, had been placed in a wardrobe in a bedroom on the first floor of the house.

An Army surveillance operation had been mounted to keep the cache under observation. While rural operations allowed the soldiers to take cover in a nearby hedgerow or ditch, the built-up nature of the area had posed particular problems for the SAS men, who had gone into position in the house nearly two days before Duffy appeared. Two soldiers were in another bedroom on the first floor of the same house, another was hiding in the attic. The soldiers entered the house in civilian clothes. Once inside they opened holdalls containing camouflage uniforms and a variety of weapons.

One had an Armalite, another a 9mm Sterling sub-machine-gun and the third an American-made Ingram 9mm machine-pistol. All three had attached torches to their weapons, a technique used to assist aiming in darkness or low light. A back-up team waited in a nearby street in a red van.

At about 9.20 p.m. on 24 November Patrick Duffy pulled up outside the house. His daughter and her baby waited in the car as Duffy climbed the stairs. He approached the wardrobe. Soldier B says he shouted a warning and began to move forward from the room at the rear of the house to the front room where Duffy was standing. Soldier B said that Duffy 'spun round to face me bringing his right hand up'. The two SAS men opened fire with their machine-guns. Duffy was hit by at least a dozen bullets and fell mortally wounded. Duffy's daughter heard the shots, moments later the red van raced up to the house and she watched as the back-up team, dressed in a mixture of civilian and military clothing, rushed into the house. She only found out later that her father had been shot.

Although the building contained an impressive horde of weapons, Duffy himself had not been armed as he climbed the stairs. Edward Daly, the Roman Catholic Bishop of Derry, commented: 'The shooting dead of a person merely because that person enters a house or place where illegally held arms or explosives are stored is quite unjustifiable.'

As more facts emerged about the incident, it became apparent that, as in many other cases involving special forces, the SAS men had intelligence which they did not share with the later inquest court. Their commander stated that he had ordered his men to enter the premises, search it and keep any arms found under observation. But statements by the soldiers indicated that the weapons had been placed in the wardrobe nearly twenty-four hours *after* they had taken up position in the house. No explanation was given as to why they had not attempted to apprehend the men who placed the guns there, nor why they had not left after finding no weapons there in the first place. Clearly the men were sufficiently confident of their intelligence to know that it was worth staying in the house.

Forensic evidence cast doubt on the soldiers' claim to have shot Duffy because he spun round. Duffy's autopsy report indicated that he had been shot from a few feet away and that the bullets had entered his body 'from his left and or behind and to his left'. This was consistent with him having been shot as he stood facing the wardrobe, with his left side and back towards the soldiers, rather than having turned towards them.

This incident did nothing to dispel the impression that the SAS were not subject to the normal legal restraint of using minimum force, and tended instead to shoot first and ask questions later. SAS soldiers had killed three uninvolved bystanders in six months. As 1978 drew to a close the practice of using intelligence to set up lethal confrontations between special forces units and suspected republican terrorists came under increasingly critical scrutiny, particularly at RUC headquarters, Knock. Some of the personalities in the security forces hierarchy who had encouraged the use of the SAS in such operations had little time left to serve in Ulster. Given both the public relations penalties and the legal repercussions of an incident like the Dunloy shooting of John Boyle, it was time for a rethink.

# Undercover Soldiers and the Law

The conflict in Northern Ireland was complicated by the uneasy accommodation between two cultures, that of the soldiers on the ground, and that of the senior officers and politicians, concerned to maintain the appearance of a rule of law. A soldier is trained to think in terms of doing battle with an enemy and attempting to gain victory by eliminating as many of his foes as possible. During the conflicts that preceded independence in some of Britain's colonies, soldiers had often been able to dispatch 'restless natives' with few questions asked. However, on the streets of Northern Ireland they found themselves constrained by the principle of the minimum use of force which had evolved during centuries of mediation between the police and courts.

The belief that the problem could be solved by shooting IRA ringleaders is a common one in the Army. 'We've all basically got the same idea of how we could end this, but world opinion wouldn't stand for it', as a sergeant serving in Ulster puts it.

For all the bar-room bravado it is apparent that in recent years the average soldier has had little opportunity to do battle with the Provisionals. The information most likely to lead to a confrontation is jealously guarded by the secret élites of the RUC and Army. For the ordinary member of the 'Green Army', rushing across the streets of Northern Ireland, the everyday threat is from bricks, spit and abuse. Training emphasizes the need on the part of troops on patrol for tolerance, because over-reaction to taunts can produce incidents which play into the hands of the IRA, feeding the nationalists' stereotype of the British Army as a brutal occupying force.

The soldiers and police in Ulster are bound by the same rules on the use of force as any other citizen. In 1975 a soldier shot dead Patrick McElhone, a farmer with no paramilitary connections, when he tried to run away. In acquitting the soldier, the judge said he had reasonably believed McElhone to be a terrorist. He also said Ulster counted as a 'war or semi-war situation'. The House of Lords upheld the judgement saying that the soldier had been right to open fire if he thought the person was a terrorist because he might 'sooner or later' have become involved in an act of violence.

The McElhone judgement was a landmark, providing a definition of what was reasonable force that caused alarm among many lawyers, civil rights activists and ordinary citizens. It effectively allowed people to be shot on sight as long as the soldier concerned could argue later that he or she had thought his or her target was a terrorist.

In practice the Northern Ireland Director of Public Prosecutions, the person responsible for deciding whether to press charges against people, including soldiers, involved in such incidents, found this concept to be too broad. The SAS men who shot John Boyle were charged with murder despite the McElhone judgement. Several years later RUC men were put in the dock after the killings which prompted John Stalker's 'shoot to kill' inquiry. The law places the responsibility on the soldier who pulls the trigger, rather than the officers who have gathered the intelligence and ordered him there.

The apparent conflict between the law of minimum force and the behaviour of some soldiers and police officers is at the root of allegations of a 'shoot to kill' policy in Northern Ireland. There are three broad dimensions to the question of whether a 'shoot to kill' policy exists:

- Why are the security forces at the incident in the first place? If it is as a result of foreknowledge of a terrorist attack there may be ways to stop it other than through armed confrontation.
- Once a confrontation between soldiers or police and terrorists begins, is it necessary for firearms to be used? This includes the important matter of whether the terrorists are armed and whether they are warned that force is about to be used.
- Last, once the soldiers or police have decided to open fire, how are the bullets aimed? Are they told to fire at a person's vital organs and to keep firing until the target is out of action, usually permanently, or are there other ways to use a weapon?

On this last point, that of shooting to kill in the most literal sense, there has never been any real question that both police and Army firearms training emphasizes the need to use a weapon in just this way, once the firer finds himself or herself in great danger. So it is on the other two elements of the 'shoot to kill' controversy that inquiries have normally centred.

The Army manual *Counter-Revolutionary Operations* says: 'A person, whether soldier or civilian, may lawfully use such force as is reasonable in the circumstances in the prevention of crime and in making lawful arrests.' This echoes the civil law as embodied in the Criminal Law Act (Northern Ireland) 1967.

From 1972 the Army issued guidance to its soldiers as to what reasonable force actually was, in the form of a Yellow Card. These were given to every soldier, some being taped to rifle butts. The Card, amended in 1980, stressed that, 'Firearms must only be used as a last resort.' It told soldiers that they must challenge somebody unless an engagement had already begun or if doing so 'would increase the risk of death or grave injury to you or any other person'. Opening fire is correct only if the person 'is committing or about to commit an act likely to endanger life and there is no other way to prevent the danger.'

While senior officers are always at pains to stress the Army's adherence to the law, attitudes to the Yellow Card and the principles of minimum force which it embodies tend to vary lower down the chain of command. According to one officer, 'The Yellow Card rules are typical of the sort of things which are repeated so often in the Army that they become meaningless.'

Soldiers who have been involved in operations in Ulster often consider the rules to be unrealistic. In particular, many believe that the idea of first challenging armed terrorists is a lawyer's nicety which can be applied in the real world only at grave risk to themselves. They sometimes cite the case of Lance-Corporal David Jones as evidence of this.

Late one night in March 1978 Lance-Corporal Jones and another soldier were in an OP in the Glenshane Pass area of County Londonderry. The troops saw two armed men wearing camouflage clothing appear. The men apparently had a flash with the word 'Ireland' sewn on to their combat jackets. Lance-Corporal Jones stood up and challenged them, believing they could be members of one of the British Army's UDR units. But they were Provisional gunmen and they opened fire. Jones, though mortally wounded, returned the fire, injuring one of the terrorists, Francis Hughes. The other man escaped. Hughes went to prison where he became one of the H-Block hunger strikers.

Both Army and RUC press officers mention this incident when seeking to explain security forces behaviour on other occasions where warnings may not have been given. Three *Sunday Times* journalists, in their book *Ambush*, claim that Lance-Corporal Jones was a member of the SAS and that the incident had a 'lasting psychological impact on the Regiment'. The authors argue that Lance-Corporal Jones' fate went some way to explaining the actions of SAS men in Gibraltar ten years later.

It is worth remembering, however, that Lance-Corporal Jones appears to have issued the challenge not because he had a benign view of how terrorists would behave but because, as a professional soldier, he did not want to open fire on what he thought might be friendly forces. Whether or not the Lance-Corporal's death had a profound impact on the SAS, Jones was not a member of this organization. His name does not appear on the plaque on the clocktower at Hereford where the names of other members of 22 SAS who have fallen are inscribed. Lance-Corporal Jones was listed in his death notice in *Pegasus*, the journal of the Airborne Forces, as belonging to '3 PARA'. It is likely that he was a member of the Close Observation Platoon of the 3rd Battalion, the Parachute Regiment, which was serving in Ulster at the time.

Many soldiers who have been involved in undercover stake-outs believe it is simply not practical to issue challenges. One describes the mood on operations: 'You have to remember the fear. If someone has been waiting all night in an ambush they are going to be shitting themselves. If someone appears in the shadows who looks like they are carrying a gun they are not going to ask a lot of questions, they are going to let them have it.'

Officers who were interviewed for this book, particularly those who had been involved in ambush-type operations, consider there to be an unspoken bargain. 'I always told my soldiers that nothing would happen to them so long as they could justify their actions by the Yellow Card,' says one. The implication is that the justification for opening fire can be pieced together afterwards.

An SAS officer argues that the soldier fighting terrorism must be given extra leeway compared to the ordinary citizen: 'You are putting a hell of a lot of responsibility on young men to make split-second decisions. The armed forces have got to have a "fudge factor". Do you penalize Soldier A who may have made a mistake? If you start prosecuting soldiers in dubious situations, you will start causing problems for yourself.'

The difficulties he envisages are that soldiers will not be prepared to take the same risks. Certainly there have been occasions where both police officers and soldiers in Northern Ireland have objected to operations on the grounds of the risks involved. The 'bargain' between soldiers and the British Army hierarchy, that it will resist prosecution, cannot always be maintained. In some cases, usually those where the greatest errors have been made like the Boyle incident, or where there is great political sensitivity, undercover soldiers may find themselves in the dock.

A fear of prosecution and dislike of red tape made Northern Ireland an unpopular place with some SAS men. 'Soldier I', the SAS sergeant who published his memoirs, wrote: 'With its sinister streets and alienated population, Belfast was no place for highly trained special forces operators. This was a job for armed police – switched-on operators who knew the law and could pick their way through the minefield of regulations.'

Many SAS soldiers sum up their attitude to the use of lethal force in situations like Ulster saying: 'Big boys' games, big boys' rules.' In other words, any IRA man caught with a rifle or bomb can expect to be shot, whatever the Yellow Card may say. The saying is, according to a member of the Regiment, their 'justification for killing people'.

Although the progressive amendment of laws in Northern Ireland has not gone far enough for many special forces soldiers, it has aroused criticism in liberal quarters. Even before the Troubles, there was a separate legal tradition in Ulster. Coroners' Courts had lost the ability to deliver a verdict of unlawful killing at inquests some ten years before troops went on to the streets of Northern Ireland in 1969. Many other changes were introduced once the Troubles had started. Internment without trial was permitted for a limited period from August 1971. Then, in 1973, juries were dispensed with in terrorist trials, leaving only the judge in what became known as Diplock courts, a step taken largely because of fears of intimidation. Juries are now in use only at inquests and in defamation proceedings.

Some terrorist-related legal measures were adopted throughout the United Kingdom. The traditional right of a suspect to be charged or released within forty-eight hours was changed under the Prevention of Terrorism Act (first passed in 1974) to allow detectives three or seven days to prepare a case against alleged terrorists. However, most changes were confined to Northern Ireland itself.

The concepts of the 'bargain' and 'fudge factor' are the result of realism about the courts, as well as loyalty between members of the special forces. Officers know it is highly unlikely that the juryless trial courts in Northern Ireland will convict a soldier for murder, since they are bound to make allowances for the person who has killed in the line of duty. The Army argues that in any case it is highly undesirable to allow prosecutions to go ahead: they are unlikely to result in convictions; they damage the soldier's morale in the process; and they fail to satisfy nationalists who believe the legal proceedings have been a whitewash.

Many officers are cynical about the legal process, often as a result of seeing men and women whom they believe to be guilty of terrorist crimes walk free or receive light sentences. These officers regard many of the lawyers representing suspects or the families of people shot dead by the Army as unofficial agents of the IRA. They suggest, for example, that a lawyer may agree to pass a message from a terrorist to his commander, or might use cross-examination of a security forces witness in an attempt to probe whether an operation had resulted from a leak within the IRA. Although specific allegations have been made to me, they remain uncorroborated and concern no more than a small proportion of those undertaking such legal work. Army sensitivities about the courts increased with the trend towards more covert operations. One senior officer who served at Lisburn in the late 1970s remarks, 'If you go into undercover warfare, you know that you will never be able fully to explain that side of life.'

This created pressure for changes in the law designed to protect undercover soldiers, their informers and the technical means used to gather information. General Frank Kitson, commander of the Army's 39 Brigade in Belfast early in the Troubles and one of its theorists of counter-terrorist operations, argues: 'Everything done by a government and its agents in combatting insurgency must be legal. But this does not mean that the government must work within exactly the same set of laws during an insurgency which existed beforehand.' Apparently following Kitson's advice, the Army went to some lengths during the Boyle case to prevent the court learning the identity of the SAS men.

SAS shootings, like others, were followed by inquests, so the government took measures to change inquest procedures. In 1980 an amended set of rules for coroners in Northern Ireland was introduced: inquests in Ulster could no longer return an open verdict where coroners believed that someone other than the deceased person was responsible for his or her death, but instead were directed simply to issue 'findings' saying when, where and how the person had died. Lord Hailsham, then Lord Chancellor, had described the open verdict in Northern Ireland as a 'potent source of difficulty'.

With the introduction of 'findings' rather than verdicts any decision to prosecute members of the security forces would rest with the Director of Public Prosecutions – and would be based on a police investigation. The possibility of an independent-minded coroner influencing such a decision was removed.

The 1980 change was part of a general review of procedures

recommended for England and Wales in the Broderick Report. However, it was put into effect only in Ulster: inquests in England and Wales always had been and can still return open verdicts and verdicts of unlawful killing.

The new rules also removed from coroners in Northern Ireland the obligation which still applies to their colleagues in England or Wales to call everybody considered 'expedient' to the death. The 1980 rules meant that soldiers who had carried out a fatal shooting could no longer be compelled to attend. And, unlike the rest of the United Kingdom, coroners' juries in Northern Ireland are picked by the police.

The effect of these rules was that the Army and RUC were able to submit their version of events with the expectation that there would be little scrutiny by the jury, particularly of those who had carried out the operation. After the confusion following the shooting of Peter Cleary in 1976 (see chapter one), about how the SAS should be dealt with after such an incident, Lisburn put into place extensive machinery to protect its people.

Officers of the Army Legal Service were specially trained in the law of minimum force and it became routine for them to meet soldiers before interview by the CID, which has the responsibility for following up fatal incidents, and to remain with the soldiers throughout their interviews.

Soldiers' statements given to courts were therefore prepared in consultation with Army legal officers on a routine basis. The need to satisfy the court that the amount of force used had been reasonable and necessary, resulted during the 1980s in statements which sounded remarkably similar from one incident to another, despite the obvious confusion that surrounded some of the deaths.

At the inquest into the 1978 Ballysillan Post Office depot shooting, held two years after the event, the soldiers had to justify the killing of William Hanna, the local resident who was killed on his way home from the pub. One of the two SAS men who had approached Hanna told the inquest, 'Suddenly he moved in a twisting motion and we thought he was going for a gun so we both opened fire.'

Patrick Duffy, the unarmed IRA man killed in Londonderry in November 1978, had appeared to reach for a weapon, according to the deposition of Soldier B at an inquest in 1980. Duffy had 'spun round' and brought his right hand up, the soldier claimed.

At the inquest into the shooting of three unarmed IRA members in Gibraltar in 1988 the SAS soldiers who carried out the shooting, who gave their evidence in person rather than in the written form which has become the norm in Ulster inquest courts, also referred to turning and reaching movements, assumed to be attempts to grab either guns or a remote control device for a bomb. Soldier A said Danny McCann moved his right arm 'aggressively across the front of his body'. Soldier C related that Sean Savage, another of the terrorists, 'spun round very fast', and 'went down with his right arm to his jacket pocket'. Hanna, Duffy, McCann and Savage all seem to have had the urge to reach for weapons which they were not carrying.

Attempts to keep the whole truth from courts were often motivated by a desire to protect prized informers. But there was another, more basic factor at work. Senior officers and politicians were aware of the importance of maintaining an appearance of the rule of law. Some believed that the best way to do this was to soothe nationalist unease after an incident by allowing inquests or outside police inquiries to proceed but to limit the damage which could be done by restricting the information given to outsiders attempting to scrutinize sensitive operations. But the principle of maintaining an appearance of legality, so important in undermining support for terrorism, is not apparent to many soldiers.

One NCO who served in intelligence in Ulster says, 'I do not object to capital punishment or this policy of shooting without warning at armed terrorists, I just wish the government had the balls to admit it.' He reveals an attitude to shooting an armed terrorist which would never be endorsed publicly by the Army. Again, the 'policy' he alludes to is that of 'big boys' games, big boys' rules', not a code of conduct publicly recognized by the government. The comments of an intelligence officer who said he provided information for this book partly because, 'I can't see why we can't admit that we are shooting these terrorists,' underline the point.

Both the officer and NCO were referring to ambushes mounted by special forces, usually on the basis of foreknowledge supplied by the intelligence services and involving a small, highly trained cadre of soldiers. They – and soldiers generally – would accept that walking up to a known IRA member in the street and gunning him or her down in cold blood is unacceptable.

Senior Army officers understand the culture of the soldier who wants to open fire immediately if he sees a suspected terrorist during an operation, and the pressures which may lead him to do so in error when he is lying in wait in a lonely field late at night. But they also appreciate the need to control the use of force and to avoid publicly embarrassing ministers. 'At the end of the day,' says one officer who held a senior position at Lisburn, 'what it is all really about is public relations.' Manipulating the perception of the nationalist community about whether or not the security forces act within the law is one of the keys to the republican movement's effort to maintain its support. In this context, the Army in Northern Ireland has not just been concerned to put the best frame on potentially embarrassing incidents, but has also attempted at various times deliberately to mislead journalists.

During the 1970s the Army's Information Policy Unit was responsible for disseminating disinformation about the IRA and loyalist paramilitary groups. The unit was also involved in printing fake leaflets and posters intended to discredit these organizations. It is not illegal to lie to the press, something which senior Army and RUC officers have at various times pointed out in private conversations.

Colin Wallace, the civil servant who served in the Army's Information Policy Unit, later made allegations about Army press officers co-operating with MI5 to spread smear stories about leading politicians, including those connected to terrorist groups in Ulster, as well as members of the Labour government of the day who had become unpopular with senior security forces officers. In January 1990 the government set up an independent legal inquiry under the Queen's Counsel David Calcutt into allegations that Wallace had been dismissed from his job unfairly as part of a cover-up. Calcutt found that Wallace *had* been unjustly dismissed, recommending compensation, and went beyond the inquiry's terms of reference in revealing that the information officer's appeal against his dismissal to a civil service board had been rejected following representations to the board from officials of the Ministry of Defence.

Despite the Calcutt verdict, Whitehall rejects claims that Wallace was framed for a killing of which he was found guilty and convicted of manslaughter in 1981. The issue of just who was smeared by Lisburn's 'black propaganda' unit in the 1970s remains more complex. The government continues to reject Wallace's allegation that intelligence officers in Ulster conspired to smear Harold Wilson, the Prime Minister of the day. But it admits that such activities were carried out against people associated with extremist politics in Ulster.

In the parliamentary answer which announced the setting-up of the Calcutt inquiry, Archie Hamilton, minister for the armed forces, said: 'It has not, since the mid 1970s, been the policy to disseminate disinformation in Northern Ireland in ways designed to denigrate individuals and/or organizations for propaganda purposes.'

By referring to policy from the *mid* 1970s, this statement, constructed in meticulous civil service fashion, implies that the kind of information-gathering which Wallace says was being undertaken by MI5 for use against loyalist extremists suspected of sexual abuse at the Kincora boys' home could indeed have been going on in the early 1970s, although Whitehall will not confirm it. It also leaves open the possibility of disinformation for purposes other than that of denigrating 'individuals and/or organizations for propaganda purposes'. Two days later during a debate on the Wallace affair, Tom King, the Secretary of State for Defence and previously for Northern Ireland, was happy to specify such other purposes. He told the Commons that disinformation was still being used in Ulster 'where it is necessary to protect lives and for sound and absolutely honourable security reasons'.

Although the circulation of versions of events which were known to be false, as after the Ballysillan shooting, was to become routine after operations by police and Army undercover units, disinformation activities of the kind carried out by Colin Wallace certainly did become rarer, if they did not end altogether, during the late 1970s and early 1980s. This resulted partly from the growing role of the police in directing public relations strategy. Whereas Army commanders in the early 1970s had regarded information as a legitimate weapon, particularly in trying to stir up factional rivalries within paramilitary groups, the philosophy at Knock was different.

The shift in the Army towards a more sincere and thoroughgoing acceptance of Police Primacy in the early 1980s was to be accompanied by the emergence of a closer accord on public relations. It was decided that the best way to proceed was to get the conflict out of the headlines. Attempts to plant disinformation about politicians and the general security situation were reduced in the belief that no publicity was good publicity.

# PART TWO: 1979-1982

# 8

# A Change of Mood

In late 1978 the Army reviewed its policy on the deployment of SAS troops and ended, for the time being at least, the use of these highly trained troops for mounting ambushes. This followed intensified scrutiny of and gathering unease about the conduct of SAS soldiers in undercover operations, on the part both of the public and of the RUC. From 1976 to 1978 the SAS had killed ten people. Seven of them were IRA members, but three were mere bystanders. Even some of those at Lisburn and Knock who believed that the SAS could legitimately administer an unofficial brand of capital punishment found the Regiment's propensity for 'miscarriages of justice' unpalatable.

One senior officer who served at Lisburn at the time denies that it was the number of errors which caused a rethink. Another notes, 'One is not in the business of embarrassing ministers.' In some of its public statements about gunfights involving special forces, the Army tries to project an impression that these are chance encounters. An SAS party may be referred to, misleadingly, as a 'patrol'. The intention is to create the impression that there was no foreknowledge on the part of military commanders of the whereabouts of specific terrorists. However, it is clear that information can be exploited to allow ambushes by the SAS, as it had been in the period from 1976 to 1978.

In December 1978 the ambushes stopped and for five years, until December 1983, the SAS did not kill anybody in Northern Ireland. Of course during this period IRA members were killed by normal Army patrols, the RUC and, in one incident, by 14 Intelligence Company. However, an analysis of all published sources on deaths in Ulster, including Sinn Fein's own 'Roll of Honour' of fallen volunteers, shows that during 1979 to 1980, for example, only one IRA member was killed by the entire Army in Northern Ireland.

But if the SAS had been reined in, who was responsible? The answer appeared to lie at the top of the security forces command structure. During the days when SAS operations had been confined to south Armagh control of operations was wielded at a relatively junior level. The commanding officer of the Army's battalion in the area was often in charge, sometimes seeking higher authority – from 3 Brigade in Portadown for certain operations.

With the extension of operations throughout Northern Ireland in 1977 arrangements had changed. An SAS sabre squadron, about seventy-five soldiers, has a headquarters and four smaller units called troops. A troop is commanded by a captain, usually in his late twenties, and should consist of sixteen soldiers, although there are often less.

One troop remained at Bessbrook in south Armagh in the area controlled by 3 Brigade, but the other three were placed elsewhere. One went to 39 Brigade, the Belfast area, another to 8 Brigade in Londonderry. The fourth troop remained at a central location under the personal control of the CLF. Although the other troops were notionally attached to the three brigade headquarters, this was largely an administrative convenience. One officer describes the arrangement: 'It made sense to dot them around, from the point of view of getting places faster. If CLF had nothing for them to do, they went to the brigade commander.' However, in most cases the SAS were under the control of the CLF. This system of command and deployment was conceived late in 1977 and probably remained in effect until late 1980 or early 1981. The advantage of the system was that it gave the regions their 'own' SAS men, ready to respond rapidly in an emergency. The problem was that it dispersed SAS efforts, when they might better have been concentrated at the place where the best intelligence was available.

After 1978, the CLF still had opportunities to use them for ambushes, had he wanted to. One officer holding a pivotal position at Lisburn says, 'There were a lot of occasions when we knew what the terrorists were going to do.' But the key personalities, and with them attitudes to the use of lethal force, had changed.

In February 1979 James Glover, the General Staff brigadier who had written several influential intelligence reports when in Whitehall, arrived at Lisburn as CLF, after promotion to major general. Major General Glover argued against ambushing the IRA. He was acutely aware of the importance of funerals in sustaining the republican movement and he wanted to get killing out of the headlines.

The tradition of martyrdom is a long one and it plays an important role in confirming the status of model republicans on families who have lost a member fighting for the IRA. The funerals of volunteers become set-piece demonstrations of solidarity in which the precise circumstances of the person's death are often forgotten as the mourners succumb to emotion. The funeral of a Provo volunteer, maybe still a teenager, in which thousands marched behind the coffin, was important in confirming the status of people who might otherwise have never earned any kind of respect in their community.

The idea that martyrdom increased the IRA's support and should therefore be avoided at all costs had been expressed by several officers at Lisburn between 1977 and 1978. But others had argued more forcibly that ambushes were worthwhile, principally because they deterred others from carrying out terrorist crime. Now the balance of power in the argument shifted.

James Glover had already written a highly classified paper spelling out his belief in the need for significant changes in the organization of military intelligence while he was still a brigadier in London. He knew that intelligence was the key to preventing terrorist outrages and that it was going to be harder to get it following the IRA's evolution towards a cellular structure. Major General Glover summed up his preference for agents rather than ambushes years later in an interview with the BBC TV programme *Panorama*: 'I always used to say, "Bring me a terrorist who can work for me and don't give me a dead terrorist".'

Although Major General Glover worked in 1979 for the same GOC who had advocated the aggressive use of special forces before, Lieutenant General Creasey, there were other changes at senior levels. Roy Mason, the Secretary of State who believed in putting military pressure on the IRA had been replaced, following the Conservatives' general election victory in May 1979, by Humphrey Atkins. And while Chief Constable Kenneth Newman had initially agreed with the deployment of the SAS he had become increasingly sceptical about what they could achieve in the complex circumstances of Northern Ireland. Many RUC officers considered the Boyle episode at Dunloy to have been an extraordinary display of ineptitude by the Army. And while Lisburn considered Ballysillan a 'success', RUC officers saw the episode as a propaganda disaster for the security forces.

A consensus emerged between the new CLF and the RUC that the SAS should not be deployed in ambushes. Instead, their skills of concealment would be exploited to allow them to take a greater role in the burgeoning surveillance effort.

There was an element of self-interest in the RUC's position. Newman, with his emphatic belief in Police Primacy, wanted RUC undercover squads to assume the responsibilities of the Army. But many Army officers felt that most of the police were unsuited to such work: sitting in a ditch for several days, soaking wet, was too much like hard work for a member of the police force, they would say. They regarded the RUC as having more of a 'nine-to-five' mentality. Some, remembering the strongly Protestant flavour of the Special Patrol Group police squads, wondered whether the force would behave impartially in situations where its members confronted terrorists. One senior officer says of the RUC's acquisition of special units, 'What they didn't appreciate initially was the degree of professionalism which was required to be successful.'

The police felt that they *could* train men in undercover work, even if this required them to recruit many ex-soldiers. A senior RUC officer says he thinks it is right that a member of the police should be involved in such work because 'he has more sense of the legal consequences of his actions, a different training'.

All of this debate about special forces and the integration of intelligence took place in the context of a broad and unresolved tension between the RUC and the Army, which had simmered away since the outset of Police Primacy early in 1976. While still agreeing to the principle, Lisburn felt that control of operations had been handed over to the RUC too quickly. The danger of expressing such views openly at weekly meetings of the Security Policy Committee must have been obvious to Lieutenant General Creasey, the GOC – doing so could precipitate a row which would damage the whole anti-terrorist effort. But, in any case, the rivalry between the Army and the RUC was about to be forced into the open by a devastating series of events in a single day.

# 9

# Warrenpoint

The events of 27 August 1979 caused the tension which had been deepening between the RUC and the Army over the past few years to erupt. It was a day which saw the Army's worst ever loss in Northern Ireland and the assassination of a member of the Royal Family – a day which, in the words of a senior security forces official, 'brought to a head the crisis which had been brewing between the police and the Army'.

Soldiers from 2nd Battalion, the Parachute Regiment, were travelling from the Army depot at Ballykinlar in County Down towards Newry. The men were riding in two four-ton lorries and a Land Rover. They had no more protection than was offered by the canvas sides of their vehicles.

The IRA had chosen to ambush them at a place called Narrow Water, near Warrenpoint. Here, the road comes close to the sliver of water which marks the international boundary between the Republic and the North and connects Newry, via a canal, to the Irish Sea.

In its conception and planning, the attack showed how far the Provisionals had come from their early, chaotic, bomb-making days. About 1500lb of explosive were used in the attack. Attacks in rural areas often involve huge amounts of explosive because the IRA knows the chances of catching innocent bystanders are much less than in the city and because it is much easier for them to conceal large quantities in the open country.

Some 500lb of explosive had been packed in milk churns, placed on a lorry trailer and covered with hay bails. The trailer was left in a lay-by beside the road. The people who planned the attack exploited local knowledge and experience to the full. In 1976 the Provisionals had attempted to ambush the Royal Marines in exactly the same place. But the troops whom they wanted to catch had noticed the wires through which the command detonating the bomb was to be sent. The Royal Marines, realizing the danger, had sought cover 400m away, behind the granite masonry of the gateway to Narrow Waters castle.

Three years later the Provisionals decided to do things differently. There would be no tell-tale command wires. Instead, the bomb on the trailer was to be triggered by remote control, using a small transmitter unit of a type manufactured for model aircraft enthusiasts. A second bomb, twice as powerful as the first, would be placed at the castle gateway. Just to make sure the soldiers took cover there, snipers on the other side of the water, in the Republic, would open fire after the detonation of the first bomb.

At about 4.30 p.m. the trailer bomb went off, catching the second lorry. It was ripped apart by the blast and six of the paratroopers inside were killed. The IRA members opened fire as dazed paratroopers tried to disentangle mutilated comrades from the twisted metal. A passer-by was also killed on the road. As the IRA had reckoned, the paras sought cover behind the castle gates. Everything went according to the IRA's plan.

The battalion based nearby at Bessbrook, the Queen's Own Highlanders, was alerted. A Wessex helicopter took off. Lieutenant Colonel David Blair, the Highlanders' CO, took off in a Gazelle light helicopter to investigate.

At 4.59 p.m., with Lieutenant Colonel Blair conferring with the paratroopers behind the gates and a Wessex lifting off with injured men, another radio signal was sent. The 1000lb device at the gates went off. Another twelve soldiers, including the Lieutenant Colonel, died.

In Mullaghmore in the Republic, the IRA struck on the same day. Lord Mountbatten, the Duke of Edinburgh's uncle, and three other people were killed by a bomb concealed on their pleasure boat. Once again, it was a highly sophisticated attack. Careful intelligence had been used to pinpont the target. About 50lb of explosive had been hidden beneath the boat's deck and, as at Warrenpoint, a radio control transmitter had been used to detonate it.

At Lisburn and Knock there was consternation. If this was the revamped IRA, officers wondered, how would they cope? The Provos had staged two 'spectaculars' in one day. Either of them – killing a large number of paratroopers or striking a member of the Royal Family – would have been a major coup in itself. Together they were sufficient to bring the differences over security policy to a point where the Prime Minister had to become involved.

Margaret Thatcher had been elected Prime Minister only three months before. She found herself facing her first real crisis. As before and since, the mounting of a 'spectacular' by the IRA produced many calls for tough action. Mrs Thatcher went to Northern Ireland to meet the GOC, CLF and Chief Constable. The events of 27 August, coupled with the killing by INLA terrorists of her old friend and political helper Airey Neave earlier in the year, meant that Mrs Thatcher went to Northern Ireland with the desire to bring in measures which would really hurt the IRA. But she soon found herself caught up in Army/RUC rivalry.

Lieutenant General Creasey, the GOC, decided the time was right to check what he believed had been the RUC's premature assumption of responsibility for security. During a working lunch attended by the Prime Minister and senior Army officers at the headquarters of 3 Brigade in Portadown, Lieutenant General Creasey inserted what was, in bureaucratic terms, the dagger. He suggested that there should be a single security supremo for Ulster, and implied that it should be a military man. The GOC said the Army should regain operational control, at least for a limited period. At first he asked for twelve months, later reducing this to six. He also advocated a closer integration of intelligence – something which was, in fact, already underway.

The Prime Minister went to Crossmaglen to talk to troops and then by helicopter to Gough Barracks in Armagh, where Kenneth Newman and the RUC team were waiting. There the Chief Constable asked her to authorize the expansion of the force by 1000. The Prime Minister agreed to this on the spot. In the days following her return to London, Newman defended the RUC's assumption of control of all security operations, resisting the Army's call for a temporary reversal of Police Primacy.

In London Frank Cooper, a senior Ministry of Defence civil servant with some experience of Ulster, was given the task of evaluating the Army and RUC proposals. Cooper soon realized the difficulties involved in abandoning Police Primacy, even temporarily. But the Army's attempt to regain the direction of operations could not be wished away. Cooper came up with the idea of appointing someone to soothe the tension between police and Army and to chart the way ahead in security policy. It was decided that Maurice Oldfield, chief of SIS (MI6) between 1973 and 1978, should be appointed as Security Co-ordinator. Oldfield – sometimes described as the model for John Le Carré's fictional character George Smiley – had retired to All Souls College in Oxford, where he had intended to pursue his interest in mediaeval history. Such was his sense of duty that Oldfield felt he could not refuse the Prime Minister's personal appeal to go to Northern Ireland.

His appointment as Security Co-ordinator was announced on 2 October 1979 and, less than one week later, he had arrived. Oldfield, a bachelor, lived in a flat above his offices in Stormont House, which adjoins the castle which was once home to the devolved Northern Ireland government. The Security Co-ordinator was not given the authority to run actual operations; neither was he given any power to compel the RUC or the Army to accept his judgement. Instead he and his staff were briefed to draw up reports which analysed what was going wrong in the government's handling of the situation. Some of these studies dealt with particular matters of security policy, for example the organization of intelligence. Others set out political, economic and security strategy for each of Ulster's six counties. The aim was to present these reports to ministers and officials who might then implement further improvements in security based on Oldfield's recommendations.

Oldfield was assisted in his task by a group known as the Planning Staff. It contained two Army, two RUC officers and two civil servants. Its members were rising figures within their respective organizations. Brigadier Robert Pascoe, the Army's senior member, was a Royal Green Jacket officer who had commanded a battalion in Ulster and would go on to become the GOC there. Assistant Chief Constable John Whiteside was considered one of the rising stars of the RUC. Before joining the Planning Staff he had spent several years as a chief superintendent in charge of Belfast CID. When the Planning Staff's eighteen-month assignment was complete he went on to be Head of CID.

The Security Co-ordinator earned the respect of most of the people he came into contact with. As a senior figure at Lisburn recalls, 'He had no executive powers, but with his great presence and experience he was able to persuade and cajole people down the right path. He was really a sort of Solomon-like figure: everyone thought they could trust him and go to him. People were prepared to accept his adjudication. He really took the steam out of it.' Small, with thick spectacles, Oldfield had the bearing of an academic. Someone who worked at Stormont remembers, 'He was almost a teddy bear of a man. Very unimposing – a delight – most of us became very fond of him.'

At the same time as Oldfield and the Planning Staff were preparing their reports, Whitehall was preparing to put the reins of security into new hands. Kenneth Newman was coming towards the end of his time as Chief Constable and was to go on to become Commandant of the police staff college and later Commissioner of the Metropolitan Police. Newman had seen through the advent of Police Primacy. In the process he had earned the respect of many ordinary RUC men, a breed not noted for their easy acceptance of the ideas of 'outsiders', which as an Englishman Newman had been. One veteran RUC man says of Newman, 'He was highly esteemed here, very well liked. We can only speak in the highest terms of him.'

His successor in 1979 was Jack Hermon, who for some years had been groomed for a senior position having sat on the Bourn Committee which had produced the idea of Police Primacy. Hermon had grown up in Larne in North Antrim, a strongly Protestant area. After considering a career as an accountant, he had joined the police, serving initially in the religiously mixed areas of counties Londonderry and Tyrone.

In 1963 he had become the first RUC officer to be sent to the police staff college at Bramshill in Surrey. After returning he was involved in the policing of a tense sectarian period in west Belfast. During this posting he was involved in a riot when constables were ordered to remove an Irish tricolour from the window of a Sinn Fein election candidate's shop. He was convinced the police should have stayed away and not done the work of local unionists, who considered the flag's presence an offence. Coincidentally, the incident was regarded as something of a watershed by the young Gerry Adams.

As a Chief Superintendent, Hermon was put in charge of retraining the force after its twin maulings of 1969 – first from the Bogside rioters and then from the Whitehall inquiry which had followed. He later served in Britain, broadening his perspective.

During the years that followed his appointment, Chief Constable Hermon and the RUC were to become virtually synonymous. A strong-willed man, he moulded the organization in his own image, as had John Reith at the BBC or J. Edgar Hoover at the FBI. His style was appreciated by many who felt the force needed strong leadership able to withstand the assaults of local politicians. He won considerable independence for both the RUC and the Army in operational matters, something for which many senior officers were grateful. But like any forceful leader he was not without his critics: some officers felt he had a tendency to meddle, and was a poor delegator who became increasingly set in his views and intolerant of the opinions of outsiders.

At the outset Hermon was perceived as a moderate in some ways. He was considered sincere in his desire to boost the number of Catholics serving in the force. A senior Army officer who worked with him says, 'He may have faults, but bigotry is not one of them.' After taking charge he gave a speech to RUC cadets at a passing-out parade in Enniskillen. He told them that he expected the highest personal standards from them. But parts of his message were considered by some police officers to be naive:

'I have been fortunate enough in my career to walk down a street on my own, meeting and talking to people, without a flak jacket, without a gun. I want to see the day when you too can do the same.'

Experience led Hermon to set the preservation of morale in the RUC as one of his main objectives. He became deeply suspicious of attempts at outside scrutiny: he had seen the problems which outsiders could cause – from the Hunt Report (into RUC handling of the 1969 riots) to the Bennett Report in 1979 (into interrogation practices at Castlereagh). He held many politicians, particularly those unionists who expected the RUC to act as the strong arm of loyalism, in contempt. Hermon was subsequently seen as a ruthless street-fighter in seeing off outside scrutiny of his force and as a man who could be dictatorial in attempts to impose his personal beliefs on others. He tried, for instance, to remove women from active positions in the RUC and brushed aside officers who he thought drank or gambled too much.

Like Kenneth Newman, Hermon wanted to rein in offensive operations by Army special forces, according to senior Army officers. But like his predecessor, Hermon was also motivated in part by simple, institutional self-interest rather than repugnance for those types of operation. He was keen to continue the development of RUC special units. He well understood that his predecessor had fought the tough battles necessary to establish Police Primacy and that he would enjoy its fruits, in terms of real operational power and control of an intelligence establishment which was in the process of integration.

Lieutenant General Creasey was also about to depart. His failed attempt to roll back Police Primacy in the wake of Warrenpoint, despite Whitehall's polite unwillingness to label it publicly for what it was, had in any case made his position very difficult. He was to be replaced in 1979 by Lieutenant General Richard Lawson. In one sense Lieutenant General Lawson did not, at first sight, seem like ideal material for the role of GOC. He was not an infantry officer but came from the Royal Tank Regiment and, short of embracing the measures demanded by the loyalist lunatic fringe, there seemed little scope for the use of armour in Ulster. However, his cool, self-effacing manner allowed him to establish a good working relationship with Chief Constable Hermon. Both men had been left in little doubt by Whitehall that any further disagreements would be unacceptable. In the uncharacteristically direct words of one mandarin, 'Lawson and Hermon had been given firm instructions that they had to work together and there should be no frigging about.'

The GOC and Chief Constable established a close rapport, trying to shape the overall direction of security policy and leaving the resolution of operational matters to their respective deputies. After the shocks of August, the Prime Minister maintained close contact with both men through frequent phonecalls and occasional meetings. With these new appointments the crisis in Army/police relations had passed.

# 10

# Special Branch in the Ascendant

When the Troubles began in Northern Ireland the RUC's Special Branch had been small, numbering only around eighty, and somewhat disorganized. The Branch, like that of police forces in Britain, was meant to provide intelligence on terrorism and subversive groups. But at the beginning of the 1970s, at the time of internment, much of the information it provided on republican paramilitary groups had been hopelessly inaccurate. In particular the SB had overestimated the importance of the Official IRA and known little about the emerging power of the Provisionals.

Intelligence, particularly that gained from informers, is the lifeblood of anti-terrorist operations. The SB had the largest network of informers of the various information-gathering agencies in Ulster – that in itself was enough to give it considerable power. But the RUC's assumption of overall control of operations in 1976 gave the branch a pivotal role in the struggle against the Provisionals.

During the early 1970s the SB had taken a series of blows following inquiries into its interrogation methods. By the mid 1970s many Army officers had a low opinion of it. To one battalion commander the SB were 'emasculated'; while to the Chief of the General Staff they were a force with poor morale and the taint of association with Protestant terrorist groups.

As a result of the SB's disgrace, the CID had taken over interrogation at the main centre, Castlereagh near Belfast, and at subsidiary points at Gough Barracks in Armagh and Strand Road police station in Londonderry. The CID had improved the organization of interrogation and the collators of the information thus assumed a highly important role in the campaign of the mid 1970s.

Castlereagh attained a fearsome reputation among republicans. Many police officers, to this day, argue that most prisoners were treated fairly there; however, not all police officers have taken this view. Michael Asher, the SPG man who later wrote about his experiences in *Shoot to Kill*, remembers the reaction of one suspect: 'Taggarty blanched when Castlereagh was mentioned. It had a grim reputation. Suspects were held there in windowless cubes for up to one week. They might be denied sleep, stripped, beaten or humiliated. No one wanted to be taken to Castlereagh.'

Just as the CID's bureaucratic fortunes had been boosted by outside inquiries into their rival, so they would themselves be diminished by them. In 1978 Amnesty International, the independent human rights monitoring group, published a report which was highly critical of the methods employed in police interrogation centres. Following its appearance Kenneth Newman and the government agreed that they should open the doors of Castlereagh to an inquiry headed by Harry Bennett QC, a respected judge. The Bennett Report was published early in 1979 and did not give the clean bill of health for which Newman had hoped.

It stated that most police officers were carrying out their duties correctly but came to the conclusion that some prisoners had injuries which 'were not self-inflicted and were sustained in police custody'. Following this admission that some prisoners were being beaten up, steps were taken to protect suspects' rights. Closed circuit TV cameras were fitted in interrogation rooms and prisoners were given medical checks. The RUC took such steps well before most of the British police forces – albeit a change which was forced on them. Subsequently new legislation under the PTA gave detectives three or even seven days to interrogate suspects and elicit information or confessions, reducing the pressure on them to resort to illegal and violent means. Allegations of ill-treatment did not end but there was a recognition – even by many republicans in private – that physical coercion became rarer in the holding centres.

But the benefit that the SB gained from the CID's reversal of fortunes in the late 1970s was only one of the reasons why it was beginning to inspire new confidence. In 1976 Assistant Chief Constable Mick Slevin took over as Head of Special Branch (HSB). He had served previously as a chief superintendent in charge of plain-clothes work in Belfast. Slevin had become something of a hero among his fellow detectives: during the early days of the Troubles he had personally defused two bombs, receiving a gallantry award and, in 1973, an OBE. He had already been in the force for thirty-one years when he was appointed HSB.

Assistant Chief Constable Slevin, an Ulsterman, did much to rebuild the department. He increased its resources and brought it to the centre of the intelligence establishment as refashioned in the late 1970s. After several years of bitter conflict with British Army intelligence, the new HSB soothed the atmosphere. A senior figure at Lisburn comments, 'We had excellent relations with him.'

During the late 1970s and early 1980s the RUC SB, or E Department, was split into its current five divisions. E1, Administration Division, carries out routine administrative functions: it maintains the Department's cars, vets its personnel and ensures the security of its buildings. E2, Legal Division, is closely involved with the CID in preparing cases against suspects and in overseeing the remaining SB contingent in interrogation centres. E3 is the Intelligence Division, the central organizing and analysis body of the Department. E4, Operations Division, carries out surveillance, runs the Department's library and collects relevant press cuttings. E5, Collation Division, updates the data on suspects and incidents, and analyses it in an attempt to establish connections between individuals as well as incidents.

Of these divisions E3 and E4 are the most important. The Intelligence Division is subdivided into E3A, E3B and E3C which oversee operations respectively against republican groups, loyalist organizations, and leftist groups which are considered subversive. E4A became well known as the surveillance group within the Branch – the watchers who follow suspects and mount observation posts. It is backed up by E4B which is involved in technical surveillance, installing bugging and tracking equipment. E4C and E4D are believed to be involved in specialist photographic surveillance.

The central organization is augmented by a headquarters in each of three regions and the divisions are grouped under them. The Regional Head of Special Branch (RHSB) is normally a chief superintendent and the divisional one a chief inspector or superintendent. It is the organization at the regional level, with its officers in police stations around Ulster, which is engaged in the SB's most vital work. These elements control the informers in various communities and paramilitary groups. The Army's Special Military Intelligence Unit (SMIU) interacts with SB at each level, both with its headquarters at Knock and via a force of about thirty military intelligence officers in the police divisions.

With the success of the three Regional Crime and Intelligence Units founded by Kenneth Newman in improving general police work in the mid 1970s, security chiefs decided to extend the system to cover co-operation between the police and Army by establishing a new integrated intelligence centre called a Tasking and Co-ordination Group (TCG). The setting-up of the TCGs was probably the most important of all the steps taken during the late 1970s towards enhanced information-gathering.

Each Group combined CID, SB and Army specialists; but while the CID had been in charge of the Regional Crime and Intelligence Units, the TCGs were commanded by an SB officer. Despite its imposing title, the TCG was not an extensive nerve-centre with ranks of police and soldiers watching screens and poring over maps, but consisted of a much more basic collection of portakabins or rooms. When it was not organizing any operations the TCG was often staffed by just one person, a duty officer sometimes as lowly as a detective constable. When operations were on, as many as twenty to thirty people may have become involved, according to interviewees with experience of such activity.

The first TCG was created in 1978 at Castlereagh to serve Belfast Region. It was followed in 1979 by one at Gough Barracks to serve South Region, and later by another in Londonderry for North Region. Although there have been some changes in the function of different regions during the last ten years, the centres at Castlereagh, Gough and Londonderry were normally known as TCG Belfast, TCG South and TCG North respectively.

The TCGs attained a critical role in what security chiefs called 'executive action' – locking together intelligence from informers with the surveillance and ambushing activities of undercover units. The Army's TCG Liaison Officer (TCGLO), a captain or major, is almost always a veteran of an SAS or 14 Intelligence Company tour in Ulster, whose duty is to act as go-between and advise senior detectives on the Army's capabilities. The Army and the SB have people permanently delegated to the TCG, but the Security Service (MI5) does not, according to people who have worked in this field. Security Service personnel may, however, join the TCG for limited periods during operations in which they have a particular interest, for example where one of their agents is involved.

As a result of this initiative, Regional Heads of Special Branch, operating through their TCG, were able to eliminate duplication of effort by Army and police surveillance squads. They ensured 'de-confliction', declaring areas where covert operations were underway out of bounds to prevent accidental confrontations with uniformed patrols. The new arrangement also lessened the chances of the Army or police arresting one another's informers by mistake.

The founding of the first TCG preceded the examination of intelligence-gathering efforts by Maurice Oldfield and his Planning Staff. They were impressed with the system as a key step in the integration of security forces intelligence activities, and in their report to Whitehall recommended the establishment of a similar system of joint operations and intelligence centres at the RUC division/Army battalion level. These lower level groups had a less formal structure and concentrated on the co-ordination of patrolling activities rather than on the response to sensitive intelligence.

The centralization of activities in the TCGs carried certain risks, however. For example, the TCG commander was permitted to hold back information. An informer might allude to the identity of terrorists who were about to carry out an attack. The TCG commander might pass on to the Army information about the likely target and timing of the attack without referring to the would-be perpetrators, feeling that doing so could put the informer at risk by revealing the small group in which he or she moved. But in omitting this information, the commander might himself be committing a crime because he would leave the soldiers with no option but to confront armed terrorists, when they might have had a chance of arresting them before their attack. Working in the TCG forced SB officers at times to make difficult decisions: should they compromise the security of their source in the interests of making possible preventive action against terrorists, or should they keep their informer's identity secret and thereby run the risk of endangering the lives of soldiers and possibly bystanders?

Such responsibilities required the officers who ran TCGs to display the utmost judgement and integrity. In fact, as the events which followed the shooting of six people in the Armagh area by RUC undercover units late in 1982 were to show (see chapter sixteen), some of them were incapable of living up to these exalted standards.


Although the SB developed the most extensive network of informers, other organizations such as the Army and MI5 also used informers – or 'human sources' as they were termed. The traditionally close relationship between the Branch and MI5, though not as intimate as in many British forces, provided a further boost to the RUC SB.

The Security Service became more involved in Northern Ireland in 1973. The government had initially favoured the use of the Secret Intelligence Service (MI6) because it was believed to be more adept at running networks of agents in a foreign country, namely the Republic of Ireland. However, after the IRA's initial bombing campaigns in Britain in 1972, MI5 was able to convince ministers that its efforts to protect the realm from acts of this kind required an expanded presence on the far side of the Irish Sea.

During the mid 1970s, while the Security Service was 'empire-building', there was a period of rivalry between MI5 and MI6, and between MI5 and the RUC SB and Army intelligence-gathering organizations too. By the late 1970s SIS liaison officers had been displaced from Lisburn and Knock and most of its agents taken over by MI5 or the SB, although SIS retained a vestigial presence with an office at Stormont.

The Security Service's expansion, particularly of its agent-running operations, was bound to cause friction. As MI5 had little presence at first in Northern Ireland most of its informers could only be acquired by relieving other organizations of them. Most agents were recruited during questioning by the RUC or the Army – MI5 simply could not get this kind of access to large numbers of people from republican areas.

Security Service agents became known as 'national assets' – a phrase which was meant to reflect their importance to national security, as opposed to the local anti-terrorist effort. According to intelligence officers who have served in Ulster, MI5 is in theory concerned with trying to recruit and observe people involved only with the IRA campaign outside Ulster. In practice, it has muscled in and tried to run any good agent it can find.

The Service's relationship with the RUC SB is apparently different to that between MI5 and the SB contingents of other police forces in the United Kingdom. In some parts of the country SB are still regarded by MI5 as little more than errand boys, carrying out arrests and serving warrants on MI5's behalf. The Security Service used to be technically unable to carry out such routine activities since it was barely supposed to exist in any legal or constitutional sense. In 1989, however, the government passed legislation – the Security Service Act – which regularized its position. But in Northern Ireland MI5 remains too dependent on the SB, in terms of exploiting its extensive informer network, to treat it with the same disdain.

MI5's activities in Northern Ireland are run by the Director and Co-ordinator of Intelligence (DCI) at Stormont. The DCI's duties include the overall direction of intelligence policy in Ulster as well as the supervision of an MI5 force numbering sixty to seventy. Although Army and RUC intelligence officers do not consider themselves subordinate to the DCI, there are several elements of the intelligence effort under the DCI's direct control. MI5 has a Security Liaison Office at HQNI, Lisburn and another at RUC headquarters, Knock. It also possesses one unit for running agents and one for technical surveillance specialists. The DCI is supported by a group of officers at Stormont sometimes referred to as 'The Department'.

Those who have worked alongside MI5 in Northern Ireland say that their people come from a variety of backgrounds. Some are Ulstermen and women who have been recruited either direct from the populace or from the ranks of the RUC. Others have come from a more conventional intelligence service background, joining the agency after completing a university degree. And some have served in the British Army. The Security Service's personnel divide into 'officers' – who make up about one in five of its numbers – and 'support staff'.

Because of its highly secretive nature, and its role in combating subversion (often broadly defined), MI5 is regarded with deep suspicion by many with liberal convictions who question the range of its activities and consider them a threat to civil liberties. However, many in the Army and RUC who have had contact with MI5 during this period are not in awe of it. One person says of the MI5 officers who ran 'national assets' in the late 1970s, 'Some of them were laughable.'

Despite the scepticism of their colleagues in rival intelligence-gathering organizations, the Security Service gradually improved the running of its Ulster operation. Many high-flying officers were sent to Northern Ireland where the value of the work was readily apparent. 'Ireland, like the operations against Eastern Bloc diplomats in London, was considered worthwhile,' says one former intelligence officer, adding, 'Everybody understood the reason for doing it.' Among those who served there in the late 1970s was Patrick Walker who, in 1989, became Director General of the Security Service.

Although the DCI's authority was enhanced during the intelligence reforms of the late 1970s and early 1980s, the holder of this office still had no powers to compel the RUC SB or Army to do things they did not want to do. The DCI therefore had to derive power through the exercise of great tact and persuasiveness in the running of high-level intelligence committees at Stormont. On the other hand, the relationship between the resident MI5 chief and the secretary of state was critical. Several ministers were to use the DCI as a personal adviser on intelligence matters from the state of terrorist groups to the areas where the security forces needed to make a greater effort.

The Security Service Act, passed in 1989, made the DCI responsible to the secretary of state for Northern Ireland rather than to the Home Office, as is most of MI5. In practice, MI5 officers tend to communicate frequently with their colleagues in London.

From 1977 to 1980 an MI5 officer called Michael Bettaney worked at Stormont. Bettaney suffered a personal collapse which in turn brought profound changes in the Security Service. Bettaney spent much of his time in Northern Ireland running agents. He later told MI5 colleagues in London that he had had a number of close escapes in Ulster. Once, he said, he had narrowly avoided being caught in a bomb blast. On another occasion he claimed to have hidden in one part of a house as paramilitaries broke the kneecaps of someone suspected of informing in another. I have been unable to confirm whether these incidents actually took place.

What is known is that Bettaney began drinking heavily while at Stormont and that he converted to Catholicism during the same period. At the same time he underwent a change of political heart – the right-wing views he had held in his early twenties were abandoned as he became interested in the political left. He was later to say that his tour in Northern Ireland caused him to re-examine government policy for the first time. Posted back to London, from 1980 to 1982 he gave training lectures as his personal problems worsened. When he began working in MI5's K Branch, which is responsible for counter-espionage, Bettaney saw the opportunity to pass information to the Russians. Despite the fact that his attempts to do so were bungled to the point of being comic, in 1984 Bettaney was sentenced to twenty-three years in prison.

While he was on remand in Brixton jail, a light-hearted story appeared in the diary of the *Guardian*, suggesting that the authorities had gone to great lengths to keep Bettaney apart from an IRA suspect in the same wing. However, during the preparation of this book I was told by an intelligence officer that the Security Service believed Bettaney had actually succeeded in giving the IRA information in prison. He added that MI5 had assumed that the names and addresses of senior officers, including those involved in anti-IRA work, had been compromised, and that the people concerned had taken increased security precautions, some moving house. The alarm at MI5 had followed the discovery that Bettaney had indeed been able to associate with IRA prisoners or suspects. At the time of going to press, neither Bettaney nor his solicitor had chosen to comment on letters sent them by me setting out this extraordinary allegation.

A period of profound turbulence followed Bettaney's sentencing and the security commission investigation which came after it. MI5 followed numerous other British institutions in receiving what one Whitehall insider calls a 'hand-bagging' from Mrs Thatcher. John Jones, Director General of the Security Service, was replaced by Anthony Duff. Whereas Jones was a career MI5 officer, Duff was a diplomat whom Mrs Thatcher had used to run the Joint Intelligence Committee, the intelligence steering group which is part of the Cabinet Office. Several other senior MI5 officers were forced into retirement, including the director of the branch which should have discovered Bettaney's problems during its vetting interviews.

The service was reorganized under Duff, followed by another shake-up since his departure in 1987. The principle result of these changes, from the point of view of the Northern Ireland conflict, was a substantial increase, by the late 1980s, in the importance attached within MI5 to combating terrorism.

During Bettaney's time at Stormont, F5 – the London-based section of the service which gathers intelligence on Irish terrorism – was simply a part of F Branch, MI5's counter-subversion empire. In the mid 1980s the media paid considerable attention to F Branch, and in particular to its definition of 'subversive' – wide enough to encompass organizations like the National Council for Civil Liberties.

By the late 1980s counter-terrorism had been given its own branch which combined the activities of the old F5, F3 – which investigated other (mainly Middle Eastern) terrorist threats – and some sections of C Branch which was responsible for the security of MI5 and other sensitive government installations. The director of counter-terrorism was elevated to sit on MI5's 'board' – a position of equal importance to that given, for example, to the director of counter-espionage.

Northern Ireland remained a separate operation, with the DCI also accorded the director-level privilege of sitting on MI5's board. The job of DCI and director of counter-terrorism were considered to be of the same rank; and late in the 1980s the director of counter-terrorism was even transferred to Stormont to become the DCI.

The emergence of a powerful counter-terrorism branch in the Security Service and indeed of a considerable reduction in its counter-subversion staff were products of the post-Bettaney rethink and of the Service's desire to redefine itself as tensions between East and West ebbed, following Mikhail Gorbachev's assumption of power in 1985. In the process the Service was to interest itself in areas of counter-terrorism which, in the early 1980s, had been the province of the Metropolitan Police Special Branch and of various other intelligence and counter-intelligence bureaucracies in Europe, as we shall see in chapter thirteen.

# 11

# Human Sources

The importance of the informer to the security establishment, which had been growing since the outset of the Troubles, reached its zenith in the late 1970s and early 1980s. It has never been in the interests either of the British government or the IRA to publicize the degree to which the republican heartlands are penetrated by informers. The security forces wish to protect individual sources and keep from the public eye the fact that the informer campaign requires unenviable moral judgements on the part of those in charge of intelligence. For the Provisionals the issue highlights the degree to which many people, even in the most deprived Catholic areas, despise them to the point of being willing to betray them.

Some security chiefs saw the entire campaign to isolate the IRA from the community in terms of the contest for informers. 'The crucial line to be crossed', says a senior Army officer, 'is one where a passive acceptance in the Catholic community moves to a readiness to betray.' The intelligence given ranges from a general call on the security forces confidential phoneline to readiness by comparatively senior IRA personnel to turn on their colleagues.

But the campaign to extract information from the republican heartlands sometimes flounders because of the strength of informers' ties within the community. Very few informers are prepared to stand up in court, and thus identify themselves. Declaring oneself as a 'tout' invites assassination by the IRA and ensures the enmity of almost everybody one has grown up with and known. It also brings scorn and anger on the heads of relatives.

An informer's handler must make difficult judgements about how the information is exploited, not the least of which is the duty to protect the source's life. The IRA knows that the number of people aware of any forthcoming operation is limited. A decision may have to be taken to bring the informer out of the community, into protective custody and to a new life away from those seeking revenge. The close personal ties in the Catholic community mean that some informers who have been taken into protective custody cannot stand the isolation and take the decision to return, despite the considerable personal risk this involves.

Following the reorganization of the IRA into cells during the late 1970s the security forces stepped up their efforts to recruit informers. In 1980 this prompted the IRA to set up its own Security Department, tasked with hunting out the moles. The IRA Army Council was well aware that there was a growing war-weariness among nationalists and boosted political work by Sinn Fein to maintain the power base. At the same time, they realized coercive measures were needed to prevent people moving from weariness to betrayal.

Killing touts – 'nutting' them in IRA slang – had been going on for years. The first had been slain in 1971. However, from the late 1970s onwards the number increased. During 1979 to 1981 the IRA killed eight people for informing, seven of them members of its own units. This was more than the number of Provisionals killed by the police and Army (five) during the same period. In the ten years from 1978 to 1987 at least twenty-four informers or alleged informers were killed by the Provisionals – almost the same number of republican activists as were killed in Northern Ireland by the SAS during this period.

According to a number of journalists who have written about the subject, several of the murders followed the discovery by the IRA of an informer named Peter Valente, a volunteer and organizer of protests in support of the H-Block inmates. Valente told his SB handler that the IRA had an agent inside the RUC. Accounts of the policeman's motives differ: some say he was selling the information for profit; others that he had taken an extraordinary personal decision to cultivate his own IRA informers as a means of convincing his superiors that he was suitable for acceptance into the SB.

The guilty police officer was arrested in October 1980. Valente and his handler came to the fatal conclusion that he could remain within the IRA. However, following a raid on a house in west Belfast, which police had, on a tip-off from Valente, believed was going to be used in a terrorist attack, the IRA set to work to find the source of the leak. They put the few people who had known of the operation under surveillance, and Valente was followed to a meeting with his handler. After interrogation Valente is said to have revealed the identity of others and four killings were reportedly connected with the IRA's discovery that Valente was an informer. Maurice Gilvary, a member of the Ardoyne IRA – believed by some to have provided the tip-off which led to the SAS ambush in June 1978 at the Ballysillan postal depot – was killed in January 1981. Eugene Simmons, an IRA quartermaster, was shot dead in the same month in south Armagh. Paddy Trainor, another Belfast Brigade member, was killed in February 1981; and Vincent Robinson was killed in June of that year.

However, key facts about the IRA's discovery of this block of informers remain unclear. Just how Valente knew the identity of the informers remains unclear, although it is thought that the treacherous RUC man may have given him the information. But how had the RUC man known who they were, given that the identity of informers is probably the most closely guarded secret in Ulster?

More importantly, why was there a gap of around a year between the supposed discovery that Valente was an informer and his own killing in November 1981? Perhaps he had been led to believe that his life would be spared if he delivered others: Gilvary, Simmons, Trainor and Robinson were all killed before Valente himself.

The discovery of several touts within the IRA and of the corrupt police officer were shameful enough to their respective organizations. It may be that the idea of linking separate events with Valente was part of a security forces disinformation ploy designed to obscure other errors on their part. The period in which the deaths took place coincided with the failed attempt by some middle-ranking Special Branch officers to gain control of Army agents.

This case is not the only one to have involved recruitment of agents within the security forces by the IRA. Some people close to the republican movement claim that there have been other instances where senior RUC men have provided information in return for promises from the IRA not to harm them. It is impossible to verify these claims but it is apparent that some police and prison officers have been threatened by the IRA and have sometimes agreed to allow the Provisionals special favours. Early in 1990 a prison officer was convicted of providing information to the IRA which was used to murder one of his colleagues. Although the Provisionals have succeeded in penetrating the RUC on occasions, the evidence suggests that the security forces have far more agents in the republican camp than the other way round.

Senior Provisionals were aware that killing informers might lose them support in the nationalist community and carrots were tried as well as sticks. In January 1982, for example, the IRA announced an amnesty by which informers were given a fortnight to turn themselves in. Articles appeared regularly in republican newspapers in an attempt to demonstrate that the organization was capable of forgiveness. A typical example in 1985 was headlined 'Never Too Late'. It related how an unnamed man from the New Lodge had been working as an informer for the Army for several years. 'When picked up he was usually taken to a number of "safe" houses or carparks in Holywood, Lisburn and Ballykinlar,' the article said. Eventually the anonymous informer had been unable to stand the strain of his double existence. He had apparently told the paper, 'I thought it was too late, I thought there was nothing I could do. Now I realize it's never too late. You're better coming forward.'

The offer of clemency applied only to those who confessed their treachery; the organization continued to kill other informers who had not come forward, often after lengthy interrogation. They were left, sometimes with a folded bank note in a pocket, without shoes and with masking tape over their eyes, and a bullet through the back of the head. Tape recordings were sometimes made of their confessions and played to relatives or others who complained about the punishment.

As well as killing touts, the IRA also carries out punishment attacks on petty criminals. During the 1970s hundreds of people were knee-capped. The aim is not simply to convince people that the Provisionals can provide an alternative system of justice on the estates; there is also a practical recognition of the fact that criminals are particularly susceptible to recruitment as informers by the security forces.

Informers are usually recruited in police stations or Army bases following arrests. Some inform out of hatred for the Provisionals while others within the organization have apparently used informing as a means of disposing of unwanted members. But most prospective touts range from the taxi driver stopped on a motoring charge to the IRA member caught with a gun. They are offered the chance to walk free in return for information. Most refuse to co-operate. Republicans claim that when such approaches fail, people are often blackmailed by the authorities. They could be threatened, for example, that if they do not become informers the IRA will be told that they are indeed 'touts'.

Those who have been involved in attempts to recruit 'human sources' confirm that the techniques used to persuade people often are unscrupulous. Sometimes information gained by surveillance teams can be employed as a means of coercion. An Army intelligence officer relates that on one occasion an IRA member was shown photographs of his wife committing adultery with his ASU commander. But the basis for recruitment 'is usually black-mail', says an intelligence officer.

By the late 1970s, this had become so widely known as the standard method of recruitment that anybody who had gone free after an arrest was liable to fall under suspicion within republican communities – it became common for people to announce the fact that they had been approached by the police while in custody in the pages of nationalist newspapers as a means of trying to dispel suspicion about themselves. During the 1980s agent-recruiters refined their methods, putting more time into targeting suitable people and more ingenuity into setting up a situation in which an approach could be made.

The Secret Intelligence Service, Security Service and to some extent the Army, have gone to great lengths to recruit agents because, unlike the police, they do not have easy access to republicans in holding cells. During the 1970s, SIS set up a fake holiday firm so that it could tell a number of leading republicans that they had won free trips to Spain. When they took these holidays they were approached by intelligence officers who asked whether they would work as agents. Subsequent journalistic inquiries traced Caruso, the front company, to SIS's London Station which deals with operations in Britain.

In 1985 Gerry Young, a Sinn Fein activist, revealed how he had been approached by plain-clothes police officers during a visit to his children who were living in Birmingham. Young says the officers threatened him with an exclusion order, separating him from the children, unless he agreed to work for them. This is believed to have been an operation carried out on behalf of MI5 by the local Special Branch.

Much effort goes into targeting people whom the intelligence specialists believe are suitable for recruitment for whatever reason. If they agree to provide information they are given a code-name and details of how to contact their handler.

Meetings normally take place in areas away from republican strongholds. There is a preference for the haunts of the respectable Protestant establish-ment – the carpark of a golf club, the area around Queen's University in Belfast or outside a school in a middle-class suburb. Most informers are paid small amounts, often only £10 or £20 each week. A successful tip-off, about an arms cache for example, may lead to a bonus of £200 or £300. But top sources – people within the upper echelons of Sinn Fein, the IRA or INLA – have been paid thousands of pounds. The money is often banked in mainland accounts and it is frequently not possible for the informer to use it, because to do so would attract attention.

Meetings with handlers are often set up by telephone. The agent will ring a local police station or Army base on an unlisted number and ask to speak to his or her handler. Arrangements will then be made to meet. Agent-runners may arrange the rendezvous so as to be able to follow the source prior to the meeting in order to make sure that he or she is not being followed by the IRA.

Agent-running in Northern Ireland has taken the security forces into many profoundly difficult moral areas. The dangers of using informers are well known to intelligence officers. The information itself may be unreliable. The source may be fabricating evidence to get even with someone. They may even be involved in serious crimes and, by providing information on others, may thereby seek to remove themselves from police scrutiny. The security forces dilemma is often, most simply, that they find themselves developing uncomfortably close relationships with people intimately involved in terrorism. As one senior Army officer with experience of undercover operations in Northern Ireland explains, 'for the informer to be any good, you can almost guarantee that he is going to be part of the operation'. In the battle for intelligence, SB or Army agent-runners found themselves developing close working bonds with people whom they suspected or even knew to have been responsible for killing their colleagues.

In 1982 a case came to the courts which highlighted the close ties between an informer and his handler. Anthony O'Doherty and his one-time SB handler Charles McCormick were charged with carrying out a series of crimes, including the murder of a police officer and a bank robbery. As a detective sergeant, McCormick had been O'Doherty's contact during the early 1970s. O'Doherty had gone on the run after coming under suspicion within the IRA. He relied on the detective sergeant, who felt a bond of loyalty to his ex-agent, for protection and help. O'Doherty was to claim in court that McCormick had joined him in the series of crimes.

The judge in the case cast doubt on some of O'Doherty's allegations, warning of the dangers of accepting uncorroborated statements which implicated the former police officer. Nevertheless, McCormick was found guilty of robbing a bank, hijacking cars and of firearms offences. He was sentenced to twenty years but was released after a successful appeal in 1984.

O'Doherty himself came out the following year, leading many to speculate whether further unknown deals had been done with the authorities.

British police forces are bound by Home Office guidelines on the use of informers, but the RUC is not – another measure of the degree to which it does not operate under the same rules as its British counterparts. The guidelines say the police should not let a serious crime go ahead if an informer has told them about it, that they should not mislead a court to protect an informer, and rules out the granting of blanket immunity to an informer. All of these principles have been breached in Northern Ireland. RUC officers regard this as a necessity in the fight against terrorism but many outsiders are critical of some of these practices.

The confident tone adopted by many Army and RUC officers when discussing the actions of individual terrorist suspects is often founded on little more than the half-truths, self-interested speculation and pub gossip provided by low-grade informers. This may be the product of a syndrome well known in intelligence work whereby the agent's handler paints an overly optimistic picture of the reliability of his source in order to enhance his own position. Running a high-grade source can, after all, make the career of an SB or MI5 officer. In other cases well placed informers may allow them to assemble considerable genuine information about the activities of individuals.

Particular efforts are made to recruit quartermasters – the IRA's weapons supply experts. These people can pinpoint arms caches which can then be watched, allowing the intelligence specialists to learn the identity of cell members. Since weapons must be issued before an attack, the quartermaster may play a critical role in giving the SB or the Army foreknowledge of a terrorist attack.

Eugene Simmons, whose body was only found four years after his murder in 1981, was believed to have been a quartermaster whose information on the location of dumps of bomb-making materials led to the arrest of several Provisionals. Frank Hegarty, forty-five years old, who was killed by the IRA in 1986, worked in the Derry Brigade quartermaster's department. Hegarty's knowledge of large supply dumps in the Republic marked him out for handling by MI5 as a 'national asset'. On the night before the Gardai were due to raid a dump containing dozens of rifles, Hegarty was taken into protective custody. He went to a Ministry of Defence-owned safe house in Sittingbourne in Kent. He was visited there by his girlfriend, and told her that his minders were MI5 men. After one month in hiding he could not bear being away any longer. He returned home, pleading his innocence of any treachery, a ploy which failed to save his life. The IRA interrogated him, saying he admitted to having worked as an informer for seven years.

Sinn Fein made plain what lessons others should draw from the Hegarty case. In an interview with Peter Taylor of BBC TV's *Panorama*, Martin McGuinness, the Derry republican leader and one-time Chief of Staff of the IRA Army Council, said that if republican activists 'go over to the other side then they more than anyone else are totally aware what the penalty for doing that is'. 'Death?' asked Taylor. 'Death, certainly,' McGuinness replied.

By the late 1970s attempts to gain more information and to process it more efficiently through the TCG joint operations centres were yielding results. One area where this was evident was in arms finds. Most finds are normally the result of the SB passing informer information to the Army, which then conducts the search. A battalion intelligence officer says, 'We get Special Branch information that a house is worth searching. They don't really tell us why, but they give us a few hints as to what we might find.'

Finds of explosives and guns fell steadily from 1974 to 1978. However, in 1979 – although the number of houses searched was cut to one-third as many as in 1978 – the amount of explosives found was almost the same. The cut in searches was ordered by Kenneth Newman, who understood that better intelligence could help the security forces in their relations with the nationalist community, which bitterly resents house searches.

Although important progress had been made in intelligence collaboration, one major issue remained unresolved between the SB and the Army. With the advent of Police Primacy, during the years 1977 to 1980, the RUC tried to reduce Army agent-running to the minimum, hoping that it could take over the Army's sources. In fact, it does not appear that Assistant Chief Constable Slevin, HSB, endorsed the argument for closing down the Army's entire agent-running operation, but rather that this was the prevailing view held at the middle levels of command within the SB.

Predictably, their moves were strongly resisted by the Army. Partly as a result of RUC pressure, Major General James Glover – both in his role as CLF and in his previous intelligence post in London – had tried to improve the efficiency and professionalism of Army agent-running. Until 1977 each battalion had run its own agents, passing them on to its successor after four or more months in Ulster. But it had become clear that many of the unit agent-runners were inexperienced and inept. Their sources must have questioned the wisdom of placing their lives in the hands of these young men, most of them English, who went around trying to look like civilians but who quickly revealed their ignorance of Northern Irish ways. At the same time Lisburn accepted that suspects could no longer be interrogated or 'screened' by battalion intelligence officers, and that the amount of time they could hold people before handing them on to the RUC was reduced – all of which made recruitment of sources by the Army more difficult.

Major General Glover, in his reorganization of military intelligence in Northern Ireland, stopped battalions running their own agents and transferred this responsibility to brigades, the next level up in the chain of command. Each of the three brigade headquarters had what was called, rather coyly, the Research Office, which consisted of full-time agent-runners. This arrangement did not last long, however, and in 1980 Glover established a centralized human source handling group known as the Field Research Unit (FRU) at HQNI, Lisburn. The FRU joined 14 Intelligence Company and the SAS in forming the trinity of Army undercover operations units in Ulster. It has remained more secret than either of these organizations and this book is the first to discuss its role.

Like the surveillance unit and SAS, the FRU took recruits from various branches of the armed forces and trained them for tours in Northern Ireland. But its Commanding Officer and several other key figures were drawn from the 'green slime', so that the FRU has remained more closely under the direction of the Intelligence Corps than 14 Intelligence Company or SAS. The FRU, like MI5's agent-runners, had only limited access to people in holding cells, and thus needed to use greater ingenuity when deciding how to make the first approach to potential agents.

Despite this initiative, SB men often saw the Army's agent operations as a waste of effort. A senior police officer says, '80 per cent of the valuable intelligence sources belonged to the RUC.' An Army man says this charge is 'balls' – a measure of the passion which the issue still arouses. Other soldiers considered many of the SB's agent-runners to be time-servers and that the Army was carrying out more imaginative agent recruitment efforts.

Maurice Oldfield, in his role as Security Co-ordinator, was soon drawn into these rivalries. Oldfield had found the pace of work difficult to handle. He was more suited to analyzing papers at Stormont House than constantly climbing in and out of helicopters to visit remote bases. And, more importantly, by early 1980 he was beginning to succumb to stomach cancer.

The Army argued that it was important to maintain its own human sources because, as one officer puts it, 'Many Catholics feel much happier talking to a Brit than to a policeman.' There was another related but more basic reason for the Army's position. Informer intelligence was so important that Lisburn was reluctant to trust the SB with it all. The misgivings of some officers, that the SB had in its ranks too many Protestant 'hard men', meant that the generals did not want to be completely dependent on Knock for their information of what was going on in the IRA.

MI5 took the same attitude. It maintained its agent-running unit partly because it saw dangers in allowing the SB a monopoly of human source intelligence, according to an important figure at Stormont during this period. Oldfield apparently agreed with the Army and MI5 on this, realizing the dangers of putting too much power in the hands of the SB.

Early in 1980, shortly after it had become clear that he was seriously ill, Oldfield's positive vetting security clearance was withdrawn. This step – remarkable considering he had been involved in some of Britain's most sensitive covert operations during the previous forty years – was taken because he had not declared his homosexuality during positive vetting interviews at various times in his career.

He returned to England, terminally ill, to face a series of interviews with senior MI5 officers. They had been ordered to find out if Oldfield's homosexuality had been exploited by any foreign power. In March 1981 at the age of sixty-five, he died of cancer. At about the same time Oldfield's replacement as Security Co-ordinator, Sir Francis Brooks Richards, completed the studies ordered by Whitehall. Sir Francis returned to London and the Planning Staff dispersed. The reports completed by the Security Co-ordinators and their staffs were circulated to senior civil servants and ministers. Although Maurice Oldfield's mission had begun with much publicity as a government attempt to address problems in the security edifice following the Warrenpoint 'spectacular', its effect was, in the end, largely to endorse the status quo. The reports backed the Police Primacy policy and the centralization of intelligence, but preserved the diverse information-gathering activities of the Army, RUC and MI5.

Six years later, the reasons for Oldfield's removal became public in a newspaper article which suggested that his Special Branch guards in London had alerted their superiors to the fact that the chief of the Secret Intelligence Service was having casual sex with young men. An article by the Northern Irish journalist Chris Ryder in the *Sunday Times* said Oldfield had been removed from Ulster after an incident in which he had approached a man in the toilets in a pub not far from Stormont.

Mrs Thatcher made a public statement confirming that he had 'confessed' his homosexuality and had, as a result, been removed from his position as Security Co-ordinator. Many in SIS and at Stormont considered the Prime Minister's behaviour to be a betrayal of a man who had forsaken the short-lived pleasures of his retirement in order to serve her. They found it hard to understand why, when governments normally never comment on the security and intelligence services, she had needed to be so explicit about a man who was dead and in no position to defend himself.

Some people have detected the hand of MI5 or the RUC's Special Branch in Oldfield's fall. If a senior SIS officer had been taking young men to his flat, why hadn't it been noticed before? The allegations about the incident in Northern Ireland itself are puzzling. One of Oldfield's colleagues from Stormont says the story about the pub is wrong, and that the former SIS chief was questioned about an incident which had happened well before he arrived in Northern Ireland. The possibility exists that the 'security and police sources' cited by Ryder as the providers of the information in his story had known about Oldfield's homosexuality for some time and that they chose to use the information because he would not back the middle-ranking SB detectives who wanted to take over the Army's agents in Ulster.

# 12

# 'Jarking' and the Technology of Terror

Although informers remained the prime source of intelligence for the RUC and the Army, the use of technical means of gathering information was on the increase. By 1980 both the security forces and their republican opponents had invested considerable resources in new technology. From state-of-the-art surveillance equipment to sophisticated bomb detonators, both sides tried to give themselves an advantage by exploiting the evolving technology.

The IRA had learnt from its early disasters in bomb-making and was able to produce devices of much higher quality, using more stable explosives and more reliable timers. And radio-controlled bombs, with which the organization had experimented since 1972, also became common during the late 1970s. Notably, the Provisionals used them in the bombings at Warrenpoint and of Lord Mountbatten at Mullaghmore.

A standard device would be triggered by a transmitter known as a McGregor, designed for use with model aircraft and boats. At first this was used to activate a simple switch, also often acquired in model shops, which would then set off the detonation. It was not long before the Army began to explore the possibility of sending jamming signals on the 27Mhz wave band used by this transmitter. This tactic presented risks, however, in that there was a chance that the Army, by transmitting on the same frequency, would cause the bombs to go off prematurely, possibly injuring innocent people.

As time passed, the IRA made various changes to its radio-controlled devices. Advanced electronic equipment, obtained overseas, was used to modify both transmitters and receivers, by means of a coded signal to activate the bomb. As a result Army jamming, based on transmitting a constant frequency, would no longer be able to set the bomb off or disarm it; and the security forces were not able to find out which modulations in the signal were necessary to arm the bomb. Although this represented a significant technological development for the IRA, both sides were to progress beyond simple coding.

Ministry of Defence scientists at research establishments in England were constantly pitting their wits against IRA bomb-makers, and the adoption by the IRA of coded arming signals for their bombs forced the scientists to consider new ways of protecting soldiers. They came up with the idea of 'inhibitors' which would prevent the bomb from functioning – an intervention which would save many lives.

By the mid 1980s soldiers had been equipped with a family of portable counter-measures packs designed to meet different threats. The IRA was aware of the function of the devices carried by soldiers on patrol and later tried to blame Army counter-measures for triggering the explosion in 1987 at the Remembrance Day service at Enniskillen which killed eleven people. In fact it was set off by a timing device.

Perhaps inevitably, IRA experts found an area of the electronic spectrum in which inhibitors would not operate – the 'white band'. From 1985 onwards, several soldiers and police officers were killed, notably in south Armagh, by bombs set off using a radio signal in the white band. Defeating this threat became the subject of urgent effort at a Ministry of Defence establishment in southern England. After more than a year of intensive effort, the scientists came up with a successful counter-measure to transmitters operating in the white band. Having been chased across the electronic spectrum, increasingly the IRA reverted to an old-fashioned and unjammable method – the command wire.

Under its strategy of long war, the IRA became more aware of the risks to its men and women and of the need to avoid reckless operations. Republican areas, particularly in the inner cities, were intensively patrolled and subjected to undercover surveillance activities by the security forces, which increased the chances of IRA agents being intercepted. Because of this, the IRA had to put greater effort into the preparation of attacks to ensure that snipers or bombers would get a free run at their target. The IRA developed the skills of its own intelligence organization, scoring some coups which were to cause dismay in the security community.

During the early days of the Troubles, women had banged dustbin lids whenever an Army patrol entered the estates. As the 1970s went on, the IRA shifted towards more subtle forms of communication. Telephones were used to pass cryptic messages. Sympathizers living in tall blocks of flats would spot patrols with binoculars and then hang a towel on their balcony or open a window. These warning posts made it safer for the IRA to stage attacks or move weapons and, in turn, forced an increase in undercover surveillance by the security forces. These were mainly plain-clothes operations which were more likely to catch people out. Attempting to counter this new surveillance activity, the IRA employed their own teams of watchers, known as 'dickers' or 'dicks'. They were often recruited from the youth or women's branches of the movement and took part in attacks, by observing the security routine or by finding the home of a police officer, as well as observing the home turf.

The Provisionals also soon made attempts to intercept their opponents' communications. The small tactical radios of soldiers on the street were easily listened to. Attics or spare rooms were kitted out by the IRA as eavesdropping posts. Those who ran them quickly learned how to interpret the basic code words used by soldiers and police in an attempt to disguise their actions. It did not take long, for example, to establish that a soldier mentioning 'Felix' on the radio was talking about a bomb disposal officer or that 'Sunray' referred to a unit commander. This kind of information could be valuable in setting up 'come on' ambushes where the IRA would stage an incident and attack those who responded to it. Simple direction-finding equipment could also be used to trace the location of the transmissions.

However, intelligence gathered by listening to the communications of foot patrols remained fairly basic. The IRA realized that it would gain far more important information if it were able to break into the higher-level communications used by senior commanders. In 1979, as part of a major police intelligence operation code-named HAWK, the RUC raided a house near Belfast which had been converted into a bomb factory and sophisticated listening post. The police deduced that the Provisionals had succeeded in tapping in to the landlines which carried the phone conversations of senior officers. During the same year, sympathizers in England had succeeded in stealing from a mailbag the so-called Glover Report on future terrorist trends in Northern Ireland. The loss of this secret document was a profound embarrassment to Whitehall.

The tapping of their communications led the Army to devise a new, more secure system. One, code-named BRINTON, which was deployed in the early 1980s, was intended to provide encrypted telephone and data lines between various headquarters. However, doubts were raised recently about BRINTON. In late 1989 someone with extensive contacts in the republican movement alleged to me that the IRA had succeeded in breaking into this high-level

network. During the same month, the Ministry of Defence contracts bull-
etin, a publication circulated to defence contractors, contained an invitation
to tender for an extension to project BRINTON – possibly a recognition that
the system needed enhancement.

By the late 1970s, in tandem with the new cellular structure, more effort
was put into giving formal training to IRA volunteers, often at camps in
Donegal and other remote areas of the Republic. They became more expert
at sidestepping advances in crime detection. This 'forensic awareness', as
the police call it, included several new measures: the use of balaclavas was
increased to prevent identification from photographic surveillance; it became
standard practice to use rubber gloves when handling weapons, keeping
prints off guns and oil and powder from the hands; and boiler suits or other
garments were put on top of normal clothing to prevent them picking up
traces of explosive. These clothes, balaclavas and gloves were hidden away
from IRA members' homes, often with the weapons themselves. Volunteers
bathed soon after handling explosives so that no traces could be found
on their hair or skin. The IRA's inventiveness prompted many counter-
measures from the security forces which sought, also through technology
and improved forensic practice, to gain more convictions.

Another area where technology was used to combat the IRA was in the
checking of car number plates. In 1974 the security forces introduced the
first computerized vehicle number plate system, code-named Operation
VENGEFUL. This project was developed by the Army, the main-frame computer being based at Lisburn. And it had been the Royal Military Police in
Londonderry, not the RUC, which had made the first attempts to link
vehicle checkpoints to the agencies holding records so that instant checks
could be made. VENGEFUL terminals, many of them at checkpoints on the
border with the South, could be used to obtain information on a car in
about thirty seconds.

The IRA soon realized its vulnerability to such a system, but it too
developed counter-measures. IRA operatives toured the streets of prosper-
ous areas, whose inhabitants would be listed in VENGEFUL as being of no
interest, and took the precise details of cars. They would then find a similar
model, change its number plates and ensure that it was identical to the
first, even down to stickers in the window. In this way a soldier or police
officer checking the number by computer would assume the car belonged
to a respectable suburbanite. However, the use of 'ringers', as the IRA
called them, involved the organization in a great deal of extra effort and
was not possible in many cases. But equally it took the Army some time to

discover the most effective way to use the computer – at first a great deal of time was wasted in checking vehicles belonging to the bulk of the population, uninvolved in terrorism. In 1977 the VENGEFUL computer was modified to deal mainly with suspect vehicles.

During the 1970s most Army and RUC records were held on index cards at headquarters from local through to national level. These cards listed suspects, houses and firearms, often in considerable detail. Soldiers arriving to search a house would know the location of the furniture within it and other details – like whether the building had a cellar or a blocked chimney. This data had been compiled on house cards from previous raids and sometimes by the simple expedient of looking through the window. Security forces could obtain other information about a house from the Post Office or from the Northern Ireland Housing Executive.

Inevitably, the houses of people innocent of terrorism were sometimes subjected to such scrutiny. The searches were deeply unpopular and were criticized by some Labour MPs in London, who felt that Ulster was turning into a 'Big Brother' society in which ordinary people were subject to an unacceptable level of surveillance by the security forces. As a result of this, in 1976 Harold Wilson announced the setting-up of a personal records computer. Compiling this kind of information causes concern among civil liberties activists, although Army officers argue that it allows Lisburn to establish, at the press of a button, the many people who definitely were not involved in an incident, removing the innocent from suspicion. Security chiefs hoped this would enable them to focus their efforts more effectively, lessening the unwelcome attention given to those uninvolved in violence.

The police and Army had realized for some time that there was considerable scope for mishandling of information held in the system of card indexes and that the amount of time required to keep the information up-to-date was escalating. They introduced a computer known simply as '3072', its model number, which was intended to improve the situation. Like many early experiments with computers, it soon became apparent that the machine did not have the memory or speed to be effective. As a result police stations and Army bases retained their card indexes, and the computer had little real impact on their intelligence-collating activities.

During the early 1980s a new system was developed to replace '3072'. In 1987 125 Intelligence Section, the data-processing department of 12 Intelligence and Security Company based at Lisburn, took delivery of a new computer. The new machine, which had a memory many times the size of

'3072' was code-named CRUCIBLE. The Army hoped that CRUCIBLE would at last allow it to exploit the possibilities of the information revolution.

CRUCIBLE does not only store information on people and incidents but also contains data on the *movements* of individuals, fed in from dozens of terminals in the intelligence cells of units around Ulster. The introduction of the new computer brought some complaints from intelligence officers who resented the amount of time which their men had to spend feeding information into it. Luddite elements in the intelligence world felt the input of information into the computer absorbed more time and effort than was necessary with a system of cards and a skilled collator. Although it may reduce the number of people subjected to the attention of the intelligence-gatherers, computerization of information can compound mistakes, and the consequences – being detained at roadblocks or having homes searched – for people entered erroneously in the computer as terrorist suspects are potentially very damaging to the security forces.

Computerizing records has not brought any miraculous changes to intelligence work. CRUCIBLE has various levels of access, with those at the lower levels spending much time putting information in, but not being able to access the best intelligence themselves. According to an officer who has used the system, only the highest level of access provides the user with information significantly better than written records.

In 1973 the Reconnaissance Interpretation Centre (RIC) was established at RAF Aldergrove in Northern Ireland. The RIC is used to channel requests for aerial photography. This work is often undertaken by high altitude passes by RAF Canberra aircraft flying from England. The pictures are useful for simple mapping purposes but can also be valuable for establishing whether equipment in an enclosed area has been moved or if large weapons storage pits are being dug.

The Army Air Corps has also deployed Gazelle helicopters equipped with a specially stabilized TV camera mounting. These 'heli-telly' missions became a near constant presence over Belfast and Londonderry and at events such as republican funerals. Heli-telly pictures were used in 1989 in the successful prosecution of several men who had killed two corporals after they had accidentally driven into a republican funeral.

During the late 1970s and early 1980s the Army Air Corps ran an operation to find command wire bombs and arms caches through the use of infra-red imaging equipment which could detect disturbances in the earth. The equipment was too sensitive to work properly in a helicopter because of the vibrations. Instead it was fitted in the Corps' ancient Beaver spotter planes, small propellor aircraft with several seats. Such sorties from Aldergrove went on through the early 1980s, often over border areas where the IRA mounted command wire bomb attacks. The Beavers were retired in the late 1980s, for by then a new generation of thermal imagers was being carried in helicopters. One model, often used by special forces, provided high quality images at night at a distance of several miles.

Technology was also used to reduce the burden of running covert OPs. This task presented serious risks and the number of people trained to do it was limited. Newly invented sensors, which did not require personnel to run them, appeared to offer help. Devices which sensed approaching foot-steps could be planted in the ground. Special cameras were developed which could be left by one of the many unstaffed border crossings and would be triggered by movement. These devices could then be recovered several days later. Cameras were also fitted in the headlight cavities of cars which were left parked opposite a suspect's house or other area of interest.

Provisional newspapers revealed that the cumulative effect of physical surveillance, heli-telly, spotter planes, bugging and computerization was making many IRA volunteers fearful of carrying out operations. A senior IRA member said in an interview with the newspaper *An Phoblacht/Republican News*:

> There is their vast array of forts, barracks and spy-posts which bristle with antennae and communications masts, listening devices and other hi-tech equipment. Behind this visible presence there is also the fright-ening level of undercover and covert surveillance. Recently [1989] on this front there has been a dramatic increase in the use of hidden surveillance cameras in both urban and rural areas ... there is also the bugging of cars and even certain open locations in republican strongholds.

The IRA member concluded, 'Ultimately it is a battle of wits, every oper-ation must be meticulously planned, taking account of the obstacles.'

Hi-tech bugging equipment offered extraordinary possibilities to the covert operators especially as, by 1979, the security forces faced a dilemma over what to do when they found an arms cache. The policy of using the SAS to confront terrorists at arms caches or at the scene of a planned attack had been abandoned, as previously related in chapter eight, largely because those in charge of security felt that killing terrorists under such circumstances resulted in the dead IRA or INLA members being seen as martyrs in the republican community. Intelligence specialists came up with the solution of planting miniature transmitters inside weapons found in such dumps. The idea was that the devices would be activated when the weapon was picked up and that the terrorists' movements could be monitored as they went towards their target. Later, more sophisticated devices were developed which not only allowed the location of the weapon to be tracked but also acted as microphones, enabling intelligence officers to listen to the IRA members' conversations.

The task of fitting these devices was entrusted to specially selected officers and NCOs belonging to the Weapons Intelligence Unit (WIU), a joint Army/RUC outfit which pooled all information on ballistics and arms finds. Within each brigade headquarters there is a Weapons Intelligence Section and it was often these officers who were summoned to fit the devices to weapons, an act known in the secret argot of covert operations as 'jarking'.

The heyday of this type of covert operation was to extend from the late 1970s to the early 1980s. On numerous occasions experts succeeded in jarking IRA weapons. In several cases there were spectacular successes resulting in the arrest of IRA members who planned to use the weapons. For years these results were achieved for comparatively little risk.

A well-planned operation to bug IRA weaponry required several preconditions, the most important of which was the ability to gain access to the guns without the IRA becoming aware of it. In some cases caches were discovered in remote areas. Under these circumstances weapons could sometimes be removed to be worked on under laboratory conditions while the cache was kept under surveillance. In other cases the guns were hidden in built-up areas, sometimes even inside people's houses.

On occasions the SAS and 14 Company were used on 'covert search' missions, sometimes gaining access to a republican household while its occupants were not at home. On these missions they were able to plant listening devices of various types, including those used inside weapons. At other times people acting as agents of the security forces allowed soldiers and police access to weapons stored in their houses.

Another requirement for a successful jarking operation was that the IRA should plan to make some use of the weapons in which devices had been planted while they were still working. This factor was clearly beyond the control of the security forces. Monitoring listening and tracking devices required a base close to the site of the cache. The small transmitters used inevitably had a limited range. The bases used for such operations ranged from a local police station to an unoccupied house. In the case of a barn bugged in Armagh in 1982, where events central to the subsequent investigations of John Stalker took place, the devices were monitored from a specially placed portable cabin nearby.

Ultimately, it was inevitable that the IRA would discover that its weapons were being jarked, no matter how clever the experts were at disguising their work. It appears that the first time an IRA member noticed that a gun had been tampered with was late in 1983 or early in 1984. The discovery led to the death of James 'Jas' Young, an IRA member and police informer.

Young had been recruited as an agent following a car accident in August 1981. The police apparently threatened to return Young to jail to serve the remaining four years of an eight-year sentence for terrorist offences given to him in 1976. Young agreed to help the police as a means of keeping his liberty, and was active in the County Down IRA. In the first days of January 1984, he allowed his Special Branch handlers access to a sub-machine-gun which he was moving to Belfast. After this Young's career as an informer came to an abrupt halt. The IRA appear to have discovered the presence of an electronic device in the gun soon after it was dropped off and Young was abducted and subjected to interrogation.

Under the questioning of his former colleagues in the Provisionals, Young apparently admitted to his activities as an informer. The IRA say he confessed to providing advance warning of several bomb attacks as well as revealing the presence of stores of weapons and explosives. He was shot once through the head and his body left on a roadside near Crossmaglen in south Armagh. Young himself had reportedly not been told that the weapon he handed over to his IRA colleagues had been bugged. The exact reason for the Provisionals' curiosity about the weapon remains obscure even today.

In the wake of the Young incident, the Provisionals began to examine their weapons much more carefully. After years of success, jarking became a mixed blessing for the intelligence operators, because it provided the IRA with a method of uncovering informers. Despite the threat to agents which continued use of jarking represented, the Army, SB and MI5 carried on doctoring weapons. The experts at the government laboratories which developed the bugs put greater ingenuity into disguising them. The units which placed them also tried to improve their procedures to lessen the chances of discovery.

Jarking was not a perfect system. Placing a transmitter in a weapon brought an opportunity to monitor IRA members for a short time. Like other types of bugging device, the ones used in jarking weapons were powered by batteries with a limited life. And although WIU experts would take large numbers of polaroid photos of a cache before touching anything so that they could ensure that everything was left as they found it, they suspected that in some cases the IRA had become aware that a cache had been compromised and the weapons were never recovered.

Another possibility open to the WIU was to sabotage bomb-making materials found in the caches. Peter Wright, in his book *Spycatcher*, says that MI5 studied the possibility of booby-trapping terrorist weaponry found in arms caches, but decided not to do so. Fred Holroyd suggests that this was in fact done on one occasion, leading to the death of an IRA man in south Armagh in 1974. People who have been involved in intelligence work in Ulster say that they do not booby-trap weapons because of the risk to innocent parties.

However, a solution *was* found by interfering with weaponry to render it harmless. Bomb-making materials can be made harmless. Minute transmitters can also be planted to allow them to be tracked. The identity of an informer who has pinpointed the bomb can thus be protected because the IRA knows that it has dud ordnance from time to time. This type of operation left the IRA profoundly unsure whether its bomb-making materials had been neutralized or whether it was simply a bomb that didn't work, although the Provisionals knew that on occasion its explosive devices were being tampered with and said so publicly in 1988 when a device failed to go off in Londonderry.

The Jas Young case had alerted the IRA to the dangers of jarking. In 1985, things went wrong again, when an IRA man noticed something unusual about his gun. It was examined by Provo technical experts who realized what they had found. The weapons had been stored by Gerard and Catherine Mahon, a couple in their twenties living on Belfast's Twinbrook estate. The Provisionals launched a counter-intelligence operation.

The couple were followed to meetings with Special Branch handlers. They were subsequently abducted and interrogated, during which it was established that they had agreed to work for the SB the previous year in return for being let off prosecution for unpaid fines. They had allowed SB technical experts to go into their house and jark the weapons stored there.

The SB had given them a 'panic button' to press if they felt they were in danger of being caught, but they had been unable to use it.

In the middle of one September night in 1985 a taxi stopped on the Turf Lodge estate. The Mahons and their executioners got out. Mrs Mahon was forced to watch as her husband was shot in the face and back of the head. She was then cut down with a burst of machine-gun fire. The Special Branch had been paying them £20 a week.

1 *Above* Derry Brigade members appear on a Catholic housing estate. By the mid-1980s the Provisionals could obtain the best firearms on the market; the central figure carries the highly effective Belgian FNC assault rifle and those on either side German-made G-3s.

2 *Top* Royal Marine Close Observation Platoon members in south Armagh
displaying a variety of non-standard weapons. Such units carried out
surveillance missions and prepared soldiers for more elite duties. One of those
here went on to 14 Intelligence Company, another to the SAS.

3 *Above* A member of D Squadron 22 SAS in an observation post in south
Armagh shortly after the unit arrived there in 1976.

4 *Top* Members of Parachute Regiment units played an important role in early undercover operations. This member of a Parachute Regiment Close Observation Platoon carries the Armalite rifle, favoured by the SAS and soldiers in these units during the late 1970s and early 1980s.

5 *Above* Army Lynx helicopters provide a vital service for Army patrols in the border area. The IRA became preoccupied with the idea of shooting one down, finally succeeding in 1988.

6 *Top* Members of one of the RUC's special firearms units providing protection for a visiting member of the Royal family. During the early 1980s, more dangerous duties were assigned to such units.

7 *Above* The RUC was transformed in the years following its assumption of control of security operations in 1976. But even during the late 1980s, two officers patrolling west Belfast required the protection of 16 soldiers.

8  *Top* These republican suspects were searched after troops in a covert observation post called for a patrol to stop their car. This photo, taken by soldiers hidden in the observation post, shows the quality of photography possible.

9  *Above* Another surprise vehicle checkpoint (VCP), this one set up at night in Fermanagh, and captured on infra-red film. Republican leaflets were found on the driver.

10 *Top* Overt observation posts are equipped with computers linked to vehicle registration and suspect intelligence collation centres, as well as with high quality surveillance cameras.

11 *Above* Specially designed vehicles were deployed to protect patrols from radio command bombs. The trailer contains powerful transmitters, designed to jam any detonation signal.

12 *Above* The aftermath of the SAS ambush of two IRA gunmen at the Gransha hospital in December 1984. Their covered bodies lie beside the motorbike. The operation was based on informer intelligence that the IRA intended to kill a part-time UDR member who worked at the hospital.

13 *Top* An aerial view of Loughgall police station after the gun battle which left eight IRA men and one bystander dead. The effects of the bomb can clearly be seen.

14 *Above* Loughgall: the aftermath of the ambush before the press were allowed to see it. Patrick Kelly lies dead, a G-3 rifle across his chest. Just visible behind the wheel, the slumped figure of Seamus Donnelly. The IRA men who fell between the van and fence can be seen, covered on the far right.

# 13

# Beyond Ireland

During the 1970s the IRA developed contacts abroad to provide it with arms and money, although at this stage it was not using these contacts to help attack targets on the continent. Early shipments of weapons from America – where there was a strong Irish Catholic community with links with the IRA – had been followed by deals with Libya and with Palestinian guerrillas. The IRA gained a bewildering variety of weapons from these and other deals with arms merchants: weapons recovered by the security forces included Venezuelan army surplus self-loading rifles, 0.357 magnum revolvers bought over the counter in American gun shops and Chinese-made assault rifles. In addition to standard sniping weapons, the IRA also acquired RPG-7 anti-tank rocket launchers and heavy machine-guns.

Attempts to thwart these shipments had met with limited success. In 1973 five tons of arms from Libya on board the freighter *Claudia* had been intercepted and in 1977 a consignment from the Middle East was seized in Antwerp. This included seven RPG-7 launchers and thirty-six rockets. Both of these operations had involved collaboration between various intelligence services. In spite of such examples, many more shipments were still slipping through customs, as the variety and quantity of weapons turning up on the streets in Northern Ireland showed.

In the United States and many other parts of the world Britain's Secret Intelligence Service attempted to intercept these shipments. But the IkA had well understood the difficulties facing SIS. As each country protected its sovereignty jealously, the ability of MI6 to act on any information received was limited. The IRA had only to spread its activities across several frontiers to multiply the number of intelligence bureaucracies searching for them, decreasing the likelihood of any co-ordinated effort to detect its operations.

These weaknesses could also be exploited by attacks on British targets overseas. Sinn Fein had become aware that another bomb in Northern Ireland was less likely to make headlines than one in London. The IRA had consequently committed ASUs to various campaigns in Britain, and, during the early and mid 1970s the organization pulled off a series of bloody attacks on pubs and other targets in England: in Birmingham in 1973, and at Guildford and Woolwich in 1974. The British police were ill-prepared to meet the threats of these outrages and, under political pressure to find the culprits, moved against the Irish community in Britain. The result was a number of false convictions. In 1990 the 'Guildford Four' were freed after serving sixteen years for bombings which they did not commit. Then, less than a year later, six men who had been convicted of the IRA's bloodiest murder of the mid 1970s, the Birmingham pub bombings, were also freed. In both the Guildford and Birmingham cases convictions were secured on the basis of confessions which the prisoners later claimed were beaten out of them.

Chris Mullin, an investigative journalist and later MP who championed the Birmingham Six, claimed in 1990 to have uncovered evidence that the police knew for years who the real culprits were. One man was even alleged to have gone on to take part in subsequent bombing campaigns in England.

After this early wave of violence in Britain both the IRA and the police refined their methods. The Metropolitan Police Special Branch had a supervisory role in co-ordinating the activities of smaller SB detachments around the country. Increased contact with the RUC SB, directly and via the Security Service, allowed the Metropolitan Police SB to act more effectively in monitoring individuals as they moved between Ireland and Britain, where greater efforts were also made to establish informer networks in Irish communities. As the SB and MI5 became more effective, the IRA too changed its method of operation. For instance, more care was put into keeping ASUs apart from unreliable elements in the Irish community.

In another important change of strategy, the IRA Army Council decided in 1979 to carry the fight to British targets on the Continent, where the security establishments were still temptingly disorganized and unco-ordinated. In March 1979 the IRA killed the British ambassador to the Netherlands. A simultaneous attack aimed at a senior British diplomat in Belgium went wrong, claiming the life of a businessman. Shortly after, a bomb attack was made on a British Army mess in West Germany, but there were no casualties.

During 1980 several more attacks were directed at British military installations in Germany. A British Army colonel was shot dead. Then several shots were fired at a group of military police. In another attack a British

officer out jogging was fired on, but survived. These events naturally triggered counter-moves by British and West German intelligence, but as in
Northern Ireland a few years before, the lack of clear lines of control and
responsibility was a recipe for rivalry and unscrupulous behaviour.

In 1980, SIS, under the direction of the Cabinet Office Joint intelligence
staff, started an operation code-named SCREAM to establish agents in expatriate Irish communities in various parts of the world. It was an 'offensive
penetration operation', meaning that those agents taking part were meant
to involve themselves actively in republican movements in the countries
concerned. It is known that one SCREAM agent arrived in Düsseldorf late
in 1981.

At the same time, the Army Intelligence Corps started its own activities
in Germany. Neither organization knew what the other was up to. The Int
Corps attempted to recruit agents in the Irish expatriate community in
Germany, which numbered more than 100,000, on the assumption that
IRA cells would need support from these people. Unfortunately, the British
Army omitted to tell the West German government about these operations
– a breach of the understanding between Western nations that they will not
carry out intelligence operations on one another's territory without seeking
permission to do so.

To confuse matters further, there was yet another player seeking to
influence events. The Security Service, the domestic counter-intelligence
and counter-subversion organization, also had a presence in West Germany
– its Security Liaison Office in Cologne – a relic of the period of British
occupation after the Second World War. And sitting organizationally
between MI5 and the Army Int Corps was yet another body, the British
Services Security Organization (BSSO) which originated from the days
when Germany was the world's foremost spy battleground. BSSO has
headquarters at Rheindalen in the same camp as the commanders in chief
of the British Army of the Rhine and Royal Air Force in Germany. It is
meant to uncover plots by Warsaw Pact intelligence services or German
fifth columnists to subvert British service personnel. BSSO is part of the
Ministry of Defence and its members are classified as civil servants within
that department, although their relationship with the Security Service is
close.

BSSO and MI5 discovered the Army operations and realized that it could
cause offence to the Bonn government. Despite MI5's reputation in some
quarters as the most ruthless and 'cowboy' of Britain's intelligence organizations, its chiefs realized that the whole matter would have to be put on a

legal footing with Bonn, whatever the difficulty in admitting what had been going on.

Just as MI5 had in the mid 1970s used the threat of Irish terrorism in Britain to gain an operational foothold in Ulster, squeezing out its rival MI6, so now it was presented with an opportunity to extend its role on the Continent. Although SIS enjoyed close ties with Bonn's foreign intelligence service, the *Bundesnachrichten Dienst* (*BND*), this agency was forbidden by the West German constitution to adopt any role in internal affairs. SIS was therefore forced to approach the equivalent of MI5, the *Bundesamt für Verfassungsschutz* (*BfV*) or State Office for the Protection of the Constitution, for intelligence on Irish terrorist activity. As the *BfV* had already developed much closer ties with the Security Service, the IRA continental campaign of 1979 to 1980 came as something of a gift to MI5 in pursuing its traditional competition with the Secret Intelligence Service. Having vanquished SIS in Ireland, MI5 was now ready to position itself as the central force by bringing together the various agencies hunting the IRA in Europe.

In the United States the constitutional position also favoured MI5 since the Central Intelligence Agency (CIA) – SIS's counterpart – is constrained from carrying out operations against the Irish-American communities in the United States which support the Provisionals. This task falls to the Federal Bureau of Investigation (FBI) which is organizationally closer to MI5. Liaison with the FBI is sufficiently important for the Security Service to maintain a liaison office at the British embassy in Washington. Despite MI5's involvement in Germany and the US, SIS remained responsible for operations in many other countries. And, in an attempt – at least at an official level – to co-ordinate their efforts and pool information, the agencies had founded a group of experts called the Irish Joint Section.

A new operation, code-named WARD, was set up in 1981. It took the informers recruited by the Army and placed them under a Control Group of bureaucrats, including representatives of Army intelligence in West Germany, the BSSO and the Irish Joint Section. In belated deference to the West Germans, it was stressed that they were not running 'agents' but 'listening posts', people who could give the British early warning of a forthcoming IRA campaign. The *BfV* were to be kept fully informed of any good intelligence coming from the informers.

The introduction of WARD, however, was not enough to stop unconstitutional behaviour by Army intelligence. In June 1982 members of 28 Intelligence Section, an Army unit, were discovered by the West Germans mounting surveillance on an Irish expatriates' political meeting in Düsseldorf. It was all the more embarrassing since the official duties of 28 Section were to tail the Soviet military liaison officers living in West Germany, a hangover from the old occupation arrangements. As a secret BSSO memorandum put it, 'The use of 28 Section in a WARD context was certainly not envisaged in the acceptance of WARD as given by the President of the *BfV*.'

At some point after 1984, the IRA succeeded in obtaining several documents relating to these operations, papers which included the identity of several informers recruited under operation WARD. They were published and this account is based on them. When it resumed its attacks in West Germany in March 1987, the IRA was therefore able to steer clear of the informer network. Members of its ASUs in the later campaign were to avoid Irish expatriates in general, dealing mainly with West Germans.

The loss of these sensitive papers represented a shocking breach of security. While there have been instances of documents and photographs relating to suspects having been lost in Ulster, this was of a different magnitude. The papers relating to WARD and SCREAM represent the only written insight into the anti-IRA activities of agencies like MI5, SIS and BSSO ever published. Their content is more likely to leave the reader believing in the stereotype of Britain's intelligence officers as factional bureaucrats who cloak their failures in a heavy mantle of secrecy, rather than as acute architects of perfect conspiracies.

All the effort of establishing an agent control system acceptable to the Bonn authorities and various British organizations would have been worthwhile if terrorists were apprehended as a result. But of the total of sixteen people recruited as agents under WARD, the secret BSSO papers said, 'Only two can be said to be active in the sense of reporting anything at all.' The remainder provided nothing or proved an embarrassment to their handlers.

Two of the agents were arrested by the West German authorities for working illegally. One was dropped after he was caught lying to his handler. Another two fell under the suspicion of the Irish expatriate community and were excluded from the group. After several years of effort, BSSO concluded, 'Operation WARD has not so far produced any worthwhile intelligence.'

The people responsible for the killings of the British ambassador, the businessman and the Army officer were never caught. In fairness to the intelligence operators, IRA continental operations then stopped for several years. This, of course, provides the most important indication as to why, even if better organized, WARD would have produced little.

In 1989, following the publication of the secret BSSO documents, a leak inquiry was launched at the organization's headquarters in Rheindalen. The initial suspicion was that a German civilian employee might have obtained the papers and given them to republican sympathizers. The best efforts of BSSO, Army intelligence and MI5 failed to prove this hypothesis, according to someone involved with the inquiry. That person also told me that by late 1991, at the time of writing, British intelligence still did not know how the IRA had obtained the sensitive documents.

Early in the 1980s the IRA hatched a number of sophisticated plans to obtain weapons from the United States. The collaboration between the various agencies involved in frustrating these activities was of a more impressive nature.

The IRA had become increasingly preoccupied with the idea of shooting down British helicopters. Republican propaganda likes to emphasize that the IRA is able to strike anywhere and that nobody in the Army is safe, but in practice helicopters were being used to move soldiers around freely, particularly in the border area, often allowing them to forsake their vulnerable vehicles.

In the early 1980s the IRA developed a plan to design and produce its own anti-aircraft rockets in America. Developing an anti-aircraft missile is a multi-million pound undertaking, and even though the IRA intended to cut the costs, it would still take years of effort. The project showed the degree to which highly qualified sympathizers were prepared to get involved with republican terrorism. Richard Johnson, an American electronics engineer working with top-level security clearance at a defence contractor, was one of them. Another US citizen involved was also qualified as an electronic engineer.

Two Republic of Ireland nationals were also in on the project: Martin Quigley lived in America; Peter Maguire in the Republic where he worked as a systems engineer for Aer Lingus. Quigley and Maguire provided the know-how in explosives and detonator design and the team designed a rocket which was to be fired from a six-foot tube and would be radio command-guided on to its target. They even test-launched a prototype.

But from 1982 onwards the FBI was aware of their plan and put the group under surveillance. They kept track of them for seven years. The operation only ended in the summer of 1989 when Johnson entered his garage to find FBI officers wiring his car for sound. By then, however, the authorities had accumulated a wealth of information on the conspirators: Martin Quigley was sentenced in 1990 for eight years; and Peter Maguire was indicted, but remains at large, believed to be in the Irish Republic.

In 1983 John Crawley, a former US Marine who had been living in Ireland and had become close to the Provisionals, was sent back to his native country to buy arms for them. The IRA may have hoped that an all-American boy would not arouse the suspicions of arms dealers in the way that an Irish person might. Crawley linked up with arms dealers and pro-IRA groups of expatriate Irish in Boston. He arranged for a shipment of weapons to be sent on a freighter called *Valhalla*.

Crawley's shipment, estimated to have cost £1.5 million, included ninety rifles – mostly Armalites, sixty machine-guns, pistols, hand grenades and 71,000 rounds of ammunition. The FBI had become aware of the plan and notified SIS, and an elaborate combined operation evolved to thwart delivery of the consignment.

On 23 September 1984 *Valhalla* left America. It was tracked across the Atlantic by RAF Nimrod aircraft and, it was claimed afterwards, by a US spy satellite. On 28 September the arms were transferred on the high seas to *Marita Ann*, a trawler registered in the Republic. Martin Ferris, a senior Provisional – reputedly a former IRA Army Council member – was on board. The next day Republic of Ireland naval vessels intercepted the trawler and the men were arrested.

After the boat was seized, John McIntyre, a native of Boston, disappeared. His family said they believed he had been murdered by the IRA. They held the British authorities responsible, saying that a leak to newspapers that the shipment had been intercepted after an informer in the Boston Irish community had told the US authorities about the arms had led to his death. They believed that false information was given out to protect a high-level source within the IRA in Ireland.

As in so many cases involving intelligence operations against the Provisionals, it is impossible to ascertain the truth about these claims. Nevertheless, the leaking to newspapers of information which alluded in reasonably precise terms to the nature of an informer, as happened in this case, would be highly unusual under normal circumstances. It is quite plausible that it did constitute deliberate disinformation and that McIntyre may have died as a result.

# 14

# Hunger Strikers and Supergrasses

The development of the protest at the Maze prison, following the abolition in 1976 of special category status for prisoners of terrorist groups, prompted the IRA to switch more of its resources from the armed struggle into the political work of Sinn Fein. Since the change in policy from treating imprisoned paramilitaries effectively as PoWs – allowing them to wear their own uniforms, for example – to dealing with them as ordinary criminals, the jail had become the focus for a battle of wills between the inmates and their guardians.

The prisoners' first act of defiance was to refuse to wear regulation clothing, wrapping themselves in blankets instead. Prisoners' claims that they were being beaten by officers when they went for showers ended up with them refusing to leave their cells. In April 1978 the 'dirty protest' began, with hundreds of republicans choosing to campaign for the return of political status and privileges by staying in their cells and covering the walls with their own excreta. The authorities did attempt occasional cleaning of the cells but did not have the resources to do so regularly. Perhaps also they underestimated the impact on public opinion which photos smuggled out of the prison would generate.

Although the Maze had been designed as one of Europe's most modern prisons – less crowded and more comfortable than jails in Britain – conditions in the cells of prisoners on the dirty protest soon deteriorated. Maggots appeared, infesting the excreta and uneaten food. The willingness of the prisoners to subject themselves to confinement in these conditions soon caught the attention of the media and triggered an emotional upsurge in the nationalist community. The authorities' attempts to ameliorate the situation only highlighted their impotence. Cells were washed down with high pressure hoses and disinfectant, but within days would return to their putrid squalor as inmates continued their protest.

The prisoners' plight attracted media interest around the world, putting the British government on the defensive. The protest had successfully switched attention from the reason the men were in jail to questions about the sort of government that could allow them to exist in such conditions. The media campaign was spearheaded by Sinn Fein's publicity director, Danny Morrison. A veteran activist, Morrison developed an acute ability to recognize what journalists coming to Ulster wanted, and to mobilize the resources required to provide it quickly while ensuring that the republican message was not forgotten.

Gerry Adams, the former Belfast Brigade commander and one of the architects of the new IRA, had in 1979 become its overall leader, replacing Martin McGuinness as the Chief of Staff of the IRA Army Council, the Special Branch believed. Nobody was more aware of the need for political mobilization if the Provisionals were to sustain their support to fight the 'long war'. Increasingly Adams saw the value of using Sinn Fein, republican-ism's shop front, to achieve this goal. Advice centres were opened in nationalist heartlands, giving help which ranged from telling people what benefits they could claim to showing them how to find out if a son or daughter had been taken to Castlereagh. Adams, who held the title of Vice President of Sinn Fein as well as his IRA rank, backed this low-level activism because he wanted to use the electoral process to demonstrate popular support for republicanism. Adams knew success at the hustings would expose the claims of Westminster that only a tiny minority backed the IRA.

As time passed Adams, Morrison and Brendan Hughes – the IRA Officer Commanding the H-Block prisoners – became involved in a discussion about whether the protest for restoration of political status should become a hunger strike. There were ample precedents for such a move, the IRA having demonstrated its members' willingness to starve themselves to death on several previous occasions. On 27 October 1980 seven prisoners, includ-ing Hughes himself, began their fast. They hoped that they would win a concession which would allow Sinn Fein to claim that political status had been restored, while at the same time they knew the strike would have enormous value in dramatizing the republican cause. On 18 December, following suggestions from a Northern Ireland Office civil servant who visited the Maze that compromise might be possible – for example on the clothing issue – they called off the strike.

However, the republican prisoners considered this promise breached and early in 1981 a wider attempt to end the dirty protest collapsed when the prison authorities prevented the prisoners from obtaining civilian clothes.

A new hunger strike began, led by Bobby Sands, who had become the leader of the prisoners in the H-block. Others joined him a few days after each other so the authorities would be faced by a stream of prisoners nearing death.

Then the death in March 1981 of the MP for Fermanagh and south Tyrone prompted a by-election. Bobby Sands was entered as a candidate and the SDLP withdrew from the race, allowing the entire nationalist vote to swing behind the hunger striker. Sands won, giving a dramatic boost to the protest and to Adams' plans to exploit the ballot box as well as the Armalite. On 5 May 1981 Sands died, his death leading to large-scale rioting. Some 100,000 people attended his funeral. Through his self-sacrifice, which appealed to the Irish people's deep respect for martyrdom, Sands had won near universal acclaim among republicans.

One after another the IRA prisoners died and each time the republican enclaves erupted in violence. Lieutenant General Richard Lawson, the GOC, and Chief Constable Jack Hermon decided to bring in an extra Army battalion to help contain the public disturbances. The two men spent many hours discussing the situation, often late at night in the Chief Constable's flat at police headquarters in Knock. Despite the scale of the street violence prompted by the deaths, the two men remained calm throughout the strike, according to a source party to their discussions. Mrs Thatcher, who frequently consulted them by phone, remained adamantly opposed to the idea of any concessions.

More funerals did not bring any change in Downing Street's public position and, finally, on 3 October the hunger strike was called off, after the death of eleven prisoners – eight from the IRA and three from the INLA. The government then announced a deal: prisoners would be allowed to wear their own clothes and half of the remission lost as a result of joining the strike would be restored.

The most important practical effect of the strike was to strengthen the hand of those within the republican movement who favoured political campaigning. The strong instinct that the organization should abstain from elections – which had caused the original split with the Officials and which was still held by many in the Provisional IRA – had been compromised by Sands' election. After Sands' death Owen Carron, another prominent republican, held the Fermanagh and south Tyrone seat. The republicans had succeeded in showing that they could win elections and had done so largely because of the emotion generated by the hunger strikers' sacrifice. Having a Sinn Fein MP opened a new dimension for republican propagandists. It brought home to the populace in Bromley or Barrow that the strength of feeling in Ulster led, in some places at least, to the people choosing a candidate who clearly endorsed IRA violence to be their representative.

In the years which followed the hunger strike, prisoners and prison officers evolved means of defusing crises through dialogue rather than confrontation. When BBC TV's *Inside Story* was allowed to film inside the Maze in 1990 it became clear that prisoners there enjoyed privileges quite different to criminals in British jails. In one scene, evoking memories of the internment years when paramilitary groups held drill parades before the 'criminalization' of terrorist offences, a loyalist flute and drum band marched down the corridor on their H-Block to commemorate the battle of the Boyne. Prison officers confirmed that the men had 100 per cent control of their wings: the prison officers could only perform their duties with the co-operation of the inmates. Raymond McCartney, Officer Commanding the IRA prisoners in the Maze, and a veteran of the dirty protest, described it as a 'political jail'.

Just over a month after the hunger strikes ended a further drama began with the arrest of Christopher Black, a member of the Belfast Brigade, who had been mounting an illegal IRA roadblock in the Ardoyne. Black was taken to Castlereagh for questioning and, under pressure, he agreed to give information about the organization. Despite the use of cellular structures and Black's comparatively lowly position, he was able to identify many people who he said had played a key role in acts of terrorism.

There had been previous attempts to use members of paramilitary groups in court but Chief Constable Hermon and the Army hierarchy at Lisburn agreed that there should be, as one senior Army officer describes it, 'a very special effort made to persuade some CTs [converted terrorists] to turn Queen's Evidence', despite the mixed experience some years before with the 'Freds'. The 'very special effort' involved trying to protect them from the kind of pressures which had led some of the Freds to return to the ghettos. Black was to become the most celebrated of the 'supergrasses', as these informers were known. Large sums of money were allocated to give the supergrasses – often accompanied by their wives and children – a new life away from IRA retribution.

Black told the police that he would testify against several people who he said were senior IRA members. These included Gerald Loughlin, who according to the RUC was commander of the Belfast Brigade's 3rd Battalion, and Kevin Mulgrew, described as being in charge of one of Loughlin's subordinate ASUs. A total of forty-one people were arrested on Black's word, although three of them were not subsequently charged.

In August 1983, thirty-five of the thirty-eight people charged were found guilty in the Black case. During the trial Black had painted a picture of the IRA which was quite different to the idealized image projected in republican propaganda. He told of boredom, mistakes and service in an IRA unit nicknamed the 'Sweeney' which meted out punishments to wrongdoers on the estates. Although claiming that he had deliberately undermined attacks on the security forces, Black and his colleagues emerged as brutalized people who gave little thought to the purpose or consequences of their violence. It was a notable propaganda coup for the security forces.

Exploiting supergrasses offered tempting possibilities for the police. Few people would give evidence against paramilitaries, and the IRA's growing forensic awareness meant that they often left few clues. Although by the early 1980s the Special Branch informer network was giving more information than ever before on the operations of paramilitary groups and the individuals responsible for particular crimes, many RUC officers were increasingly frustrated because the number of convictions was not keeping pace. Turning terrorists against one another appealed to many intelligence officers because of the climate of suspicion which it would generate. More and more operations would be stalled while internal investigations were carried out into individuals who had fallen under suspicion. Significantly, the supergrass system was also backed by those who felt that ambushing the IRA was counter-productive and that convicting a large number of its members might break the organization.

This early enthusiasm for the supergrass system was backed by evidence which seemed to indicate that a long prison sentence was a good deterrent: government figures showed that only about 15 per cent of those imprisoned for terrorist offences were reconvicted – a much lower rate than for many other crimes. In the republican estates someone who had served time was considered to have done his or her bit, with many no longer taking any active part in terrorism. Many police officers and soldiers who support the ambushing of terrorists, on the other hand, say they find it hard to accept that the number of people returning to terrorism is so low.

During the latter part of 1981 and 1982 more than 200 people were arrested on the evidence of supergrasses. The arrests offered the RUC the chance to cut right through the terrorist infrastructure in parts of Ulster. In effect, it was a more discriminating form of internment. Supergrasses were not confined to the Provisionals: there were also several in the INLA and the loyalist Ulster Volunteer Force, organizations with less discipline and more factionalism than the IRA.

Moving against the UVF allowed the RUC to show that they were not pursuing informers in a sectarian way. Some seventy loyalists were convicted on the words of Joseph Bennett, William Allen and James Crockard, the three UVF supergrasses. Most of these convictions were upheld, all except the fourteen loyalists imprisoned on the word of Bennett – a higher success rate than that gained against republican terrorists.

In January 1982 Kevin McGrady, a one-time IRA member who had been living in the Netherlands, voluntarily returned to Northern Ireland and put himself in police custody. McGrady had killed several people, and had seen his brother wrongly convicted of the murder of one of them. His guilt about these events mounted until, having become involved with a religious sect, he could bear it no longer and chose to return. McGrady was therefore unique among the supergrasses in that he was not in police custody at the time he made his decision to inform.

Given the seriousness of his crimes, the police would not agree to grant him immunity, although he was subsequently released after serving six years of a life sentence. However, in court McGrady's testimony was patchy, several times confusing individuals who he said had been involved in crimes.

In August 1982 Raymond Gilmour, his wife and two children, left their home on Londonderry's Creggan estate, telling neighbours they were going on holiday. In fact they were taken into protective custody prior to a series of RUC swoops in which more than forty people were arrested. Gilmour, like Black, said he had evidence which could implicate senior Provisionals in terrorist crimes, including murder. Although Black became the more famous of the two, Gilmour's testimony was arguably a greater threat to the IRA since its structure in Londonderry is smaller and more closely knit.

By late 1982 many members of the IRA were close to panic. Sinn Fein began to orchestrate a closing of ranks in the nationalist community. It referred to the supergrasses as 'paid perjurers' and sought ways to pressurize them into retracting their testimony. For some people the appearance of an angry crowd in the public gallery of a court was enough to give them second thoughts. In other cases family members were told that deals could be arranged protecting the safety of the informer if he would withdraw his evidence.

In August 1983 Clifford McKeown, a UVF member, changed his mind and retracted his evidence. This was followed in September by rowdy scenes at a preliminary hearing in Belfast, following which Sean Mallon – an alleged IRA man – withdrew his evidence against several men from Armagh. As he walked from the court some of those who had earlier screamed abuse at Mallon shook his hand saying, 'We will not forget what you have done.'

Patrick Gilmour, the sixty-one-year-old father of Raymond, was taken from his home by hooded men in November. The IRA hoped that a threat to Patrick Gilmour's life might force his son to retract his evidence. The problems faced by families of supergrasses were such that his father was believed to have co-operated with the 'kidnap' plan, hoping it would end their isolation in the community. But although the ploy failed to deter his son, all the people charged were eventually acquitted. The Derry Brigade took a heavier blow with the defection of another supergrass, Robert Quigley. Ten people were convicted on his evidence.

Shortly after Patrick Gilmour's abduction, Jackie Goodman, a senior INLA man, withdrew his evidence. Goodman had been wounded in an internal feud and then arrested on the word of another supergrass. It is believed that the police exploited his feelings of betrayal by fellow INLA members and as a result he agreed to give evidence against twenty-seven people. While in protective custody in England, awaiting the trial of his associates, Goodman underwent a change of heart. His wife returned to Belfast and obtained assurances that the INLA would allow him to return to Ireland unharmed if he retracted his evidence.

Despite the collapse in the second half of 1982 of the McKeown, Mallon and Goodman cases, there were still many other cases brought as a result of supergrass evidence going through the courts. Nevertheless, by the end of 1982, many in the RUC expressed growing reservations about the wisdom of bringing any new supergrasses into play. This feeling was particularly strong in the plain-clothes branch: as a veteran detective in the RUC puts it, the problem with putting sources on the witness stand is that 'you use them up too quickly', and the overall intelligence picture suffers.

The credibility of the supergrass system received a further blow in October 1983 with the appearance at a hastily called press conference in west Belfast of the IRA member and supposed supergrass Robert Lean. He had given the slip to detectives at Palace Barracks, where he was staying pending the trial of twenty-eight people being held on his evidence. Lean said at his press conference that he had no real evidence against any of them, rather that, 'The RUC did all the writing, read it over to me and I signed it.' He said the detectives had been particularly keen for him to implicate

Gerry Adams. Lean denied that he had been a member of the IRA and said he had decided to retract his statements as soon as he had made them. Some intelligence officers were left with the suspicion that Lean had been part of a deliberate IRA plot to undermine the supergrass cases.

During the years which followed a series of appeals by people who had been convicted on the word of informers was to lead to the end of the supergrass system. Successful appeals were launched: by those convicted on the evidence of Bennett, the UVF member; by eighteen of those convicted solely on Black's word (in other words, where there was no other corroborative evidence); by eight of those named by the Derry Brigade informer Quigley; by two of those fingered by McGrady; and twenty-five people named by Harry Kirkpatrick, an INLA supergrass.

Of the sixty-five people convicted in this way who appealed, all but one were released. And of the 120 people convicted on the evidence of the ten principal supergrasses, sixty-seven were released after subsequent appeal. (Sixty-five were convicted solely on informer evidence; other evidence had been offered in the other two cases.) The appeal judges had in several cases found supergrasses to have been liars who implicated other people simply to get off serious crimes themselves. McGrady, for instance, had admitted to three murders, Bennett to one. Kirkpatrick, meanwhile, had perjured himself during the trial. The judges in these appeal cases effectively ruled out any further sentencing based only on the word of an informer.

Despite the success of these appeals many in the security forces were convinced that the majority of those released were guilty and only regretted the expenditure of informers on inconclusive court cases. Not long after the members of the Belfast Brigade implicated by Black had been released on appeal, an Army intelligence officer told me that the number of incidents in their part of the city had gone up – in his view, as a result.

Although the world of the informer had been largely discredited in the courts, it nevertheless remained the world which continued to provide the security forces with the bulk of their operational intelligence – information on which they were sometimes required to make life and death decisions.

The supergrass system had brought alarm to many republican enclaves. But the reaction to the arrests among ordinary residents varied. One Army officer recalls a humorous response in north Belfast to a painted republican graffiti which warned 'Remember Chris Black'. Somebody had added, 'I hope to God he doesn't remember me.'

# 15

# Reasonable Force

Early in the 1980s the Army rethought the deployment and operations of its SAS contingent in Ulster following the shift in early 1979 from ambushing terrorists to observing them for long periods in the hope that evidence could be gained which would lead to their prosecution and conviction. This rethink was led by Army commanders who considered the arrangements which had developed since the expansion of SAS operations outside south Armagh to be unsatisfactory in several ways. First, the deployment of one troop in each of the three brigade areas, with the Squadron's fourth troop as a central reserve, was an inflexible one. Lisburn wanted the ability to switch the entire SAS contingent from one place to another with the minimum of delay.

The SAS Regiment was also finding practical problems sustaining squadron tours in Northern Ireland. Each tour normally lasted between four and six months, with a period of preparatory training before and a period of leave afterwards. With four operational squadrons, this meant that SAS soldiers rarely had a sustained period away from Ulster. It also involved the Regiment in a constant turnover of personnel, resulting in few soldiers getting to know the complex situation in Northern Ireland really well.

This disruption, in Army jargon a lack of 'continuity', did not affect the surveillance operators of 14 Intelligence Company to the same degree. They were based in Northern Ireland for longer tours – usually for a minimum of one year. Detachments of the surveillance unit contained some soldiers on their second or third tours with years of experience of that type of covert warfare in that particular place. The SAS, on the other hand, needed to keep its soldiers proficient in a wide variety of skills from the jungles of Brunei to the Arctic fjords. There was also a feeling at Lisburn that the SAS should be drawn organizationally closer to 14 Intelligence Company.

As a result of these priorities a new structure was created to act as the executive arm of Army intelligence in Ulster. Major General Glover, who had been so influential in the development of other aspects of intelligence co-operation in Ulster, was the architect of the change. The plans do not seem to have been put into effect until late 1980 and early 1981, by which time Major General Glover had been succeeded as CLF by Major General Charles Huxtable.

The new operative group took the cover name Intelligence and Security Group (Northern Ireland) which, confusingly, had already been in use for some time by 14 Intelligence Company alone. It was more often known among its soldiers as 'Int and Sy Group' or simply 'The Group'. As with previous cover names it suggested a unit carrying out an entirely different and more routine sort of business. There are Intelligence and Security Group headquarters in Britain and Germany (the group in Germany having been involved in operation WARD described in chapter thirteen) but they are a collection of Intelligence Corps sub-units, whose daily activities consist mainly of paper-pushing. They are certainly not operational units of SAS soldiers and surveillance experts.

With the formation of the Group, the number of SAS in Ulster was reduced from a squadron strength of around seventy men to a reinforced troop of just over twenty. For the first few years these men were provided by whichever squadron was doing a six month stint at Hereford as the Regiment's Special Projects team – ready for an emergency anywhere in the world. In the mid-1980s this changed and the Northern Ireland troop separated from the squadrons. It became, in the words of one SAS man, 'a posting like any other'. The men selected went for one year, allowing greater continuity in Ulster while enabling the Regiment's four squadrons to concentrate on other types of training. However, SAS reinforcements were always available for transfer to Ulster at short notice.

Under the new arrangements, the SAS element and 14 Intelligence Company were brought together under a single commanding officer. The CO of Int and Sy Group was able to deploy the three surveillance detachments and the SAS soldiers together or separately, according to the nature of the mission. The SAS unit was to be held at a central location, ready to move quickly to any part of Ulster. Furthermore, the activities of the Group and of RUC special units were to be integrated by the Special Branch's three Tasking and Co-ordination Group (TCG) headquarters.

During 1980 to 1981 members of the Int and Sy Group were involved in a number of successful operations against the IRA. In several cases they were able to apprehend terrorists without firing a shot.

On 2 May 1980 eight IRA men with an M-60 machine gun were cornered by the SAS at a house in Belfast's Antrim Road following an intelligence operation. The security forces planned to cordon off the area around the building, but a vehicle accidentally broke the cordon and two Morris Marina Q cars went into action carrying eight heavily armed SAS troops. As they piled out, the IRA opened fire and Captain Richard Westmacott was struck by two bullets – the first SAS soldier to be killed by the IRA. The remaining soldiers then rushed into the wrong house. They were withdrawn and the IRA men later surrendered, only to escape from the Crumlin Road jail five weeks later.

In September 1980 the SAS mounted an operation at an arms cache in Tyrone. A sniper's rifle had been hidden in a hen coop. In 1978 two IRA men and John Boyle, the Dunloy farmer's son, had been killed in similar circumstances. However, in this case the weapon is thought to have been doctored by Weapons Intelligence Unit experts. When two members of the IRA, Francis Quinn and Thomas Hamill, came to recover the rifle, the SAS men therefore knew they would be safe. Quinn and Hamill were both sentenced to eight years' imprisonment.

On 14 March 1981 SAS men surrounded a farmhouse near Rosslea in County Fermanagh. Inside were Seamus McElwaine and three other IRA men. McElwaine, although only twenty, had built an extraordinary reputation for himself. He had joined the IRA at sixteen and carried out his first killings as a teenager, boosting his terrorist status.

McElwaine had carried out several close-range shootings of local members of the security forces. In February 1980 he had shot dead Alexander Abercrombie, a forty-four-year-old part-time corporal in the UDR and father of four, as he drove his tractor. Seven months later he killed thirty-six-year-old Reserve Constable Ernest Johnston as he climbed out of his car outside his house. Despite being younger than most of the other local volunteers, McElwaine soon gained command of his own unit. A subsequent biography of him in the Sinn Fein newspaper *An Phoblacht/Republican News* stated, 'Seamus gained plenty of operational experience, so much so that by the time he was nineteen he became OC of the IRA in County Fermanagh.'

Arresting somebody like McElwaine requires careful planning and excellent intelligence work. The task facing the soldiers outside the farm buildings on 14 March 1981 was made still more difficult by the fact that those inside possessed an arsenal of weapons. They had four rifles – an Armalite, an M1 carbine, a Ruger rifle like those issued to the RUC and a German-made assault rifle – as well as 180 rounds of ammunition.

Int and Sy Group had conducted an extensive surveillance operation against McElwaine and the other four members of his ASU. They decided to surround the house, but make no attempt to storm it. In a fashion reminiscent of the American police during the prohibition era, the Group called to the IRA members inside the house telling them they were surrounded and should come out with their hands up. Faced with this hopeless situation, they complied.

A fifth member of the unit was subsequently arrested at a different location, but was tied by forensic evidence to the farmhouse. In May 1982 the five-member unit received sentences ranging from ten years to life. McElwaine himself was found guilty of the murders of Corporal Abercrombie and Reserve Constable Johnston. The judge, who described him as a 'dangerous killer', recommended that McElwaine should serve at least thirty years.

The break-up of McElwaine's ASU represented something of a textbook example in the use of special forces. The reasonable use of force during these years to a large extent demolishes the notion that the SAS will open fire whenever they have the opportunity to eliminate an armed member of the IRA. Clearly, in this case the orders not to use force were well understood. It may be in the disposition of an SAS soldier to invoke 'big boys' rules', but during these years the Army clearly discouraged them from doing so.

Despite the success of this operation, Int and Sy Group remained vulnerable during their surveillance operations. The death of Corporal Paul Harman in Belfast in 1977 (see chapter four) had underlined the risks run by 14 Intelligence Company personnel when on duty in their unmarked cars.

On 28 May 1981, at a time when tensions were high due to the hunger strikes, a young Army officer belonging to the Londonderry Detachment of 14 Intelligence Company climbed into his unmarked Opel Ascona car. According to an intelligence officer, he went through the city to conduct a reconnaissance for a forthcoming operation on the other side of town. It was only on his way back that his journey was interrupted.

The car's progress had been noticed by a group of IRA members. George McBrearty, the twenty-three-year-old leader of an ASU from the Creggan, and three colleagues set off in a hijacked Ford Escort to intercept the Opel.

As the Opel approached a road junction the Escort swerved in front of it and two men carrying Armalite rifles got out. The young officer, armed with a 9mm Browning pistol with a 20-round magazine cannot have felt he had much hope against four men carrying more powerful weapons. McBrearty went to the front of the car and Charles Maguire went to the back. The officer got out of the car and stood behind the open door.

McBrearty turned his back and the officer grasped his moment. He drew his pistol and fired nine times at him. All but one of the rounds went into his back. He then turned and faced Maguire, who was still standing at the back of the car, stunned. He shot Maguire in the head twice. Jumping into the car, the soldier fired at the Escort, hitting a third IRA man, Edward McCourt, twice. As he pulled away one of the IRA members opened fire at the Opel shattering two of the windows and peppering its side with bullet holes. The officer escaped, unlike Maguire and McBrearty who both died from their injuries, and he was subsequently decorated for his actions.

Shortly after the incident an RUC patrol arrived on the scene and came under sniper fire. The police returned fire but are not believed to have hit any IRA members.

The incident was followed by deliberate attempts to disguise the truth of what had happened. The IRA, smarting from the death of two men and the capture of another because of the actions of a single soldier, claimed that there had been two more cars containing five more 'SAS men' who had opened fire on its unit.

Those critical of the Army version of events have cited several possible indicators that more soldiers were involved. Several weapons were handed in for testing besides the officer's 9mm pistol. But these were found to be Ruger revolvers and an M1 carbine belonging to the RUC patrol which was ambushed on the scene later. It was also pointed out that there was a discrepancy between the soldier's statement to police investigators that he had only fired eleven times, whereas the IRA members appeared to have been hit by more bullets. It is possible that the soldier's statement was mistaken on this point. I am confident that the officer was the only member of the security forces involved. Unusually, I was able to confirm this with both republicans and soldiers. A senior republican admitted to me during the preparation of this book that their version of events was entirely false, and they had known it to be so at the time; they maintained instead that the IRA members had died because they had exercised soldierly restraint, not opening fire immediately on somebody of whose identity they were unsure.

Maguire and McBrearty were the only IRA men killed by Army under-cover units during the five years from December 1978 to 1983. Even some republicans recognized that the shoot-out was started by the IRA – one man with a pistol would hardly have wanted to get involved in a fight with four men with assault rifles.

At the inquest in 1988 into the deaths of the three IRA bombers killed in Gibraltar, an SAS officer – 'Soldier F' – who was called as a witness suggested that the arrest of Seamus McElwaine's unit and of Quinn and Hammill proved that their Regiment did not gun people down. Soldier F told the court, 'The ratio between arrests and kills is 75 to 25 in percentage terms in favour of arrests.' People who have served in covert operations in Northern Ireland suggest that the great majority of those arrested by the SAS were apprehended prior to December 1983, pointing to a significant change of tactics after this date in favour of aggressive ambush operations.

One joint police/Int and Sy Group operation which to my knowledge has not been revealed before as an episode involving undercover units occurred in July 1982 in Belfast. According to an officer who was closely involved, the operation was mounted after intelligence was received that the IRA intended to blow up the RUC band.

Intelligence led the covert operators to believe that the terrorists would attempt to detonate a bomb close to a bridge across the River Lagan in Belfast. At about 5.30 p.m. on 9 July 1982, surveillance teams sighted two vehicles – a Datsun and a Cortina – in a lay-by off the Annadale embankment. The cars moved off crossing the Lagan on the Governor's Bridge and heading along Stranmillis Road. A police vehicle checkpoint (VCP) had been set up at the end of Stranmillis Road. Before it got to it, the Datsun stopped and its driver, Bobby Brown, aged twenty-two, got out. Special plain-clothes police firearms units then moved in, arresting Brown and the occupants of the Cortina – twenty-eight-year-old Thomas McKiernan and Siobhan O'Hanlon, aged twenty-one – which was stopped at the VCP at the junction of Stranmillis and Malone Roads. Police recovered a pair of gloves from the scene which were later shown to have traces of explosive.

Shortly after the arrests a bomb in the Datsun exploded, causing extensive damage to property. There was no loss of life because the area had been cleared. It is not clear from accounts of the trial whether the terrorists intended to detonate the device with a remote control unit, and the blast was caused by a fail-safe timer, or whether it was only fitted with a timer, as was the case in Gibraltar.

There were further arrests during the following days and Brown came under police pressure to testify against his accomplices. Brown's wife was abducted from their home on the Twinbrook estate, apparently by the IRA as a means of pressurizing him not to give evidence. She subsequently returned home and Brown did not turn Queen's Evidence.

One of the occupants of the Cortina, Siobhan O'Hanlon, was released on bail, only to be arrested a few days later with three other women, in possession of explosives and other bomb-making materials. When the trial of those accused of plotting to kill the RUC band came to court, O'Hanlon was acquitted. Police officers claimed to have seen her throw the pair of gloves recovered from the Malone Road out of the Cortina's window, but the judge said he did not believe them. Although O'Hanlon was sentenced to seven years in prison for her part in the other incident, she was released after serving only part of the sentence. The *Sunday Times* later claimed that O'Hanlon was one of the IRA members to have survived the Gibraltar operation in 1988 – an allegation which she has denied.

Brown and McKiernan pleaded guilty to conspiracy to murder the police band when they were tried in 1985. Daniel Quinn, one of those arrested shortly after the abortive attack, also pleaded guilty to attempted murder. Four others pleaded guilty to lesser charges of involvement with the Active Service Unit. During the trial it emerged that the ASU had carried out several other operations during the summer of 1982: an attack on an Army patrol on the Twinbrooks estate in May; a mortar attack on Woodbourne police station in June; and, in the same month, a shooting at an Army patrol on the Springfield Road.

Although the operation succeeded in its basic aim – saving the lives of the police band – it could be criticized for several reasons. In presenting their evidence to the court, the police claimed that the bombers had been intercepted by a routine police patrol which became suspicious of the two cars. This, on the evidence of the officer involved with the operation, was clearly untrue since the operation was mounted on the basis of informer intelligence. The surveillance operators failed to tie O'Hanlon to the bomb plot through photography or forensic evidence, and were reduced, in the opinion of the judge, to lying about having seen her drop the gloves.

In the end the RUC were forced to rely on Brown, the bomber himself, to try to implicate the others. Since the whole RUC/Army operation was mounted on the basis of informer intelligence, it is open to speculation that their original informer may have been one of those arrested, since knowledge of the precise details of the plot would clearly be confined to a small number of people. It could further be speculated that the security forces knew in advance of the ASU's operations throughout that summer, but had allowed them to proceed to keep suspicion from falling on their informer.

What the whole episode showed was the difficulty of carrying out an intricate covert operation without resorting to an ambush. To the outsider it would seem that the security forces tactics were still worthwhile – after all, the operation produced several convictions and prevented the police band from being blown up. But if the police knew about the IRA operation in advance, they might have had the option of preventing it entirely, so ensuring that the lives of fellow officers were not put in jeopardy. Some of those in undercover units were left wondering whether it had really been worth risking the lives of so many people for the convictions gained, especially given the failure of the case against O'Hanlon. 'It wasn't a very glorious incident', the man involved with the operation comments; and alluding to the O'Hanlon episode, he says, 'It was that sort of thing which did lead to frustrations.'

The Belfast case was similar to the Gibraltar case in that intelligence indicated a car bomb attack on a band. But in July 1982, there was a strong reluctance on the part of security chiefs to authorize anything resembling an ambush. The Belfast incident shows the difficult dilemmas facing those mounting undercover operations, not the least of which was their decision to let the band continue with its concert engagement despite the fact that they were confident that it was under a considerable threat. But it was also an example of a successful joint police/Int and Sy Group operation: Brown and his accomplices were successfully apprehended by a force made up of both soldiers and specially trained police officers.

The existence of élite police firearms units like that used at Governor's Bridge resulted from the advance of Police Primacy. These units were intended to carry out operations based on sensitive intelligence much in the same way as the SAS. The Special Branch E4A unit and Bronze Section of the Special Patrol Group had been largely restricted to surveillance duties, although they were occasionally involved in operations, as in the · Ballysillan Post Office depot incident. In early 1980, soon after Jack Hermon became Chief Constable, the SPG had been disbanded, to be replaced by a hierarchy of mobile support units. This was largely a presentational change carried out to overcome the negative public perception of the SPG.

Each police division had a Divisional Mobile Support Unit (DMSU) of at least one squad of twenty-five to thirty. In inner city areas the DMSU controlled more squads. The DMSUs were trained in riot control, basic observation post techniques and firearms. They could be used to cordon off areas, mount checkpoints and disperse rioters. Several hundred police were drawn into the DMSUs.

In addition it was decided that there should be special units in rural areas. The two RUC operational regions outside Belfast were given their own special units, known as Headquarters Mobile Support Units (HMSUs). The function of the two HMSUs was to give back-up in the RUC's two rural regions where there were fewer DMSUs than in Belfast, and where the need for highly trained firearms squads was perceived at Knock to be greater. Each of the squads consisted of twenty-five to thirty police who received more advanced firearms training than those in the DMSUs and operated more often in plain clothes in response to SB information.

At the apex of the new structure was the Special Support Unit (SSU). Although it is believed many HMSU members were given firearms training by the Army, only the SSU sent men in any numbers to be trained by the SAS. The SSU is, says a veteran RUC man, 'the back-up, they were trained up by the SAS to be the Special Branch's own Reserve'. Many of those who had been in Bronze Section were apparently drafted into the SSU. When they were set up, the HMSU's and SSU's members received advanced training at Army camps such as Ballykinlar and at Aldershot where they were instructed by paratroopers and the SAS.

At a later trial the RUC's Deputy Chief Constable Michael McAtamney described the training undergone by HMSU members. He said they were given four weeks of special training during which they were shown how to respond to various threats if they were seated, standing or walking. 'Their training is on the basis that once they have decided they are entitled to open fire, that they should fire, in order to put their assailant out of action as quickly as possible,' he added.

The soldiers who trained them formed the impression that the quality of SSU recruits varied widely. One says that while they regarded many as being reasonably professional, some were 'Orange nutters' about whom they harboured serious doubts. These reservations were not confined to soldiers' bars in Aldershot or Hereford. One senior Army officer says that, in forming the SSU, the RUC failed to understand the complexities of such operations.

But the early 1980s saw the high summer of official optimism about what could be achieved under Police Primacy. The RUC's special units were being formed at a time when the Army thought of itself, to some extent, as disengaging from Ulster. The number of regular battalions had decreased from fourteen at the beginning of 1978 to ten by the end of 1980. One of the brigade headquarters, 3 Brigade, was also disbanded as the Army's strength fell below 10,000.

Despite its reservations, the Army leadership at Lisburn accepted that the RUC should develop its own covert units and that the SAS should help them do it. According to one observer at Stormont, 'The SAS were reined back a bit to give the police a bigger role.' Among ministers and generals confidence in the RUC was high; there was a feeling that it should have the ability to confront terrorists on the basis of its own intelligence, without Army help. This confidence was to be shattered in November 1982.

# PART THREE: 1982–1984

# 16

# Stalker

Just after midday on 27 October 1982 three police officers were blown apart at the Kinnego embankment near Lurgan in County Armagh. They had been travelling in an unmarked car which was wrecked by a large bomb placed underneath the road.

A fortnight later three IRA members: Eugene Toman, Sean Burns and Gervaise McKerr, were intercepted by members of an RUC firearms squad, near Lurgan. Even years after the event the precise identity of the unit is still uncertain. Some sources speak of it as being part of the Special Support Unit, others say that it was the Southern Region Headquarters Mobile Support Unit (HMSU). The confusion may be due to the fact that the squad, one of two based at Lisnasharragh near Belfast, was under the administration of the SSU but was controlled from day-to-day under different command arrangements.

The police, riding in unmarked vehicles, were expecting Toman, Burns and McKerr, who had been under E4A surveillance. The overall operation was being run by Special Branch officers of the regional TCG at Gough Barracks, Armagh.

The police chased after the car, opening fire on it. Later examination was to indicate that 109 shots were fired at the three men, who were unarmed. As their riddled car came to a halt Eugene Toman stumbled from the vehicle, but was shot through the heart by a policeman. All three IRA men died.

On 24 November another group from the HMSU saw two young men approaching a hayshed near Lurgan. The police were keeping the building, which they believed was an arms dump, under surveillance on orders from the TCG. Shortly after Michael Tighe, aged seventeen, and Martin McCauley, nineteen, had entered the shed the police opened fire. Tighe was killed and McCauley seriously injured.

The incidents in Armagh continued on 12 December, when Seamus

Grew and Roddy Carroll, members of the INLA, were waved down by police after crossing the border from the Republic. This was also an operation directed by the TCG, in which members of the security forces had mounted surveillance operations against INLA members inside the Republic. A car pulled up behind the two men as they returned to the North.

In the unmarked police car was a Special Branch inspector and Constable John Robinson, a member of the HMSU. Constable Robinson got out of the car and walked towards the passenger side of the suspect vehicle, where Carroll was sitting. He fired his pistol through the window, killing the INLA man. Constable Robinson then walked around the front of the car, reloading his pistol as he went, and fired four times at Grew, slaying him as well. Neither of the INLA men was armed.

These three shootings, in which the police had killed six people in a small area of Ulster in just over one month, were to prompt a series of inquiries. They caused great alarm at the Northern Ireland Office and in Westminster. Someone serving in a key position at HQNI, Lisburn at the time remembers, 'It came as a big shock to me as it did to any other citizen.' However, his statement needs to be treated with some caution, as Army surveillance operatives of 14 Intelligence Company were believed to have been involved in the events leading up to the Grew/Carroll shootings.

The killings became known as the 'shoot-to-kill' cases, because of the belief in the nationalist community that there had been a police conspiracy to murder the suspects. Many nationalists could not see how it was possible to justify the shootings. McKerr's widow, Eleanor, said at a press conference, 'If they thought they were suspected terrorists, why didn't they come to my home that night and lift Gervaise?'

The 'shoot-to-kill' affair was to become the greatest crisis of Jack Hermon's nine-year tenure as Chief Constable, a running sore which over a space of years allowed republican propagandists to exploit the Catholic community's darkest fears about the police. Matters were compounded when it emerged that the police had concocted cover stories to explain what had happened in each incident.

Journalists were told that the three IRA men had gone through a roadblock, injuring a member of the police and that the RUC had been there as part of a routine patrol. In the Grew and Carroll case it was also said that their car had run through a roadblock, again injuring a member of the police. None of this was true. While many soldiers and police do not regard the use of cover stories to the press as wrong, some would have objected to the fact that the officers had also been instructed to give the same versions to CID officers who were investigating the killings, as is routine after fatal incidents of this kind.

Following an internal RUC inquiry by Deputy Chief Constable Michael McAtamney, the Director of Public Prosecutions (DPP) decided to bring murder charges against three policemen involved in the first shooting and against Constable Robinson for his role in the Grew/Carroll incident.

Chief Constable Hermon responded by attempting to block the murder charges. He said in a later television interview, 'To prosecute these officers would be quite disastrous: a) because they would never be convicted of any crime and certainly not of murder, and b) that the resultant outcry from certain elements of the community could have damaged our sources of intelligence.' Apparently he threatened to resign if the charges went ahead, something he did not in fact do.

When Constable Robinson was tried, early in 1984, he revealed that SB officers at Gough Barracks had told him to give a false version of events. He and other officers had also been asked to sign forms indicating they would comply with the Official Secrets Act, something they were already bound to do as police. The SB wanted to disguise the facts that they had been waiting for the car on the basis of informer intelligence, and that Constable Robinson had been accompanied by an SB inspector, as well as the actual circumstances of the shooting. These revelations prompted the DPP to suggest that there should be another inquiry into whether there had been a conspiracy to pervert the course of justice.

The murder trial of the three officers involved in the first incident also brought to light false evidence. Lord Justice Gibson, the trial judge, found the men innocent. He criticized the DPP for even bringing the case, asking whether it had been considered what effect such a case would have on the morale and reputation of the police and armed forces generally. He commended the police for behaving with bravery and for 'bringing the three deceased men to justice, in this case, the final court of justice'.

These remarks caused consternation in Northern Ireland. What did he mean by the phrase 'final court of justice'? Was the judiciary endorsing the shooting of unarmed men in questionable circumstances? Lord Justice Gibson issued a statement a few days later saying that he had not meant to suggest any backing for a 'shoot-to-kill' policy and that he believed the police had only the same right as other citizens to use reasonable force. But with his statements the judge had lit a slow-burning fuse, one that was to consume him and others in a conflagration of violence.

Following the acquittal of Constable Robinson an outside inquiry was announced into these events. On 24 May 1984 John Stalker, the Deputy Chief Constable of Greater Manchester, was named as its head. Some RUC officers regarded the bringing-in of an outsider as a deliberate slap in the face from Whitehall. If it was the government's intention to punish the force by ordering an inquiry but to limit the damage to RUC morale by ensuring Stalker's findings were predictable and anodyne, then this was a grave miscalculation.

From the outset there was tension between Hermon and Stalker. The Chief Constable was uncomfortable at the damage which might be caused to morale within the force, while Stalker suspected a widespread cover-up. Relations between them were prickly, and soon focused on what the scope of Stalker's investigation was meant to be – his terms of reference.

According to the journalist Peter Taylor in his book, *Stalker: The Search for the Truth*, the Deputy Chief Constable's primary task was, 'to investigate the circumstances in which the three cover stories had been given to the CID'. He also had to investigate why surveillance teams following Grew and Carroll had been in the Republic, and to look in general terms at the practice of SB officers seeking to protect informers.

Stalker saw his primary field of inquiry differently. In his autobiography, he said he was 'to investigate the conduct of members of the Royal Ulster Constabulary in connection with the investigation of all three incidents'. Stalker regarded this as allowing him to look in general terms at whether the officers had tried to cover up murder.

The investigations established a link between the hayshed in which Tighe was killed, the killing of the three IRA men in the car and the earlier explosion at the Kinnego embankment. An informer had pinpointed the hayshed as an arms store and had also identified Toman, Burns and McCauley as having been involved in the killing of the three police officers in the Kinnego explosion. Stalker believed that the two incidents which followed the bombing might have been the result of an RUC plot to avenge the deaths of their three comrades.

It also emerged that the hayshed had been under technical surveillance. A Security Service technical officer had put special devices into the barn which would indicate if explosives stored there were moved and transmit any sounds from within the building. It was to the RUC's and MI5's great embarrassment that the explosives used to kill the three officers at Kinnego had been taken from the hayshed *after* the bugs had been installed, but that the devices had failed. The Chief Constable's attempts to restrict the inquiry's terms must have resulted at least in part from a desire to prevent his own officers finding out that such a terrible mistake had been made.

Stalker realized that the bugs in the hayshed which had failed had been replaced by new ones and that these might offer a vital clue as to whether the police officers who opened fire on Tighe and McCauley really had shouted a warning, as they claimed. So began an eighteen-month battle of wills between the Stalker team, the RUC and MI5 to establish whether the shooting was on tape and, if it was, whether the inquiry could have access to it.

Stalker's investigations also linked the killings of Grew and Carroll to their earlier meeting in the Republic with the INLA terrorist Dominic McGlinchey. He had been responsible for an upsurge of INLA activity in the border area, particularly in Armagh. McGlinchey, who had bragged in an interview about his preference for killing people at close range, had driven the INLA into active and reasonably effective terrorism, thus making him one of the most wanted men in Ireland. It is possible that the police thought Grew and Carroll's car contained McGlinchey and that, having been briefed to the effect that he was a dangerous killer who had evaded capture many times before, considered it their duty to open fire on the car without hesitation. Stalker discovered that SB surveillance men had followed Grew and Carroll to their meeting in the Republic.

The Manchester police officer came to the conclusion that the SB had become far too powerful within the RUC. He believed middle-ranking SB officers had organized the cover-up of the shootings and were engaged in trying to obstruct his inquiry. In his book Stalker wrote:

> The Special Branch targeted the suspected terrorist, they briefed the officers, and after the shootings they removed the men, cars and guns for a private de-briefing before the CID officers were allowed access to these crucial matters. They provided the cover stories, and they decided at what point the CID were to be allowed to commence the official investigation of what occurred. The Special Branch interpreted the information and decided what was, or was not, evidence; they attached labels – whether a man was 'wanted' for an offence, for instance or whether he was an 'on-the-run terrorist'. I have never experienced, nor had any of my team, such an influence over an entire police force by one small section.

According to Stalker, Assistant Chief Constable Trevor Forbes, Head of the Special Branch at the time of his inquiry, told him he would never be able to hear the tape of events in the hayshed. The existence of a tape of events in the hayshed emerged in November 1984, five months after Stalker's inquiry began. Assistant Chief Constable Forbes was to become an important figure in Stalker's inquiries. Not only was he head of the principal department under investigation, but he had also been the RUC's Operational Commander Southern Region in Armagh – and therefore in authority over the area in and around Armagh – until shortly before the shootings.

Forbes was regarded by many at Knock as utterly loyal to the Chief Constable. Shortly after Jack Hermon took over, Assistant Chief Constable Mick Slevin, the man who had rebuilt the SB during the late 1970s, clashed with his new boss, say RUC officers. Slevin apparently refused to brief Hermon fully on an intelligence matter, telling him, 'The need-to-know principle goes up as well as down, sir.' Chief Constable Hermon resolved to displace his independent-minded HSB, and the lifelong plain-clothes man was moved to a job which Chief Constable Hermon considered better suited to his abilities – in charge of complaints and discipline. Slevin had by that stage contracted cancer and died after a short period in his new job.

Forbes was not a career detective, but had previously run the force's traffic branch. He was promoted from the backwater of traffic to the difficult regional commander's post in Armagh. He enjoyed a close relationship with Chief Constable Hermon out of hours as well – for some years the two men had run the RUC's pipe and drum band.

As Stalker probed more deeply into the affair, Kevin Taylor, a Manchester businessman, came under police investigation. Taylor, who knew Stalker from various social functions, came under examination as a possible associate of a group of criminals in Manchester.

In May 1986 Stalker was removed from the Northern Ireland inquiry pending investigations of his relationship with Taylor. He had already delivered an interim report to Chief Constable Hermon which was strongly critical of his force. Stalker wrote that he was reserving judgement on the Tighe case until he heard the hayshed tape but that he considered that the five men who had died in the other two incidents 'were unlawfully killed by members of the Royal Ulster Constabulary'.

Stalker had decided that he needed to interview a number of senior RUC officers, including Chief Constable Hermon and his deputy, under caution. He wanted to know why the original internal inquiry had found out so little. His removal came just before he expected finally to get access to the hayshed tapes and to carry out these interviews.

In 1990 attempts by the police to prosecute Kevin Taylor collapsed. Taylor had been ruined by the prolonged inquiries into his activities and regarded his suffering as having been the price of removing Stalker. The Greater Manchester Deputy Chief Constable resigned in March 1987, convinced the investigation into his dealings with Taylor had been linked to the Northern Ireland inquiry.

Stalker later wrote philosophically about his battle of wills with Hermon: 'I respect, if not admire, the way in which Sir John Hermon took the fight to me. He protected the force and himself from intrusion by me into its anti-terrorist efforts and practices, and he succeeded.' Stalker concluded, 'I was expendable, he was not.'

After Stalker's dismissal, the shoot-to-kill inquiry was taken over by Colin Sampson, Chief Constable of West Yorkshire. Among those at Lisburn and Knock who observed the affair at first hand there is general hostility to Stalker. Senior officers, both police and Army, usually use the word 'naive' when describing him. For the most part, however, they do not deny the substance of his findings. It would seem, rather, that the Army too enjoyed the considerable operational independence which Chief Constable Hermon had won for the security forces and resented Stalker's investigation because it involved outside scrutiny of sensitive operations.

When Chief Constable Sampson delivered his report in 1988, he said that several officers had been guilty of conspiring to cover up what had happened during the three incidents. However, the government decided that no action would be taken against the men for reasons of 'national security'. Chief Constable Hermon, in his 1988 annual report wrote: 'What can now be said is that Mr John Stalker and Mr Colin Sampson both stated what the RUC had always insisted: that there was no 'shoot-to-kill' policy . . . at last the allegation so harmfully and sensationally publicised for so long has been proved false.'

The Chief Constable's confident summary of Stalker's views needs qualification. In February 1988 Stalker told *The Times*: 'I never did find evidence of a shoot-to-kill policy as such. There was no written instruction, nothing pinned up on the notice-board. But there was a clear understanding on the part of the men whose job it was to pull the trigger that that was what was expected of them.'

The idea that the police officers involved in the shootings had not been given explicit orders to kill, but had been led to think that was what was required of them, is endorsed by a veteran RUC man. He claims that senior officers, when visiting the RUC's special units, had made it clear that they were men chosen to act as the force's cutting edge in the anti-terrorist effort. The RUC man says, 'I believe that Sir John would demand the ultimate without thinking it through.'

In June 1988 the Northern Ireland Police Authority, a watchdog designed to oversee the force, discussed whether to investigate observations made by Mr Sampson about the behaviour of Chief Constable Hermon, Deputy Chief Constable McAtamney and Assistant Chief Constable Forbes. This was blocked by just one vote of the sixteen-strong authority.

In 1991 Peter Taylor reported on BBC television that Colin Sampson's recommendations had actually been tougher than Stalker's. Sampson had suggested that the RUC officers involved in the hayshed shootings should be charged with conspiracy to murder and that MI5 as well as police officers should be charged with conspiring to pervert the course of justice. In the latter case, the proposed charges resulted from the fact that Security Service officers were believed to have destroyed a tape of the hayshed shooting after they knew that Stalker had asked to hear it. My own inquiries confirm Taylor's summary of Sampson's findings. Peter Taylor used these revelations to support his thesis that Stalker's removal from the Northern Ireland inquiry was unconnected with his criticisms of the RUC. The new information shows that even if the reporter is wrong and people did conspire to remove Stalker because they feared his findings, that Colin Sampson proved an even tougher proposition.

Those who directed security policy at Stormont had undoubtedly drawn their own conclusions from the shootings. The price of admitting to serious misdemeanours on the part of the security forces is, to the mandarins of the Northern Ireland Office and the ministers they serve, usually too high. Instead, changes designed to ensure that there would be no repetitions of such killings were made, some of them put into effect even before Stalker had arrived in Ulster.

Without doubt the affair showed how powerful the SB had become by the early 1980s. A senior Army officer who served at Lisburn during the mid 1980s notes, 'Special Branch runs the intelligence operation. It is Army policy that the RUC SB has all the intelligence which we gain. The reverse is not true.' But the affair had shown the need for greater supervision of the Branch and in 1984 John Whiteside, the Head of CID, was made Senior Assistant Chief Constable in charge of both CID and SB. Understandably, some SB officers were none too happy at being placed under the control of the one-time head of this rival department.

During this period, several SB officers, of the rank of chief inspector, superintendent and chief superintendent were pushed out of the force. But the fate of at least two of them adds weight to suggestions made by some RUC officers that they had to take the blame for mistakes by the Security Service, for instance. Their untimely departure from the RUC did not appear to diminish their eligibility for other intelligence organizations: one was believed to have been recruited by the Security Service; another joined the British Services Security Organization in Germany, which works closely with the Army and MI5.

The shootings in Armagh also produced grave doubts in the minds of those at Stormont and Lisburn that the RUC could be trusted to execute specialist operations of the type performed by the SAS. The future of the HMSUs and SSU, the most highly trained of the firearms squads, therefore came under review. An officer serving in a key position at Lisburn at the time of the 'shoot-to-kill' incidents reflects: 'Police Primacy is 100 per cent correct, but when it comes to mounting specialist operations against terrorists, you've got to ask: is that a job for policemen? Police Primacy had inevitably led towards a police desire to run the whole thing, so there was a build-up of police special units. But the whole Stalker affair caused them to think twice.'

Some soldiers in the Army's special forces took pleasure from the failure of the RUC's efforts. 'Your British soldier is far more tolerant. You imagine an RUC man who gets a chance of slotting a Catholic. Will he be more tolerant than an SAS man?' says one member of the Regiment.

Senior officers at Lisburn expressed their views more tactfully. You couldn't expect the RUC to match the SAS, says one, because the SAS is recruited from a pool of people which is so much larger. This is true – the HMSU and SSU members represented about one in eighty of the strength of the RUC whereas the SAS numbers about 400 out of the British Army's total strength of 155,000 – one in almost 400. Furthermore, the SAS troops sent to Northern Ireland form a much smaller number, recruited from experienced men within the squadrons. In this sense the SAS were more 'élite', having been chosen with greater selectivity.

RUC officers looked on the whole affair with bitterness. As on previous occasions an investigation by outsiders was bringing about a fundamental realignment within the force. Many RUC officers agreed with Stalker about one thing: that the constables who belonged to the special squads felt badly let down by their senior officers. The shootings had exposed the fact that the police, unlike the Army, lacked the skills to protect their officers from difficult questions. One RUC officer involved in the affair says: 'Soldiers will be taken away to some other part of the world. You can't do that with us, we live here. You have to make sure that we uphold the law and live with it. Sometimes you wonder if the senior officers really realize what the men are going through. It seemed to us that the Army had things much better sewn up.'

Within a few months of the Armagh incidents, the will within the RUC to deploy its special units on missions to confront terrorists had collapsed. One senior officer says, 'As a result of the tremendous pressure Hermon was under he used the military more than he did before.' Training of the SSU by SAS men and paratroopers appears to have been stopped. The RUC's special units were given different tasks, often acting as back-up to the SAS, sealing off an area rather than facing terrorists themselves. The idea expressed by some Army officers at the time of the reduction of SAS strength in Ulster that they might be pulled out altogether was quietly forgotten. The TCGs were once more giving the critical role to the Army.

During an interview with a senior Army officer who had witnessed Stalker's investigation first hand, I said that what surprised me about the whole affair was not that the RUC had been caught feeding false versions of the shooting incidents to the media and the CID, but that Army special forces had done it so many more times and got away with it. He smiled and explained that cover stories were vital to protect the sources and methods of sensitive operations. Such operations, he said, must be allowed to continue 'without being held ransom to that mythical commodity you call truth'.

# 17

# 'Ambush': A Matter of Interpretation

Towards the end of 1983 the SAS did something they had not done in Northern Ireland for five years: they killed members of the IRA. Shoot-outs of a kind which had happened between 1976 and 1978 began to occur once more. The tone of spokespersons at Lisburn or Knock was often to imply that these incidents were the result of chance encounters between Army 'patrols' – the term SAS was never used on the record – and terrorists. In fact, in many cases these incidents were the result of deliberate choices by people armed with foreknowledge of terrorist crime.

Some were to assume that the government had simply ordered the SAS to eliminate terrorists. But according to people who have served at the heart of covert operations in Ulster, stark, explicit orders to kill would have been both unpalatable and unnecessary. Understanding the practical conse-quences of the change in mood which took place in the second half of 1983 requires a knowledge of Army tactics – in particular that of the ambush.

To many civilians the word 'ambush' carries no lethal connotation. One dictionary defines it as 'to lie in wait'. This might imply a mission to arrest as well as to shoot somebody. To anybody trained by the British Army, however, the word has quite a different meaning. The manual in use by the Army during the early 1980s to train soldiers in Northern Ireland-type operations, *Land Operations Volume III – Counter-Revolutionary Operations*, says, 'An ambush is a surprise attack by a force lying in wait upon a moving or temporarily halted enemy.' An attack of this kind could be against the law in the United Kingdom, in that soldiers may only use the minimum force necessary to protect life and property.

The Army manual sets out how an ambush should be mounted. The troops taking part are positioned to be able to fire into the 'killing area'. The main body of soldiers form 'assault' or 'killer' groups charged with destroying the enemy party. On either side of these groups will be 'cut-offs' – smaller groups who can prevent stray enemy soldiers escaping. Other soldiers may be positioned to stop the enemy trying to outflank the main ambush party.

These tactics are not peculiar to the SAS, but are taught to the majority of soldiers entering the Army. However, the SAS has made a speciality of the ambush. Following selection, all SAS soldiers are taken to Brunei to be trained in jungle warfare. They spend much of their time learning how to carry out 'Type A' ambushes, those limited to a particular area where it is known the enemy can be intercepted. Those who have taken part in such training say that the SAS soldiers train to rake the 'killing area' with gunfire and shrapnel from claymore mines and necklaces of grenades. An SAS NCO maintains that these jungle patrols are 'where all soldiering begins and ends'.

During the inquest in 1988 into the deaths of three IRA members in Gibraltar, the SAS officer 'Soldier F' denied suggestions that the decision to mount an ambush contained an assumption that the enemy party would be killed. He said that the aim of an ambush might also be to take prisoners. This may have been his interpretation of Army doctrine, but *Land Operations* makes clear that an ambush is an attack and implies that any prisoners, if it is part of the mission to take them, are survivors of such an assault. The manual deals with the arrest of terrorists under a different section. It goes on: 'The aim of an ambush is thus usually achieved by concentrating heavy accurate fire from concealed positions into carefully selected killing areas which the enemy have been allowed to enter, but from which their escape is prevented by fire and possibly obstacles.' It adds that such an attack would only normally be used in 'Setting 4', a counter-insurgency campaign verging on limited war in which the security forces had lost control of certain areas.

The increase in the amount of intelligence reaching security chiefs in Ulster by the early 1980s meant that they sometimes had foreknowledge of terrorist attacks. This information gives them a choice. In the words of someone who has run operations by the SAS in Northern Ireland: 'There are two options – either to arrest with irrefutable evidence on which to base a prosecution or the other, which is to go in and shoot. The chances of being able to make an arrest under those circumstances are minimal because the terrorists will be armed.'

A decision to confront armed terrorists can be implemented as an ambush. If the terrorist decides to mount an attack, and the security forces to pre-empt them then, the officer adds, 'the outcome is pretty obvious'. The change in late 1983 is therefore a shift – on some occasions at least

– to the second of his options, the shooting option. There had been many occasions during the previous few years which demonstrated a preference for the other approach – for example the arrest of Seamus McElwaine and his gang in March 1981.

The general or senior police officer who wants to arrest terrorists must create the right circumstances to do so. In the McElwaine case this involved ensuring, through surveillance, that the men were surrounded in a house on an isolated farm. Had it been necessary, the soldiers could have sat outside the farmhouse for hours or days until those inside had surrendered.

On the other hand, confronting terrorists during an actual attack is likely to produce a shoot-out. The paramilitaries will be armed and may be in a state of mind where they are ready to use their weapons. Failing to intercept them carries a risk for the soldiers that the terrorists may escape. And, most importantly in terms of the law of minimum force as outlined by the Yellow Card, a party of terrorists approaching their target may well represent that immediate danger to life which justifies the security forces opening fire.

Besides the Yellow Card's general rules of conduct concerning firearms, the specific nature of soldiers' orders can have a bearing on the use of force in a particular operation. Army officers and NCOs are trained to give orders in a standard format. Orders normally involve groups of soldiers gathered around an officer or NCO as he explains the plan. They move through various headings, for example 'friendly forces' or 'outline plan'. The most important, in seeking to understand whether such operations are within the law of minimum force, is the one headed 'mission'. The use of the word 'ambush' in this section will carry a particular meaning to most soldiers.

The only published example of SAS orders for a mission in Northern Ireland concerns an operation in May 1976, following the discovery of what appeared to be a command wire for an IRA bomb near a border crossing in south Armagh. The SAS were operating under the aegis of the 3rd Battalion, the Parachute Regiment, that night and the Commanding Officer decided to refer his plan to higher authorities for approval. His orders were reproduced in a book covering that tour. He told his brigadier that his aim was 'to insert that evening (23 May) a covert patrol to try to *ambush* [author's emphasis] the terrorists who would have to man a chosen firing point and probably lay out more wire'.

It is standard for the oral orders to SAS troops for operations in which they intend to confront the IRA to refer to the Yellow Card restrictions on the use of firearms, according to someone who has been present at such briefings. However, the soldier's understanding of his task, if the word 'ambush' is used, appears to be clear even if the Yellow Card guidelines are mentioned, as emerges from this interview with an SAS soldier:

> URBAN: What is the mission on an ambush?
>
> SAS MAN: You know what the mission is on an ambush, everybody knows what the mission is in an ambush.
>
> URBAN: Tell me what you think it is.
>
> SAS MAN: I know that when you do an ambush you kill people.

During the 1980s the term 'ambush' was replaced in SAS orders in Northern Ireland by 'OP/React', short for 'Observation Post/Reactive', according to an SAS man who served there. He says an OP/React order is 'to all intents and purposes an ambush' and believes it was a cosmetic change prompted by RUC sensitivity over the word 'ambush'. It is apparent that the soldiers concerned still believe they are involved in precisely that, so I will continue to use the term in accounts of actions which may have been officially described as OP/React missions. The key point is that when the intention is to apprehend armed terrorists, SAS men say their orders usually refer to a 'hard arrest'.

There is no shoot-to-kill policy in the sense of a blanket order to shoot IRA terrorists on sight. Rather the knack is to get IRA terrorists, armed and carrying out an operation, to walk into a trap. Killing an unarmed IRA member may create a martyr, but if the same person were carrying a gun, even committed republicans may feel the operation was, in some sense, fair. Peter Morton, the Parachute Regiment CO who later wrote about his 1976 tour in Northern Ireland, says of the death of Peter Cleary, 'it was certainly a pity that the first occasion on which a terrorist was killed by the SAS was not more clear-cut; the ideal would have been to shoot an armed terrorist.' Some of those who have carried out covert operations in Ulster refer to lethal force being used in such a way as to appear fair and within the law as the 'clean kill'.

The idea that it is the appearance of what has happened that may, in terms of undermining support for the IRA, be more important than the reality is not confined to members of the SAS or Special Branch. The Northern Ireland Office said, in a letter to Amnesty International in 1985 on the subject of disputed killings by the Army and police, 'The Government and the security forces themselves recognize that it is in their interest to avoid controversies over the use of lethal force by members of the security forces.' The Freudian slip, if it may be termed such, is that the civil servant chose to emphasize the avoidance of controversy rather than the needless use of lethal force itself.

Army commanders understand that incidents in which special forces have been involved may be subjected to intense scrutiny by the media and by republican propagandists. Someone who held a key post in the security forces recognizes that in SAS ambush-type operations against the IRA the public perception of what happened is all important and that there is no room for error: 'If we don't get them and destroy them totally or get them with the cleanest of cuts, then it is always assumed that it was not done properly. If it is not perceived to be an immaculately clean kill, it is automatically assumed to be wrong.'

Between December 1983 and February 1985, a period of just over one year, the Intelligence and Security Group was to shoot dead ten people in Northern Ireland, eight of them IRA members, following a period of five years in which the SAS had killed nobody. Why, then, did security chiefs choose the shooting option?

The answer lies partly in the activities of the IRA and the ways which security chiefs felt were open to counter them. In 1980 the number of terrorist incidents was at its lowest for many years. With the public disorder provoked by the hunger strike campaign in 1981, incidents began to climb again. The trend was not a marked one, but security chiefs were alarmed at the improved efficiency of the attacks, say those involved in policy-making at the time. The IRA was, in effect, able to kill more people in each of its attacks.

More importantly, the summer of 1983, which saw successful appeals against many of the convictions obtained from supergrass evidence, represented a depressing setback for those who believed that the courtroom was the best arena for cutting back the IRA, rather than the shoot-out. The supergrasses Sean Mallon and Jackie Goodman had withdrawn their evidence in 1982. Patrick McGurk, the Dungannon man, had dropped his evidence against eight people in October. And Robert Lean, claimed by the RUC to be a senior Belfast Provisional, had not only withdrawn his evidence during the same month, but had gone on to appear at a press conference deriding the way the police sought to incriminate people. Although the government continued with its supergrass prosecutions, the IRA had succeeded in checking them.

However, the most bitter blow had come on 25 September 1983, when prisoners in H-Block 7 at the Maze succeeded in overpowering their prison officers. One of them, who was stabbed, subsequently died of a heart attack. They had then commandeered a kitchen lorry and escaped from the prison. During the dragnet which followed, the security forces quickly re-captured sixteen prisoners. Another twenty-two escaped, among them some of the most ruthless terrorists imprisoned during previous years. The Chief Inspector of Prisons later described the incident as 'the most serious escape in the recent history of the United Kingdom prison services.'

The IRA exploited the incident fully, organizing a press conference in which several escapees took part. Some of the fugitives went abroad – the organization accepting that they wanted no further active role in the fight – but others returned to the forefront of the campaign. Among the escape's ringleaders was Seamus McElwaine, captured by the SAS in 1981, who soon returned to bring death to the countryside of south Fermanagh. Another was Gerard McDonnell who was later to be convicted of belonging to the IRA cell which attempted to assassinate the Prime Minister with a bomb which killed five people at the Grand Hotel in Brighton in 1984. Two escapees, Brendan McFarlane and Gerard Kelly, were later run to ground in the Netherlands by the Secret Intelligence Service and were eventually extradited by the Dutch authorities.

Those who served in Ulster at this time reject a specific link between the resumption of aggressive special force operations and the Maze escape, preferring instead to talk of a general change in mood at Lisburn and Knock. The new mood may have taken root independently among the security chiefs, rather than being the result of a political directive. James Prior, later Lord Prior, was Secretary of State for Northern Ireland at this time. In a 1988 interview with Tom Mangold of the BBC's *Panorama* programme, he denied ever having foreknowledge of SAS operations:

MANGOLD: Were you personally involved in the decision to use the SAS?

PRIOR: No, not at any time.

MANGOLD: Did you ever ask to be told?

PRIOR: No, I am not aware that I ever asked specifically to be told when the SAS were going to be used.

However, some senior security figures say that they did sometimes tell ministers of forthcoming operations. I have been able to establish, by inter-viewing several people who held senior positions at Stormont and in the security forces, that plans for ambush-type operations are not submitted in writing to ministers. Rather the chief constable or GOC may mention the possibility of such an operation verbally to the Secretary of State – the senior minister at Stormont. It is apparently not the practice for the minister of state responsible for security matters to be informed. Much depends on there being a cordial relationship between the Northern Ireland Secretary and his security chiefs. An informal hint in conversation of a forthcoming operation is regarded by senior police and Army officers more as a privilege than a right, says someone who has been party to such discussions. But it has also been suggested to me that senior politicians at the Ministry of Defence in London may sometimes be told in advance of a forthcoming special forces operation in Northern Ireland.

By the mid 1980s a regular system for the approval of special operations had been devised at Lisburn. The GOC would be briefed on forthcoming operations of this kind by the CLF. The commanding officer of the Intelligence and Security Group is often present in case the CLF, who has many other operational responsibilities, cannot answer all of the GOC's questions. The fact that the briefings took place once a week indicates both the scale of covert operations and that a great many of those planned as ambushes do not achieve their intended result.

The chief constable of the RUC is also regularly briefed by his intelligence chiefs on RUC aspects of forthcoming special operations. Any remarks to the Secretary of State about forthcoming special operations are usually based on the formal briefings which the GOC and chief constable have been given by their subordinates.

Talking to people who have served in senior positions at Stormont it becomes apparent that, during the 1980s at least, they did not consider themselves to be in real control either of the RUC's or of the Army's special operations. The chief constable, as overall director of security operations, succeeded in ruling specific discussion of undercover units and their activities off the agenda. A senior Stormont figure recalls, 'We just tended to hide behind the operational independence of the RUC. We couldn't be responsible for detailed operational matters, only for broad policy.'

Politicians and civil servants at the Northern Ireland Office had the responsibility to Parliament for security forces actions but little actual influence over them. One explains: 'I think why I can justify it to myself is that ministers, on the whole, spend half their time in London and half their time in Northern Ireland. Their pattern is irregular, they have other political responsibilities, whereas the soldiers – at least the ones who have to take the decisions – have to be there twenty-four hours a day.' The result was one of those compromises, typical of British government, in which real power is exercised by those who are not responsible to Parliament or the electorate who, in return, shield those who *are* responsible from painful decisions.

Another factor affecting the situation was the important changes among senior officers at Lisburn and at Knock. By 1983 Lieutenant General Richard Lawson had been replaced by a new GOC, Lieutenant General Francis Richardson. People serving at Lisburn say that Lieutenant General Richardson took a more direct role in the direction of everyday operations, leaving less latitude to his Commander Land Forces. In addition, the CLF, Major General Huxtable had in 1982 been replaced by Major General Peter Chiswell. The new CLF bore the visceral hatred of the IRA common among officers of his parent unit, the Parachute Regiment. However, Major General Chiswell was also a man of strong religious convictions who understood the harm which would come to the security forces if they became embroiled in disputes over the use of lethal force. And by late 1983 he had himself been replaced by another officer, Major General Pank. The new CLF was an infantry officer who had served in Borneo and Malaya before going on to command an armoured brigade in West Germany. From the events which followed (see chapter eighteen), it is clear that there must have been a consensus between Lieutenant General Richardson and Major General Pank about the use of special forces during the period 1983 to 1985.

Whatever was going on at Lisburn, the attitude of Chief Constable Jack Hermon must have been critical. After his Enniskillen speech in 1980, Chief Constable Hermon had attained something of a doveish reputation. Many in the force had considered his vision of an unarmed force to be foolishly, if harmlessly, utopian. After the Ballysillan operation in 1978, Hermon – then still Kenneth Newman's deputy – had apparently voiced a distaste for SAS operations, particularly in inner city areas.

Some of those who worked with the Chief Constable, however, believe his views may have hardened and changed over the years. Initially, he had taken it upon himself to be present at the funeral of every police officer killed by terrorists. In doing so, he had put himself squarely in the path of the torrent of grief which flowed from distraught spouses and children. Eventually he stopped going to all of them, sending one of his senior deputies instead. After his retirement the Chief Constable told the BBC TV's *Everyman* programme, 'I had a concern that it was eroding my capacity to perform my duty as Chief Constable with the objectivity and professionalism which was necessary.'

Whether or not Hermon's personal attitudes had altered under this pressure from the pacific idealism of his 1980 speech, as overall director of security operations he was theoretically responsible for the ambush tactics to which the Army was returning. But Hermon also presided over another change of note in the form of Assistant Chief Constable Trevor Forbes' promotion to Head of Special Branch. This office is so important for the direction of covert operations that the views of its incumbent could play a key role in the process of planning ambushes.

Perhaps the most compelling explanation for what the security forces sought to achieve when they returned to a policy of occasional ambushes is provided by a senior figure at Stormont. He says that the idea of mounting such operations 'is to give the IRA an occasional rap across the knuckles, something which may deter them from carrying out more attacks'. It would appear, from the interviews I have been able to carry out, that the initiative for that change came not from ministers who might have more qualms about the political repercussions of such 'raps', but from within the security edifice itself.

Another explanation for the use of ambushes is given by a one-time senior officer at Lisburn. He acknowledges that such operations may provide the IRA with martyrs, but believes they can offer the chance to deal with specific individuals, saying, 'The balance of advantage to us or them may be very questionable. There comes a time when we say, "We need a kill" – such and such a person is a thorn in our side and we've got to do something about him.'

Most officers involved in intelligence work in Northern Ireland tend to believe that ambushes are effective in removing particular players or units. They realize, though, that such measures may buy them limited breathing space. One RUC officer told me at a briefing, 'We give them a bloody nose but they wipe it and come back. Sometimes we hit them hard and take out an entire Active Service Unit. There's a lull, new faces appear and the whole thing starts up again.'

It is apparent, talking to those who have been present during discussions of special forces operations in Ulster, that the security chiefs and ministers themselves to some extent fall prey to the mentality of the 'clean kill'. Given that explicit discussion of eliminating IRA members was anathema to most of these people, it is worth discussing here how a typical SAS operation evolved in Ulster during the mid 1980s – a process pieced together from people who have played various parts in such dramas.

The idea of mounting a pre-emptive special forces operation against terrorists can emerge in a number of places. The initiative most often comes from a Regional Head of Special Branch or sometimes the Head of Special Branch himself, following the receipt of informer intelligence about the location of an arms cache or the target of a forthcoming attack. Information from a 'national asset' informer is often given by the Security Service to the SB, because it is they – through the TCG – who have the ability to do something about it. The SB may suggest a pre-emptive operation or may simply relay the information in neutral terms to the Army. It may be the brigade commander, the CLF or the commanding officer of the Intelligence and Security Group – a man selected for his experience of covert operations – who may then suggest that the tip is suitable for 'executive action'.

A plan will then be formulated by the Int and Sy Group in close collaboration with the TCG. Their operation, by this stage given a code name, will then be referred to the CLF for approval. He may then refer it up to the GOC and chief constable and they in turn may tell the Secretary of State. This is likely to take the form of a brief conversation in which the Secretary of State is told that there is an opportunity to deal a significant blow to the terrorists. If asked, the Secretary of State usually responds that the general or senior police officer should do what they think is right. Once approved, the plan is then passed on to the surveillance teams and SAS who must carry it out.

Many of the operations approved either at ministerial or lower level come to nothing because of the unreliability of informer intelligence. The soldiers return to camp several days later without sighting the terrorists.

The process of formulation and approval of such operations may be compared in some ways to the idea of loading the rifle of one soldier in a firing squad with a blank bullet. This has sometimes been done to allow all members of the firing squad to believe that they personally were not responsible for the death of their target. In the same way a general may distance himself from what the officer quoted earlier referred to as the 'pretty obvious' consequences of a successful pre-emptive operation by referring the matter for higher approval. The Secretary of State may feel he or she is not responsible because it is easier to accept the advice of the security chiefs than to reject it. The plan, as it is finally approved, will then switch the responsibility back to the twenty-eight-year-old SAS corporal or police sergeant who has to carry it out, because only the people on the spot can interpret the rules of engagement.

The organizational and tactical changes in the SAS in the early 1980s are also important in judging the attitudes of soldiers on whom such responsibilities fell. The move from occasional squadron tours by all four of the Regiment's sub-units to the sending of individuals to a reinforced troop of just over twenty soldiers in Ulster, which ultimately followed the establishment of the Int and Sy Group, had important consequences. There were undoubtedly benefits – notably that individuals served for longer, becoming more familiar with the Northern Irish scene. But this new pattern of sending people to Northern Ireland restricted the number of soldiers who gained experience of such operations, increasing their suspicion of outsiders, as well as the ties between them.

The captains sent to command the troop in Northern Ireland sometimes found it difficult to exercise control over it, according to a member of the Regiment. After the death of the SAS officer Captain Westmacott in 1980 it became increasingly rare for SAS officers to go out on observation duties or ambushes with their men. Officers are normally relegated to the Ops (operations) room at a local security forces base. Without them in the field, the soldiers are more likely to revert to 'big boys' rules' if they sight a terrorist. Most, if not all, of the fatal incidents involving the SAS which occurred during the period 1983 to 1985 took place in the absence of an officer.

After the Falklands War in 1982, the SAS admitted large numbers of soldiers from the Parachute Regiment. A Parachute Regiment major had become officer commanding of the Training Wing and, according to several people who served in the SAS at the time or attempted to get into it, the criteria for selection shifted towards an emphasis on the aggressive mentality of the airborne forces and away from the more traditional SAS values. The Regiment began to fail more people who could not meet its standards of selection; its numbers dropped as a result – a phenomenon known at Hereford as 'creeping excellence'. These problems brought the OC of Training Wing and Commanding Officer of the Regiment, a member of the Royal Corps of Transport, into conflict during the mid 1980s. The CO felt that too many Paras were getting through selection and too few from all other types of regiment. Even the Director SAS and his successor the Director Special Forces, the London-based brigadier with overall responsibility for such troops, intervened in an attempt to get Training Wing, dominated by Parachute Regiment NCOs who had been in 22 SAS for years, to let more non-Paras in. The consequence of these differences, says an SAS man, was that by the mid 1980s the Regiment was falling well below establishment, many troops having ten or twelve soldiers rather than sixteen. The proportion of Paras, who make up about one in seventy-five of the Army's overall strength, reached 52 per cent in 22 SAS in the mid 1980s, according to one regimental officer.

The consequences of this influx of paratroopers are hard to quantify. Those non-Para members of the Regiment who are prepared to discuss the issue maintain that the airborne soldiers are more violent, less likely to consider the consequences of force and less likely to propose alternative solutions to problems, than men from other regiments. However, an SAS soldier from the Parachute Regiment says the idea that their influx into Hereford had any particular effect is 'exaggerated'.

Michael Asher, who served in Ulster with the 2nd Battalion of the Parachute Regiment early in the 1970s, describes their mentality graphically: 'We begged and prayed for a chance to fight, to smash, to kill, to destroy . . . we were unreligious, apolitical and remorseless, a caste of warrior-janizaries who worshipped at the high altar of violence and wanted nothing more.' In the late 1970s, Asher served in the Territorial Army SAS. He comments, 'They were not truculent and sadistic, as the Paras had been. You could see that they might kill easily, but never for the love of it.' Those who were alarmed by the advent of a 'Para mafia' in 22 SAS in the mid 1980s argue that the influx of paratroopers had virtually eliminated the distinction described by Asher.

Against the background of 'creeping excellence' the change in the pattern of SAS deployment in Northern Ireland introduced a further element of selection. Individuals could not be posted to the troop in Ulster unless they passed a course lasting about three months at Hereford. Although most did go through, the Northern Ireland course provided the NCOs with experience of Ulster who ran the course with an opportunity to filter out those who were considered 'unsound'. That many of the veteran NCOs were Paras shifted the definition of what qualities were desirable, say some SAS soldiers, away from the use of stealth and cunning and more towards an acceptance of violence.

# 18

# The Group in Action

It was early on the evening of Thursday 1 December 1983 when an Army special forces officer arrived in Dungannon in Tyrone. He had been called there following a tip-off from an informer. The Special Branch asked him to organize a covert search of the area called Magheramulkenny, near the village of Coalisland. The Army's undercover specialists went into action before first light.

A senior NCO in the SAS, afterwards referred to as 'Soldier A', carried out a search of a small field surrounded by an embankment topped with a thick hedge. In the hedge he found an Armalite rifle, a shotgun and a bag containing balaclavas, gloves and other clothing. Subsequent ballistic tests were to show, according to the RUC, that the Armalite had been used in twenty-two shootings since 1979 including four killings – all of them of off-duty members of the security forces in the Dungannon area.

Several hours later, at 3 a.m. on 2 December, Soldier A briefed five other SAS soldiers on the task ahead. In a subsequent written statement he said, 'It was my intention on this mission to apprehend any terrorist attempting to take any weapons or clothing from the cache, and the members of the group were briefed accordingly.' He told them that they should only open fire in accordance with the Yellow Card rules and after he had attempted to issue a challenge.

Before dawn the six SAS soldiers had put themselves into positions around the field. They were split into three groups of two. All but one of them was armed with an Armalite AR15 rifle, the sixth carrying an HK53. The HK53 was something of an SAS favourite, being of the same compact, reliable design as the Heckler and Koch MP5 9 mm sub-machine-guns used at the Iranian embassy but firing a more powerful 5.56 mm round, like the Armalite.

Two of the groups positioned themselves overlooking the cache. They were about 30 metres away from the IRA weapons behind another part of the embankment. The third group were further away, lying in a ditch about 50 metres from the others and 10 metres from the lane which runs past the field. It is close country – small fields are surrounded by thick hedges and the ground around the field is undulating and often waterlogged.

For two days nothing happened. One soldier in each pair remained alert at all times, with the other often resting in a sleeping bag. The pair in the roadside ditch heard the comings and goings of passers-by, a few feet away from them. The soldiers had to ensure that they remained undetected by such people, who might have been scouts for the Provisionals. It is partly the skill and self-discipline of SAS soldiers, in their ability to remain undetected for days while exposed to the elements, which results in them being given such missions.

At about 3 p.m. on Sunday, a brown Talbot car with three men in it pulled up. Two of the men made their way through a gap in the hedge towards the hidden guns. Colm McGirr, twenty-two, and Brian Campbell, nineteen, were both Provisionals from the Coalisland area. The other man stayed with the car, which had been parked just off the road in a gateway.

According to the soldiers' later statements, McGirr went straight towards the hedge and pulled out the Armalite which he handed to Campbell. Soldier A used his radio to alert the others. As Campbell had turned and began to head back to the car, and McGirr was still kneeling by the cache, Soldier A says he shouted the challenge 'Halt, Security Forces!'.

The men did not reply, but McGirr 'pivoted round, pointing the shotgun in my direction', according to the SAS man, who opened fire. Campbell, now running towards the car, appeared to turn threateningly too, the SAS men said, and was also engaged. McGirr was hit by up to thirteen bullets, according to later examination, and died immediately.

Although several soldiers were firing at him from only 20–30 metres away, Campbell was hit just twice. The man at the car, realizing it was a trap, jumped in and started the engine. The soldiers fired at the car, shattering its windscreen. As the Talbot pulled away Soldiers E and F, who had been waiting in the roadside ditch, also opened fire. As the car sped past them Soldier E fired ten rounds at it, several of which were believed to have hit. The car was later found two miles away, spattered with blood, but with no driver.

The soldiers moved forward to the shot IRA members. Campbell was still just alive. Soldier D said in his statement:

There was one exit wound at the front of his left shoulder from which he was losing a lot of blood. I put a shell dressing on this. I did not dress the entry wounds as they were not bleeding. At this stage he was going into deep shock and having difficulty in breathing. I immediately inserted a plastic breathing tube in his throat to assist his breathing and placed him in the coma position. I stayed with him checking his pulse and pupils for about five minutes until he died.

At Lisburn the incident was regarded as a success. But the IRA made various allegations about what had happened, allegations designed to deprive the Army of its 'clean kill' and to outrage local nationalists. The Provisionals said that the driver of the car disputed the soldiers' claim that there had been any shouted warning. They also alleged that the men had been shot before they had reached the arms cache and were therefore defenceless. A priest called to the scene reportedly confirmed that both bodies were lying near the fence, suggesting that they were shot as soon as they entered the field.

Were the soldiers really ordered to arrest them or was it an ambush? Would the soldiers have done things differently if they had wanted to apprehend them?

During the previous few years, there had been several occasions when the security forces had found arms caches. Sometimes, for example when an informer from the County Down IRA had provided them with a machine gun, they had responded by 'jarking' weapons; at others by making them jam if fired. In certain instances, for example following the discovery of the sniper's rifle on a farm near Dungannon in 1980, arrests followed.

The IRA was aware of the possibility that the weapons might have been tampered with, saying after the McGirr/Campbell shooting that, 'In all probability the ammunition had also been removed from the weapons.' The RUC stated that the weapons had been loaded when recovered. However, it is clear from both the IRA and Army statements that the weapons had only been there for a short time: before the soldiers went in they realized that the guns were likely to be removed quickly from the hedge.

Soldier A stated that it appeared the cache 'was only a temporary location and may be moved in the immediate future'. The Provisionals said the weapons had been left there just two days before the shooting, which would mean they were put there after the soldiers were in position. Either way it would seem that the possibilities for getting in experts to doctor the weapons would be limited in such a short space of time. This would not have precluded Soldier A simply unloading the guns, but once the SAS party was in position they would have wanted to do nothing which could have revealed their presence to any observer.

There is, however, a simpler question about the soldiers' behaviour which may cast light on their orders. The soldiers could not arrest the men before they picked up the guns, since the IRA men could have argued in court that they had known nothing about the weapons and had simply been local people out for a stroll. But Soldier A could have waited for the weapons to be placed out of reach, in the car, before issuing his challenge.

If they had been armed with cameras as well as Armalites the SAS men could have photographed whoever recovered the weapons. It was mid afternoon and none of them was wearing a balaclava. The car could then have been followed by surveillance experts and the weapons recovered from their new location. Such a scheme would carry a risk that the men would shake off the surveillance team and the weapons be used in more killings. The soldiers had no guarantee, however, that conditions for photography would have been so good because the pick-up could have happened at night. Such risks had been taken between 1979 and 1982, and would be again in later years, but the commander of this operation was clearly unwilling to take them, or was under different orders.

There is one important possible piece of evidence suggesting that the soldiers were on orders to ambush and that, even if they didn't know exactly who would collect the weapons, they did know which direction they would drive off in. Soldiers E and F, the two by the road, were described in the Army version as being a 'cut-off' group. In their statements some of the soldiers referred to the task of the 'cut-off' as being to apprehend people. Soldier B said it was 'to cut off anyone trying to escape'.

First, it can be asked: why only one cut-off group when it was a through road? The terrorists could, after all, go the other way. Perhaps the Army did not tell the inquest court, to which its soldiers' statements were submitted, that there were more than six SAS men in the area. Or perhaps the soldiers had intelligence which led them to believe that the men recovering the weapons would head in that particular direction. If the latter, what else had the informer said about the people who would collect the guns? Was the whole incident avoidable?

Second, the use of the term 'cut-off group' has a quite specific meaning. It is part of the language of the ambush: *Land Operations Volume III* uses the term only in its section on ambushes, saying the role of the cut-off groups is 'to prevent the enemy escaping from the killing area' (see chapter seventeen).

During late 1983 and early 1984 the Intelligence and Security Group staged many other operations which produced no particular results. But in February 1984 undercover soldiers were, highly unusually, to find themselves out-manoeuvred in such an action. In a bloody sequence of events, the Provisionals tried to take the initiative against the covert operators. It happened in Dunloy, the north Antrim nationalist enclave where several years before John Boyle had been shot dead mistakenly by SAS soldiers in a graveyard.

Overlooking the main village is Carness Drive. The kerbstones in the Drive are painted in the colours of the Irish tricolour. There are a few houses on each side of the road and then the Drive curves uphill where, after 20 or 30 metres, there is another small group of houses. At the point where the road curves it comes close to a farmer's field. The Hogans – a strongly republican family – live at No. Ten, which is on the main part of the Drive before the curve. Intelligence specialists believed Henry Hogan, twenty-one, was a committed member of the Provisionals' north Antrim ASU. He had only come into the village one month before, after the family left its previous home following loyalist intimidation.

A surveillance team from 14 Intelligence Company was tasked to keep the house in Carness Drive under observation. The watchers chose to site a covert Observation Post near the bend in the road, behind two wooden garden-type sheds. This position put them close to the Hogans – about 80 metres away, with a direct line of sight to the front door. They were able to approach the OP from across the field behind the sheds.

Sergeant Paul Oram, a twenty-six-year-old from the 9/12th Royal Lancers who was serving his second tour with the surveillance unit, was in charge of the OP. He was close to the end of his tour with 14 Intelligence Company and had just become a father. Another soldier was with him. The IRA said there had been a third soldier in the OP, but this was not confirmed by the security forces. The surveillance operators were armed with pistols and compact sub-machine-guns for self-defence. As is normal procedure for the unit, there was a back-up team close to the OP and a Quick Reaction Force (QRF) at a nearby security forces base.

Somehow the IRA discovered the existence of the OP. According to one version of events the Provisionals became suspicious following the discovery of a transmitting device in a weapon hidden in Dunloy. But an Army special forces soldier who was serving in Northern Ireland at the time says members of 14 Intelligence Company subsequently felt that it was likely that the OP had been sited too close to a street light and that movements by the soldiers had been noticed. The mistake was a simple one, but because the men had to approach the OP from the rear, they did not have the luxury of being able to inspect their hiding place from the front – the aspect from which other people saw it.

The discovery of a covert OP is almost an everyday event in Northern Ireland. It is often a farmer's dog or children playing who find the soldiers. Words may be exchanged between the civilians and the camouflaged soldiers whom they inadvertently encounter, but the soldiers will normally radio for transport to remove them from the scene as quickly as possible. Sometimes they are barracked by local people.

A one-time member of 14 Intelligence Company describes the strain and the humour which resulted from long hours in covert OPs in constant fear of discovery:

> The unit ran on a sense of humour. Someone got pissed on by a passer-by – it actually happened. Cows started to eat things you didn't want them to eat. A period of high tension could be followed by unstoppable laughter, you know how it is when you try to stop yourself but that makes it worse.

The OP teams had their own term for coming close to discovery and getting away with it – the 'adrenalin kick'.

When the Dunloy IRA unit discovered the presence of the OP they meant not to embarrass the soldiers, but to kill them. Henry Hogan and Declan Martin, an eighteen-year-old from another part of Dunloy, produced a plan to attack the OP. According to the IRA there was a third member of the ambush party. The security forces said three weapons – an Armalite, a sub-machine-gun and a shotgun – were recovered from the scene, but they maintained that only two IRA members were involved in the assault.

At about 8 p.m. on 21 February the IRA members set out to mount their attack. Like the soldiers they chose to approach the OP from behind, across the field. This is probably why they were not seen. The Provisionals came close to the soldiers before opening fire on them. One of the soldiers, realizing what was happening, radioed for help. But it was too late for Sergeant Oram and the other soldier, who were hit many times. Sergeant

Oram died of his wounds but the other man, although seriously injured and left for dead by the IRA, made a recovery.

The events which followed remain highly confused. There was gunfire, possibly from a third member of the OP, as the IRA members tried to flee across the field. Two unmarked cars arrived on the scene very quickly. Their speed indicates that they were a back-up team already deployed on the ground rather than the QRF. The special forces soldier quoted above says they were not SAS but fellow members of Sergeant Oram's surveillance detachment.

A neighbour heard one of the soldiers shouting, 'Get the hell out of the way!' as he ran towards the scene. It was not known whether he was shouting at a bystander or possibly a surviving member of the OP team. There was more firing at the end of which Hogan and Martin were dead. The IRA maintains a third volunteer escaped.

Local people said that they had heard an injured IRA man calling for help before being 'finished off' and the IRA claimed the men had been 'surrounded by the SAS' before being shot. The allegations highlight the problem of trying to separate the truth about such an incident from the rhetoric generated by the strong passions which are aroused when local people die, almost literally on the doorstep of a republican area.

However, it is certain – even one of the soldiers who arrived on the scene later admitted it in a statement at an inquest – that the IRA men were killed as they lay injured in the field. The soldier said he had approached the men and that one had made a movement which he felt endangered his life, so he fired into Martin and Hogan.

Considerations about whether the soldiers had been on a mission to ambush the IRA do not arise. It was the Provisionals who fired the first shots – an attack which culminated in death for their own men. Dunloy had been a routine surveillance mission which had gone disastrously wrong for 14 Intelligence Company. The only legal question surrounded the issue of whether the back-up soldiers might, in 'hot blood' at the loss of their comrade, have shot men whom they could otherwise have taken prisoner.

After its initial cry of 'foul', Sinn Fein chose not to make propaganda capital out of the incident. The men had died, in the words of the IRA statement, 'in action against enemy occupation forces'. This had an heroic appeal to many republicans. When the inquest into the deaths came up in May 1986 Sinn Fein made little fuss about it. The Hogan and Martin families did not have legal representation and the hearing was hardly reported. Both sides drew their lessons from the deaths of three young men in Dunloy.

A curious postscript to the incident involves the reports of Sergeant Oram's death which appeared in some newspapers. A few days after the shooting *The Times* ran a story headlined, 'SAS Man's Courage Was Kept Secret.' It did not carry a journalist's by-line but said that Sergeant Oram had been the soldier who had killed George McBrearty and Charles Maguire in the shoot-out in Londonderry during the 1981 hunger strikes (see chapter fifteen). It added that the young NCO had been decorated with the Military Medal for this feat.

The article contained several inaccuracies. Sergeant Oram was not an SAS man – his own regimental journal had listed his assignment as 'Int and Sy Gp (NI)', whereas research shows that SAS members of this unit would more normally be listed as 'SAS', and colleagues have confirmed to me he was in 14 Intelligence Company. Oram's obituary in his regimental journal, and mentions in earlier issues of the journal, show that he was serving in West Germany at the time of the Londonderry incident. The sergeant's commanding officer said that the Military Medal had been awarded for 'supreme personal courage on an independent operation' during his second tour with the surveillance unit, which had begun early in 1983. Articles at the time of the Londonderry incident had, in any case, identified the soldier as an officer not as an NCO, a fact confirmed by my own research.

There is some evidence to suggest that the errors in the newspaper piece were the result of deliberate official disinformation. The article appears to have been written with the co-operation of the Army and quotes Sergeant Oram's 'colleagues' as saying he was 'a special kind of guy'. Three days earlier *The Times* had published a photograph of Oram. Clearly neither the picture nor the quotes, if genuine, were likely to have been obtained without the co-operation of Lisburn. It would appear highly unlikely that the author of the piece linking the dead soldier with the 1981 Londonderry incident would not have checked his or her theory with an Army press officer at Lisburn, if it was indeed their own supposition, when obtaining the quote.

As Sergeant Oram is still regarded by many in the Army as a hero, what was the point of cynically using a dead man's name in this way? The answer would seem to be that the Army had intelligence that the Derry Brigade was, even three years after the humiliation, desperate to get revenge for the Londonderry shooting. So an author of a disinformation plot might feel that linking a dead man to the incident would result in the IRA stopping its hunt for the real man who had shot his way out of the trap. The false claim that Oram was in the SAS was consistent with Lisburn's long-term policy of disguising the activities of the surveillance unit, although the Army later issued an on-the-record denial that he was in the SAS. 'The SAS always take the rap for 14 Company,' says a member of the former, explaining that this practice arose to safeguard the surveillance unit's identity and tactics.

Two days after the article in *The Times*, the *Irish News* suggested that Sergeant Oram was involved not in the 1981 McBrearty/Maguire shooting but in a fatal confrontation in Londonderry with a man called Liam McMonagle in February 1983. McMonagle, an INLA member, was killed by a plain-clothes soldier who also shot and injured Liam Duffy, another INLA member. The soldier claimed in a deposition to a later inquest that the men had been armed, but that no weapon was recovered from the scene. A CID officer at the inquest admitted that the court only had the soldier's word as proof that the INLA men were armed. People involved with undercover warfare confirm that the soldier was a member of the Londonderry Detachment of 14 Intelligence Company. So was the confrontation with McMonagle and Duffy the occasion on which Sergeant Oram had shown 'supreme personal courage' and won the Military Medal? It is not possible to answer this question with certainty, but it would seem quite likely.

In March 1984, intelligence officers were to mount a highly unusual operation. I learned of it in 1991 while talking informally at a briefing with a very senior member of the security forces. He told me that an agent high in the ranks of the Ulster Defence Association, the loyalist paramilitary group, had tipped them off about a plan in 1984 to assassinate Gerry Adams, the Sinn Fein leader. The information 'did not tell us the exact time and street where the attack would take place, but did give us the basic information that there would be an attempt on his life when he went to the court house'. An independent security forces contact has confirmed this version of events.

Early in the afternoon of 14 March 1984, Gerry Adams left Belfast magistrate's court, where he had appeared on an obstruction charge. Security considerations had already prompted the republican leader's lawyer to try to get permission for him to enter the court by a back entrance – something the authorities would not agree to. Adams was travelling along Howard Street on his way back to west Belfast in a car with four colleagues when they were overtaken by another vehicle. Two members of the Ulster Freedom Fighters, the UDA's terrorist arm, opened fire. Twelve shots were fired injuring Adams and Sean Keenan, one of the other passengers, severely. Adams' driver kept the car under control and drove to the Royal Victoria Hospital.

Very shortly after the shooting an unmarked car which had been following Adams' vehicle intercepted the UFF vehicle. Several men in plain clothes carrying 9 mm pistols apprehended the UFF gunmen. Gerald Welsh and John Gregg, who had fired the shots, were each subsequently sentenced to eighteen years in jail. Colin Gray, the driver, was given a twelve-year term.

In the aftermath of the incident, Sinn Fein said that SAS soldiers had been responsible for following Adams. The Army Press Office said that two off-duty members of the Royal Military Police and an off-duty UDR soldier had been in the area by coincidence and had taken action. Two days later the Army modified its line saying that the military policemen had been on duty but that, 'Their involvement in the incident was a complete coincidence.' The police described Sinn Fein claims of SAS involvement as 'nonsense'. These claims were maintained during the trial of Welsh, Gregg and Gray the following year.

Admitting that Int and Sy Group soldiers had indeed been there would have been very embarrassing to the Army. Why then were UFF men apprehended only after the shots were fired? Why had Adams not been made aware of the threat to him, and why was his court appearance simply postponed without explanation? How come the loyalists were apprehended alive when it often seemed so difficult for the SAS to do the same with armed republicans? None of those jailed for the incident claimed to have been put up to the crime by the security forces. The soldiers' presence and the arrest of the UFF men make it improbable that intelligence chiefs actually commissioned the attack. It is much harder to be sure that they did not allow it to run in the hope it would be successful.

In July 1984 security forces intelligence experts learned of a forthcoming IRA operation against Forbes kitchen fittings factory in Ardboe, Tyrone. A group of SAS men, at least nine strong, went to the area and were briefed on the evening of 12 July. Their intelligence appears to have been first-rate. One of the SAS men, who gave evidence to a subsequent inquest as 'Soldier F', recorded that the briefer told them that there would be an incendiary bomb attack against the Forbes factory, that it would be carried out by an ASU of four men and that they would be armed.

Eight of the SAS soldiers made their way to the village. The ninth, Soldier J, waited nearby with a QRF made up of members of 1st Battalion, the Queen's Regiment. Two of the SAS men, Soldiers D and E, took positions at about 10.35 p.m. on the Mullanahoe Road, which runs in front of the factory. It appears that their job was to act as a stop group to prevent anyone driving into or out of the area. The other five soldiers went into position about half an hour later. They appear to have been dropped off by a van in civilian colours. The soldiers were armed with a mixture of HK53 and AR-15 assault rifles. Several also carried 9 mm Browning pistols. These five men divided into two groups near the factory. The men were tense, not just because of their mission, but also because a crow scarer in a nearby field made a loud bang every two or three minutes.

Their intelligence was sufficiently accurate that little more than one and a half hours after these two teams went into position, they caught sight of two men making their way along a hedgerow behind the factory. Soldier A told a later inquest that when the two men were about 30 metres away he shouted a challenge. The nearest figure 'raised his hands up very fast' and Soldier A shot him, adding 'I heard him scream.' He had hit and injured William Price, a 28-year-old IRA man. Price and the other man ran away. Soldier A fired again into the darkness but did not stop the other man.

Two other members of the ASU – Raymond O'Neill and Thomas McQuillan – heard the commotion and decided to make a run for it. They came out of a field and onto the Mullanahoe road about 100 metres away from where Soldiers D and E were waiting. Soldier D said he shouted, 'Stop or I'll fire!' O'Neill complied immediately, standing in the road with his hands in the air. McQuillan ran on, so Soldier D opened fire. In a deposition to a later inquest he said, 'I thought he was going to escape so I took two quick aimed shots'. McQuillan fell to the ground, but was not hit. Soldier E went towards him and arrested him.

Meanwhile Soldier A and several others were searching the fields behind the factory, trying to find Price and the other man. Eventually Soldier A stumbled on Price. He told a subsequent inquest that Price made 'a sudden movement of his hands toward me'. Soldier A fired at Price, blowing off the top of his head, killing him instantly. The fourth Provisional escaped. Two loaded pistols and several explosive incendiary bombs were found in the fields.

Several points about the incident are significant. As far as we know, it was the only SAS action of the period from 1984 to 1985 in which the SAS made arrests. As such it might provide significant proof that, despite the rash of ambushes during this period, no blanket 'shoot-to-kill' edict was in effect at the time. There are several possible explanations for why O'Neill and McQuillan were arrested rather than killed.

The soldiers insisted at the inquest into Price's death that they were on an 'observation and arrest' mission. The simplest reading of the incident is that their orders were of the 'hard arrest' rather than the ambush variety. We do not know why such orders might be given but one can speculate, and it is no more than speculation, for example that the intelligence officers who set up the operation believed there was a high chance that their source him or herself would take part in the fire bombing. They might also have received such orders because their commanders did not believe an ambush against IRA men engaged in an attack against property as opposed to people would be perceived as just. The killing of three IRA men and one bystander at Ballysillan in 1978 when the IRA was also attempting a firebomb attack against property had aroused considerable hostility from nationalist politicians and significant disquiet within some sections of the security forces.

According to the republican movement O'Neill and McQuillan were not killed because Mrs Mary Forbes, a local woman, mistakenly thought one of the apprehended men might be her own son. She leaned out of her window, overlooking the Mullanahoe Road, and shouted to the soldiers not to harm the men.

An inquest into Price's death held in June 1986 was not attended by the man's family. It subsequently emerged that they had not known about it. In June 1987 a second inquest was held following a court ruling that the finding of the first inquest was invalid because the family had not been represented there.

# PART FOUR: 1984–1987

# 19

# Soft Targets

At all levels of the security forces there is a recognition of the IRA's power to intimidate locally recruited members of the RUC and Army through its policy of assassination. The problem is particularly acute among reservists – part-time members of those organizations – who can be attacked at home or at their place of work. Many of the reservists live and work in remote houses in rural areas where the two communities are intermingled and their identity as part-time members of the security forces is well known.

The Ulster Defence Regiment has been a particular target for assassination. Of the 159 members of the Regiment killed between its formation and the end of 1986, 129 were off duty. In recent years the IRA has sought to justify these attacks by drawing attention to the links between UDR soldiers and loyalist paramilitary groups. But the very fact that the UDR is such an overwhelmingly Protestant force is due in part to the fact that many Catholic UDR members were killed by the IRA in the early 1970s, with the intention of intimidating others into leaving.

Many of the killings have happened in circumstances where the victim was defenceless. A female UDR soldier was shot dead as she lay in bed. Others have been killed in front of their children or mothers. Delivery people have been ambushed on their rounds. These attacks have the effect of hardening members of the security forces, often making them callous to the plight of Catholics claiming harassment or other infringements of their civil liberties. IRA claims that members were defenceless when shot by the SAS are met by security forces members with rejoinders about the IRA's own standards of 'fairness' in shooting people dead on their front doorsteps. Although senior officers recognize the moral danger in drawing parallels between their own behaviour and that of the Provisionals, they accept that for many of the soldiers running night-time roadblocks the realities are different.

The selection of soft targets also carried with it an implicit admission by the IRA of its increased difficulties in attacking soldiers on patrol. In 1973 or 1974, for example, the number of British soldiers killed exceeded the number of locally recruited (UDR or RUC) people. But the Provisionals understood both the greater role being played by these forces as a result of Police Primacy and the fact that it had become more and more dangerous for them to take pot shots at regular Army patrols. In 1983 five regular British Army soldiers were killed, compared to ten UDR members and eighteen RUC members; and in 1984 nine regular Army soldiers were killed compared to ten UDR members and eight police officers. Most of the UDR murders and many of those of RUC members took place when they were off-duty.

Cumulatively, attacks on soft targets had the effect of 'needling' people – making soldiers and police more likely to overreact, thus handing propaganda success to the paramilitaries. The tactic would, in turn, make many others leave the UDR or police, and draw others into loyalist terrorism. The covert operators were well aware of the effect of such killings on morale but found it hard to pre-empt such attacks. The number of people who know in advance about an attack on an off-duty UDR soldier or RUC officer is small compared to that required for many other types of operation. The two or three terrorists carrying out the attack and their ASU commander might be the only people who knew who was going to be attacked, when and where. 'Dickers' might have a good idea of the target but no clue as to when he or she would be killed. Those sent to hijack the getaway car could give a clue to the timing but probably have no clue as to why the vehicle was needed. A quartermaster might know when it would happen, but not the target.

Security chiefs had decided by 1983 to devote significant resources to the task of trying to protect soft targets. The Intelligence and Security Group was involved, as were the Close Observation Platoons which were part of various infantry battalions serving in Ulster. The COPs were given their duties by the TCG operations centres. Some of their missions were based on informer intelligence identifying a specific threat to an individual, but high-grade information of that kind was normally given to the Int and Sy Group, leaving the COPs with little better to operate on than local hearsay and the guesswork of intelligence officers.

An insight into the work of the Close Observation Platoon which was part of the Queen's Own Highlanders, based at Aldergrove during the years 1983 to 1985, was provided by the Regiment's magazine. The COP commander reported: 'Tasking kept us employed, providing soft-target protection for off-duty UDR men. This was accomplished in varying styles with some patrols living on premises and others under dung heaps and hedges.'

The Highlanders did not encounter the IRA during these duties – like most covert operators their many hours spent lying-in-wait had passed without incident. Only the best intelligence could make possible a different outcome.

Late in 1984 the Special Branch obtained a very unusual tip-off. The SB learnt about a planned IRA attack on a part-time UDR member near Dungannon. In the fuzzy world of counter-terrorist intelligence, all of the details are rarely present. Intelligence chiefs did however believe the tip was sufficiently reliable to make a covert operation worthwhile.

Int and Sy Group surveillance experts and SAS men were directed by the local TCG to formulate a plan to catch the UDR man's would-be killers in the act. The area around the junction, where a haulage contractor called Capper and Lambe is based, was placed out of bounds to other units – a standard procedure in covert operations designed to keep patrols who did not need to be briefed on the operation away from danger and to prevent a 'blue on blue', an accidental engagement between soldiers or police officers. It is not possible to say with certainty why this point was chosen to intercept the IRA members, but local people say that the Provisionals intended to ambush a UDR officer who regularly drove past Capper and Lambe's yard in an armour-plated car on his way to Dungannon.

Just after 8 a.m. on 19 October 1984 the IRA team arrived in a yellow van, a vehicle which they had hijacked in Coalisland. There were at least ten SAS men in the area: a couple were hidden behind bushes near the entrance to the yard; and eight more were in three unmarked cars. As the IRA members' van went by the soldiers tried to block its path, but they failed and opened fire.

Frederick Jackson, a forty-eight-year-old plant hire contractor who was just driving out of Capper and Lambe's, having supervised some work there, was hit in the chest by a bullet fired by one of the soldiers. The car rolled back into the yard, crashing into a petrol pump. Jackson stumbled from the vehicle, calling for help and collapsed inside a shed. He died later.

In spite of the SAS presence in the area, and a fusillade of shots at the van, the Army was unable to prevent the Provisionals from escaping. They made their way by foot across a motorway bridge and, despite the presence of a helicopter in the area, were soon in the sanctuary of the strongly republican area to the north of the M1. The RUC said Jackson had been killed in the crossfire. The IRA disagreed, saying its members had not opened fire when Jackson was hit. However, the dumped van was found to contain many spent cases and the IRA did not deny that its members had engaged the soldiers.

At 8.37 a.m. a police inspector at the local station directed units to the scene, having received phonecalls from local people. He countermanded these orders after an SB officer told him that the area was the scene of a gunbattle between Provisionals and security forces 'specialist resources'.

The operation had been a débâcle. Unusually specific intelligence had presented the soldiers with an opportunity which had gone badly wrong. The reservist had been saved but an uninvolved man going about his business was dead and the terrorists had escaped. The death led to suggestions that the soldiers had mistakenly believed Jackson to be a member of the IRA team and had killed him deliberately.

It was difficult to imagine someone less likely to have appeared to pose a threat to the soldiers than Jackson, a middle-aged Protestant businessman. The dead man's family asked questions about why it had taken so long for him to receive medical attention. This left nationalists asking whether he had been allowed to die because the troops thought he was a republican. The fact that Jackson was hit by a single shot, however, would seem to support the official view – that he was hit by a stray round rather than engaged deliberately by the SAS in the belief that he was a terrorist. Regardless of whether Jackson's death was an accident or a mistake, a Protestant who witnessed the IRA members' escape from Tamnamore told me, 'I don't wish to denigrate the SAS, but they made a real bitch of it that day.'

An incident like that at Tamnamore prompted many questions which are impossible to answer either here or in a court without knowing exactly what information the SB had before the attack – and the Stalker affair shows how jealously such 'crown jewels' of anti-terrorist intelligence work are guarded. The most generous interpretation – to the TCG and SAS – is that they had no idea who was going to carry out the attack and had no choice but to stake out the area. Telling the UDR officer to stay away from work might only have endangered others. The fact that the terrorists escaped might support the view that the RUC had no idea who they were and where to find them afterwards.

The other extreme is to suppose that the SB had a very good idea about who was going to carry out the attack, because the circle of knowledge about killing soft targets tends to be so small. If they did, then they could have prevented the attack in other ways – methods which will be discussed in chapter twenty-two – but chose not to because they wanted to send a signal to the Provisionals by catching an ASU attempting to kill a soft target and obtain a 'clean kill' for the SAS. The terrorists' subsequent escape might then represent sloppy police work, in that suspects could not be tied to the incident, because the SB officers never expected to have to furnish evidence to a court.

More elaborate IRA plans carried a higher risk of compromise by informers or by simple mishap. A group of IRA members wanted to stage a 'come on' attack near Kesh in Fermanagh later that year. The plan involved placing a very large (900 lb) bomb in a culvert beneath the road outside the Drumrush Lodge, a country restaurant. A call would then be made to the police that firebombs had been placed in the Drumrush Lodge. As the security forces arrived at the scene the bomb would be detonated by an observer using a command wire.

Just after 9 p.m. on 1 December 1984 several IRA members hijacked a blue Toyota van in Pettigo, across the border in Donegal. They collected several milk churns packed with explosives, probably while still inside the Republic, and then went to Drumrush. In the van were at least four IRA veterans: Tony MacBride, a twenty-seven-year-old former Irish Army soldier who had done time for firearms offences; Kieran Fleming, who had escaped from the Maze; James Clark, another member of the Maze jailbreak who had been serving a sentence for attempted murder; and Patrick Bramley, aged twenty-four. The IRA said later there had been five men in the van; the Army that there had been only four. Republicans say there were other Provisionals in the area too, keeping a look-out.

SAS soldiers arrived in the area. Soldier A, a thirty-four-year-old SAS NCO, said in his later court deposition, 'As a result of information received we were on the look-out for a blue van of foreign make.' The soldiers had driven into the area by 11.30 p.m., according to Soldier A, which was one hour before a woman rang Kesh RUC station with the 'come on' warning about firebombs at the Drumrush Lodge. The soldiers' task was made far more difficult as there was thick, freezing fog that night, cutting visibility to a few metres.

According to the Army, Soldier A was accompanied by two other men and there was a second unmarked car with another four troops in it. According to an SAS man, their mission was to intercept the bombers following an informer tip-off. It is unclear, though, whether this was regarded as an ambush or an arrest-type mission. Certainly there were enough troops to have mounted an ambush once they had established the IRA unit's location.

Things did not go well for the soldiers. They sighted a suspicious van and the two cars went into position to block both ends of the road on which it was parked. Soldier A's car was parked further away from the van, on a narrow section of the road bordered by hedges. By simple bad luck they had stopped their car just a few feet from where two or three IRA members were preparing the firing point for the bomb. The IRA men, who were on the other side of the hedge, watched as two of the SAS men, Soldiers A and B, got out of the car and began to walk towards the van. Each of them was carrying an HK53 5.56 mm compact assault rifle and a 9 mm pistol. Another SAS man, Soldier E, stayed with the car to keep in radio contact with the others. Versions of what happened next differ.

The IRA members decided to open fire on Soldier E, after which there was pandemonium. Getting up from behind the hedge, they shot at point-blank range. Lance-Corporal Alistair Slater died. The twenty-seven-year-old soldier, who had combined a public school education with service in the ranks of the Parachute Regiment before passing selection and serving with B Squadron, 22 SAS, became the second member of the Regiment to be killed in action in Ulster.

After the shots, several of the IRA members decided to run for it. Tony MacBride had stayed with the blue van. He was not carrying a gun and it seems he also tried to run. Statements by the soldiers to a later inquest indicated that MacBride was first captured but then ran off and that the soldiers, thinking he might have taken one of their rifles, opened fire on him. The IRA claimed that MacBride had been apprehended, beaten and shot *before* other volunteers attacked the SAS, killing the Lance-Corporal and wounding two others.

Both versions are discounted by someone who is familiar with the Army's internal version of the case, who suggests that there was no struggle, as the soldiers suggested in their court depositions, but that the soldiers simply saw MacBride running away and shot him. It is important to establish when the soldiers knew their comrade was mortally wounded, because this might have led them to shoot MacBride out of a desire to avenge their fallen comrade.

The soldiers' statements make no mention of hearing the shots which killed Lance-Corporal Slater. Instead they simply say that they discovered him lying by the car after they had apprehended MacBride and before he tried to escape. The omission of any mention of having heard the shots is extraordinary, since they would undoubtedly have heard rifle fire so close. The four SAS men who were in the other car would also, surely, have heard the exchange. If there really was another SAS team, why didn't they then come forward to assist their colleagues? Soldiers A and B make no mention of them playing any role in these events.

A woman living 100 metres from the scene told the *Irish News* that she was woken by two shots. 'A flare was fired into the sky, and she heard several more shots and then saw a second flare fired. This was followed by a burst of rapid fire.' The soldiers said that they had fired warning shots at MacBride, and then a flare to see him more clearly; they had then apprehended him after which there was the struggle, escape and then the fatal shots were fired.

The other explanation for what the witness heard is this. The first shots were the IRA men attacking the SAS man. Lance-Corporal Slater's colleagues returned fire and, it would seem, fired the first flare. As one group of IRA men escaped, Soldiers A and B fired another flare and opened fire as their targets disappeared into the mist, killing MacBride.

Bramley and Clark entered a house near Pettigo, before hijacking the family car. Gardai officers saw the car stop and turn around at a checkpoint. It was pursued by a police car and the men were arrested. The British government subsequently filed for their extradition. In 1990, after a long legal battle, the Irish courts refused to extradite Clark, the IRA member who had escaped from the Maze, on the grounds that he might be beaten up by prison officers if he was returned.

Fleming disappeared without trace. After a few days the IRA issued an appeal to anyone who might know his whereabouts. On 21 December his corpse was found. He had jumped into the Bannagh River while escaping from the scene. Fleming had been wearing several layers of bulky clothing, in an attempt to keep warm on that bitterly cold night, and had drowned.

Despite the death of Frederick Jackson in the Tamnamore incident, security chiefs were still determined to catch terrorists in the act of attacking a soft target. But the kind of intelligence required to make such an operation possible could not be produced on demand – however high in the security forces command structure the officer asking for it might be. Nevertheless, two months after the bystander was killed, the Group found itself involved in a large-scale operation in Londonderry. As in the Tamnamore incident, the SB found itself with unusual information about a threat to the life of a security forces part-timer. An intelligence officer says an informer gave them 'the perfect tip-off' about a forthcoming attack on a UDR reservist who worked at the Gransha psychiatric hospital on the outskirts of the city.

It wasn't quite perfect because the security forces kept the hospital under observation for about two weeks before finally they secured a result. The operation was a large one, probably involving more than twenty-four members of the SAS, Londonderry Detachment of 14 Intelligence Company and SB. They used at least five unmarked cars.

The SB expected the attack to take place at around 8.30 a.m. when shifts changed and the man they knew to be the target arrived by bus at the hospital. The IRA team would attack in a way employed by the Derry Brigade before. On 28 March 1982, RUC Inspector Norman Duddy had left the Strand Road Presbyterian church with his two sons. Two hooded terrorists had appeared on a motorcycle. They shot Inspector Duddy as he got into his car, leaving the children with their mortally wounded father.

At 7 a.m. on 6 December 1984 a group of SAS and surveillance soldiers were briefed at Ebrington Barracks, Londonderry, by a major, later referred to as 'Soldier F'. It is probable that he was either the Army special forces Liaison Officer to the TCG or the OC of 14 Company. The soldiers must have received much the same briefing as they had during previous days, when they had been on the same assignment. Soldier F said he told them their task was 'to abort if possible a terrorist attack and to apprehend the terrorist or terrorists involved'.

The men then went to Gransha in their collection of unmarked cars – two Fiats, a Volkswagen Jetta, a Capri and a Toyota. Some were armed with a 9 mm pistol and an HK53, others with a pistol and an MP5K. The Heckler and Koch MP5K is a shortened version of the 9 mm sub-machine-gun used by the SAS at the Iranian embassy and can be concealed under clothing.

Two IRA men – Daniel Doherty, twenty-three, from the Creggan estate, and William Fleming, nineteen, a resident of the Waterside district – had drawn weapons from an IRA quartermaster. They were carrying a holdall with a revolver, an automatic pistol, gloves and balaclavas as they climbed on to their motorcycle, which had been stolen some time before. Doherty took the handlebars, with Fleming riding pillion.

As they made their way into the hospital grounds their progress was observed by the soldiers in unmarked cars, who passed information between them by radio. According to the intelligence specialist quoted earlier, another SAS man had got on to the bus on which the UDR man was travelling.

The soldiers said that, as the motorcycle came into the hospital, Fleming had a pistol in his hand. This was disputed later, at the inquest. The soldiers say they shouted at the men to stop. They did not do so and Soldier A, at the wheel of a blue Fiat, drove his car at the IRA men. The motorbike was rammed with such force that Fleming's right leg was shattered and he fell to the ground. Among the exhibits listed by the police Scene of Crime Officer was 'LS11 Sample of fleshy material', which had been 'recovered from the offside front wing' of Soldier A's Fiat.

Soldier A fired at Fleming with his 9 mm pistol. Soldier B used his pistol and then got his HK53 out of the car and fired it. Soldier B and Soldier C continued to fire at Doherty as he tried to escape on the motorcycle. Soldier C fired at the bike, 'thinking my own life and that of Soldier B was in immediate danger'. He emptied the thirty-round magazine of his MP5K at Doherty.

Some fifty-nine rounds were fired in a few moments. Doherty was hit nineteen times, falling from the bike. Fleming had taken four rounds. Both men died. Doherty left a wife and an eight-month-old boy.

There was a strong public reaction after the deaths. The IRA claimed Doherty had been hit thirty-eight times and Fleming thirty, allegations exposed as false by the post-mortem examinations. A local unionist politician described the shootings as 'an early Christmas present'. Neil Kinnock, the opposition Labour Party leader, called for an inquiry, justifying his request by saying, 'It is because of fear that there might have been a change of policy on "shoot-to-kill" and I want clarification on that policy.' Douglas Hurd, the Secretary of State for Northern Ireland, denied that there had been any change in security policy.

At the men's funerals there were scuffles and confrontations with the police. As at Tony MacBride's funeral, the RUC intervened to try to prevent paramilitary displays. A senior republican says that from late 1983 the police took a more active role in trying to prevent paramilitary 'honour guards' firing shots at funerals.

# 20

# The Strabane Shootings

In February 1985 the Int and Sy Group went into action again. It was to be the fourth occasion in five months in which members of the unit were involved in a fatal shooting incident. However, it would grow in reputation to be the most controversial of the killings. As in Tamnamore in October 1984 and in Kesh and Londonderry in December, the events which took place in Strabane resulted from the exploitation of informer intelligence.

An IRA ASU in the predominantly Catholic town of Strabane was given the assignment of attacking an RUC vehicle on patrol. The ASU was well armed for the task, with anti-armour grenades which had been specially developed and manufactured by the Provisionals' technical experts. They had also hidden near the town a variety of military weapons including Belgian-made FNC rifles, which fire rounds similar to the Armalite but are more modern. Their plan was to ambush an RUC vehicle with the grenades and shoot at any survivors as they emerged.

The Special Branch TCG North mobilized Army and RUC units to mount an operation against the ASU. During the early part of February the ASU and undercover soldiers danced a gavotte through the rolling countryside around the town. A squad from the RUC's N Division Mobile Support Unit was also sent to the area. The DMSU was there to act as a QRF for the undercover soldiers and to move in and secure an area in the event of a battle with IRA members. From time to time areas were placed out of bounds to security forces vehicles in case they ran into the IRA ambush. The manoeuvrings ended on 23 February.

On 22 February four SAS soldiers had travelled down from Londonderry after being briefed there by intelligence officers. From conversations with a soldier familiar with the case, it would appear that they had been told the probable location of the ASU's arms dump. That night three soldiers went to investigate the cache. It does not appear – despite the strength of later nationalist feeling to the contrary – that their intention was to mount an ambush that night.

The Army knew from intelligence that they might encounter anything up to five or six terrorists, so it hardly seems likely that they would have chosen to ambush them with just three men. The three soldiers in question took up a position overlooking a suspected IRA arms dump. A fourth soldier was manning the radio at a nearby security forces base, where he was in charge of the Quick Reaction Force. It would appear that the four who had travelled down from Londonderry were not the only Int and Sy Group soldiers in the area that night. There were probably two others riding in an unmarked car whose mission was to back up the team in the Observation Post. Their role seems to have had more in common with that of the surveillance team which was attacked at Dunloy, for example, than with the deployment of groups of six to twelve SAS men at incidents like Tamnamore or the Gransha hospital. Indeed, in its first report of the incident the Sinn Fein newspaper *An Phoblacht/Republican News* stated that the British soldiers had probably been engaged in 'routine surveillance work', although it gave a confused version of where they had been.

One journalist who has covered the Strabane incident suggested to me that the three men in the OP were in fact surveillance operators rather than members of the SAS. I do not believe this, having had their identity as SAS soldiers confirmed by two members of the Regiment and a senior security forces officer. Were they then SAS soldiers sent simply to see what they could find out, or were they on an OP/React mission – in other words an ambush – where they understood they would be clear to engage any terrorist who appeared?

Once again, the numbers of men committed would seem to indicate that it was a genuine observation mission. It was to become a hallmark of SAS OP/React missions that far more soldiers would be deployed than the two or three considered appropriate for a real OP.

On the same night, the IRA unit had been out trying to ambush a police car. Five ASU members spent the early hours of 23 February in a fruitless wait for quarry. When their patience was spent, Declan Crossan, twenty-one, and another Provisional took off their rubber gloves and handed their weapons to the other three for returning to a cache. Crossan and the other person made their way home. Charles Breslin, a twenty-year-old believed by the police to be the ASU commander, Michael Devine, twenty-two, and his brother David Devine, sixteen years old, walked along carrying the weapons. They were wearing rubber gloves and balaclavas. The anti-armour grenades had been placed in a holdall along with the gloves worn by the other two men. Each of the men carried a loaded assault rifle.

The area where the soldiers were waiting is in a steeply sloping field. At the bottom of the slope runs a thick hedge on the other side of which is a road. A largely Catholic housing estate, known as the Head of the Town, lies along the other side of the road, overlooked by the field. There is a house opposite the estate which nestles in a cutting in the hillside. Behind the building there is a nearby vertical six- or seven-foot slope at the top of which runs a hedge. The soldiers were lying there, looking uphill into the field. It is believed that the IRA members planned to hide the weapons at the side of the enclosure at a point which could be overlooked by the OP.

According to a soldier who spoke to me, the SAS soldiers heard the three Provisionals before they saw them, though this was not what was said later by the Army. As the IRA men walked past the SAS soldiers, only a few metres away, the soldiers opened fire without warning with their HK53 assault rifles. Soldier A fell down the steep bank into the house's back yard. In the confusion both Soldiers A and B radioed their back-up team to report a contact.

Soldiers B and C carried on firing. Soldier C said in a statement, 'At this time I heard voices in front of me saying something like "They're over there – get them".' Whether or not it is true that one of the terrorists said this, none of the IRA weapons was fired and two still had their safety catches on when examined later. The SAS men carried on pouring fire into the prostrate IRA men, who were only 5 to 6 metres away, reloading their weapons with fresh magazines as they did so. In all they fired 117 rounds, twenty-eight of which hit Michael Devine. A pathologist later said his wounds had almost defied interpretation. Before the firing was finished the QRF appeared, having come the short distance from a nearby base. There was a cry of 'Shoot out the street lights' and the soldier who was with the QRF fired a burst at some lamp posts.

Local people were to claim that they had heard cries of 'Don't shoot, don't shoot' from one of the injured Provisionals. The question of whether the SAS finished the men with a *coup de grâce* as they lay injured on the ground was to emerge as one of the most controversial aspects of the incident. Many extraordinary allegations emerged from the estate – for example, that other soldiers had opened fire with a machine-gun from a cemetery several hundred metres away. This was not borne out by any of the forensic evidence and was denied by soldiers and police.

Immediately after the shooting, soldiers and RUC officers from the QRF broke into a house, searching for other terrorists. This suggests they probably knew there were more than three men in the original ambush party. Crossan was arrested; he subsequently confessed to several terrorist crimes, and in 1986 was sentenced to twenty years in jail. The judge, referring to the fate of Breslin and the Devines, said that Crossan was lucky to be alive and that, 'They that take up the sword perish by the sword.' The fifth member of the ambush team has never been charged with involvement in the plan.

Shortly after the Strabane killings, the IRA began a hunt for the source of the leak which had led the men to their deaths. Two days later Kevin Coyle, a twenty-four-year-old republican was found dead in Londonderry's Bogside. The IRA said he had been an informer for some time, but the police denied it. Some people linked his killing with the Strabane incident, though not the IRA itself. In October of the same year Damien McCrory, a twenty-year-old Strabane Provisional, was found shot dead. The IRA said he had been a traitor who, like the Mahon couple – killed in Belfast a few weeks before – had been given tracking devices to insert in weapons. The IRA said that some people had come forward as a result of the Mahons' deaths but that, 'Where we are forced to hunt down touts, they must expect no mercy.'

Many questions remained unanswered after the Strabane incident. Some were to emerge at the inquest held from 3 February to 22 April 1987. It was to be the fullest inquiry of its kind held until then, but, despite this, it produced claims of cover-up and whitewash from many nationalists.

Loyalists did not, on the whole, object to the soldiers' behaviour. Sammy Wilson, a Democratic Unionist on Belfast Council, said after the Strabane shootings, 'Talking, reason or persuasion does not work with the IRA so the only answer is to shoot its members; this at least ensures that they will not be available to carry out any more murders of Protestants.' But while Wilson and the DUP may have their fingers on the pulse of opinion in the working-class Protestant enclaves – and therefore of some elements within the UDR and RUC – there were other Unionists who saw things differently. Enoch Powell, official Unionist MP for south Down from 1974 to 1987, challenged the idea that it was legitimate to exploit foreknowledge to catch armed terrorists in ambushes. 'I am astonished that the proposition should be put forward that because a person is suspected of preparing to commit a crime, therefore he should be shot without trial', he was to say after the Gibraltar incident.

The Strabane inquest was extensive because the solicitors representing the families understood the importance of the issues and the need to call many witnesses. In many other cases there was only the most perfunctory hearing. Oistin MacBride, brother of Tony, who was killed in the Kesh incident, remembered that his family 'were so naïve at the time'. He says the RUC had told them the proceedings were a 'formality' and the inquest, at which the MacBrides had no legal representation, was completed in three hours. Some of the inquests have been little more than minor skirmishes between country solicitors, who usually agree to represent the families for free (since there is no legal aid for inquest proceedings) but who have no real experience of such matters, and anonymous security forces witnesses.

Interviews with members of the security forces who have been involved in such incidents, or who have had access to information about them, reveal in many cases a version of events which is significantly different from that presented in court. The concoction of cover stories designed to protect informers and disguise the degree of foreknowledge of a crime had been exposed by the Stalker inquiry. The stories given to courts about incidents involving Army special forces in the period 1983 to 1985 also appear, from the evidence of interviews conducted for this book, to be designed to disguise the amount which SB and Army intelligence officers really knew before an incident. In effect they are designed to preserve not only the sources of that intelligence but also the myth of the 'clean kill' – that IRA members lost their lives because they were encountered, armed and in the middle of an operation, when the security forces had no choice but to engage them.

The inquest into the shooting of Doherty and Fleming at the Gransha hospital showed some of the problems of trying to establish the truth in such cases. Throughout the proceedings the Army maintained that the presence of the soldiers in the hospital grounds was in some sense 'routine' or part of normal security duties. But committing around ten SAS men – just under half of the total resident SAS contingent in Ulster – in a small area of one city cannot, by definition, be a routine security operation. The officers who control Int and Sy Group require hard intelligence to act on before they will use their scarce resources in this way.

The CID detective chief inspector charged with carrying out the official investigation of the Gransha shootings told the inquest, 'I can't say what information was available to the forces prior to this incident.' This issue, of exactly what they did and did not know, is crucial in forming a judgement about the ethics of how the IRA men met their deaths. Were it to emerge in a court, for example, that they had been followed from their homes, or from the cache where they picked up their weapons, to the place where they intended to kill, then serious questions would have been raised about whether the SAS soldiers had used reasonable and necessary force. It might, for example, have been possible to have 'jarked' or 'fixed' their guns previously and have captured the IRA men as they picked up the weapons.

Soldier F, the officer who had briefed the soldiers at Gransha, told the court, 'I had no specific information.' Yet a person who has reviewed the case claims the soldiers had the 'perfect tip-off'. His suggestion that they knew exactly who the IRA men's target was – and even put a soldier on the bus to protect him – never emerged during the court proceedings. Soldier F did admit it would have been better 'with hindsight' to have called in the police to have made arrests when the motorcycle was seen in the hospital grounds. This was reflected in the jury's finding at the end of the inquest, when they said the Army should have called in the police. But the overwhelming likelihood that the operation could not have happened without the knowledge of the Special Branch – through the TCG, part of the police – was not examined in court. Whatever its limits, the Gransha finding was the closest a coroner's court has come in recent years to censuring Army special forces for their role in such a shooting.

The Strabane inquest focused on a different part of the 'shoot-to-kill' conundrum: not on whether there was an alternative to the confrontation but on how the soldiers had behaved during it. This is not promising ground for those seeking to question the soldiers' behaviour. It had been shown in the Boyle case that even if SAS men end up charged with murder it is very difficult to prove to a court that their version of why they opened fire is untrue, however implausible it might sound. Much of the questioning at Strabane centred on the question of whether the IRA men had been given a *coup de grâce* as they pleaded for mercy.

Police witnesses said that the cries of 'Don't shoot, don't shoot' had come not from injured Provisionals but from a frightened motorist, when stopped by members of the QRF on the road. However, they were not able to trace the man, saying he had identified himself only as 'Kelly from Plumbridge'. They said they had not taken his full name or car registration number.

Post-mortem evidence showed that each of the IRA men had at least one shot through the head. Yet their balaclavas contained no bullet holes, leading to suggestions that the soldiers had approached them, lifted off the masks to identify the men and then delivered the fatal shots. The soldiers' statements admitted that they had taken the balaclavas off the men, but said it was after the firing had stopped. The Crown suggested by way of explanation that the bullets might have entered through the balaclavas' eye holes.

One aspect of the soldiers' depositions not raised in court was why two of them had suffered 'stoppages' (jamming) of their HK53 rifles. The chances of a weapon jamming are slim, particularly when the gun is of a German design, one chosen for its reliability. The chances of two guns jamming are even more remote. I showed an SAS man copies of Soldier A's and Soldier C's written depositions. He said he found it 'very hard to believe' that both men had had stoppages and that, given the Regiment's pride in its exhaustive firearms training, they would admit to having their weapons jam even if it had happened.

There is another possible explanation. As the SAS soldiers approached the terrorists they might have drawn their Browning 9 mm automatic pistols. A pistol is a better weapon for a *coup de grâce* since it causes less trauma to the target's body when fired very close and poses less of a risk to the firer through the impact of ricochets. Forensic evidence showed that both soldiers did use their 9 mm pistols, so they had to give some explanation for having done so.

If they had used their Brownings to finish the men off at very close range there would have been other signs. The Provisionals' clothes might have shown powder burns and 9 mm spent cases would have been found near the bodies. But examination of the clothing was impossible: the RUC had destroyed it. The forensic scientist recovered eighty-three or eighty-four spent cases from the scene. When he realized forty-two were unaccounted for he tried to go back, but was told by the RUC he could not for 'operational reasons'.

It may be that both HK53s did indeed jam. There may be some other explanation for the use of the 9 mm pistols. In the heat of the moment a soldier may have mistaken an empty magazine for a stoppage and drawn his pistol. But, remarkably, even some leading members of the security forces and of the administration at Stormont believed that the IRA men had been given *coups de grâce*. One senior figure told me, 'One thing one couldn't be sure of after Strabane was whether they were finished off afterwards . . . there was heavy anecdotal evidence that they were.'

There is another, equally curious, aspect to the evidence at the inquest. An RUC Scene of Crime Officer told the court that two crates, one of empty milk bottles, the other containing eleven petrol bombs, were found in a hedge near where the shootings took place. He said he did not think the petrol bombs were connected with the incident and consequently their existence was left out of almost all press reports on the shooting. However, during the course of our interview, the soldier familiar with the shootings mentioned the crate of petrol bombs, indicating it had an important role in the incident. He maintained his story despite my mistaken insistence, based on an initial reading of press cuttings and the soldiers' statements, that there had been no petrol bombs.

According to Soldier A, the engagement started because the terrorists heard him alerting the other soldiers to their presence – on hearing his words, 'All three gunmen swung their rifles towards us.' The person familiar with the case says things happened differently. The SAS men heard the sound of footsteps and the 'chinking' of the petrol bombs in their crate which, he says, the Provisionals were carrying. He says the petrol bombs had either been taken with the men for possible use on the ambush or were being moved from another cache. The IRA men put the crate down as they came through the thick hedge from the road into the field. It is likely that they wanted to put them into the same arms cache as the other weapons. The OP commander, although not there with the mission of mounting an ambush, took an on-the-spot decision to engage the men, which they did, without warning, as they walked past.

On the morning the inquest ended John Fahy, solicitor for the Breslin family, withdrew from the proceedings saying they had served only to rubber stamp unlawful killings. Mr Fahy says the inquest was 'a waste of time, it served no useful purpose'. There is such a thing as a lawful killing by the security forces, he adds – meaning a sincere adherence to the Yellow Card rules – but he believes that in the Strabane case, 'The police and Army got together shortly after the incident and worked out the version they were going to tell the world.'

Lawyers who have acted in such cases say they think there is ample scope for soldiers to enter into a conspiracy to disguise the true facts of an incident. SAS soldiers leave the scene of an incident almost as soon as the shooting has stopped. They have the opportunity to discuss what they will say with their officers before being interviewed by CID officers. The soldiers are normally accompanied during their interviews by an officer of the Army Legal Service, an expert in the legal use of lethal force.

While officers who have served at Lisburn are prepared – on condition of anonymity – to say that the exploitation of intelligence offers deliberate choices, to ambush or not to ambush, and to say explicitly that the policy on such engagements has changed over the years, the court depositions of SAS soldiers involved in shootings do not reflect this. Instead, they consistently attempt to give the impression that the soldiers only ever used lethal force when they were themselves in immediate danger.

There was William Hanna, the unarmed bystander shot at Ballysillan in 1978 because the SAS men said he suddenly reached for what they thought was a gun. Colm McGirr, shot at the arms dump in Coalisland in December 1983, had 'pivoted round', pointing a shotgun, according to the soldier who shot him. William Fleming, despite having been knocked off a motorcycle so hard at the Gransha hospital that his leg was shattered, began, in the soldier's words, 'raising himself' and pointing a gun. The Strabane IRA men had 'swung' their weapons simultaneously towards the soldiers.

Reading these statements, one would conclude that the difference between the periods 1976 to 1978 and 1983 to 1985 and the five-year period in between when nobody was shot by the SAS could be accounted for only in terms of the desire of IRA members to 'reach', 'pivot', 'point' or 'swing' towards SAS soldiers with real or imagined weapons. Someone who relied on the official version of such incidents would be left concluding that the years when the SAS succeeded in making arrests, despite the fact that in the cases described in chapter fifteen the IRA members were armed or near an arms cache, were the years when everybody refrained from making any sudden movements.

Officers who have served at Lisburn in positions where they had a knowledge of covert operations will readily admit to having misled the press after such incidents. 'There is a world of difference between what you say to the press, in the immediate aftermath of an incident, and what you say in a court,' said one, who nevertheless would not deny that false stories had been given to courts too.

The desire of Special Branch officers to protect informers and the nature of technical intelligence-gathering was at the root of the deception uncovered by Stalker. Among many Army officers there is a feeling that telling the court the full story would compromise intelligence sources, make their men reluctant to carry out dangerous assignments and discredit them in the nationalist community. They argue that the supporters of Sinn Fein are so entrenched in their position that gestures of openness will bear no reward for the security forces. Remaining tight-lipped about such operations may feed allegations of cover-ups and "shoot-to-kill" policies, but prosecuting people for their part in covert operations will simply allow republican propagandists to say 'I told you so', they argue.

Some officers in covert operations regard courts as a dangerous inconvenience. They feel republican lawyers use the proceedings to obtain operational information about special forces. One officer says, 'There is all this talk about "shoot-to-kill". What do you think the IRA do – shoot-to-tickle?' He argues that republican use of court proceedings is an obscenity, given the way the IRA kills its own people suspected of informing or shoots defenceless reservists in their homes. If the republican movement believes itself to be at war with the British state how does it justify using its courts in this way? Oistin MacBride, himself a Sinn Fein activist, says in response: 'We are not whingeing about the fact that he [Tony MacBride] died fighting the SAS, but he did have the right as a prisoner of war to be treated properly. I don't think there is anything immoral about us challenging the legal process. There is a certain amount of natural justice that we are due.'

Those officers who question the right of coroners' courts to pry into the world of covert operations sometimes say it is impossible to answer many questions because 'there is a war going on'. Enoch Powell regards this as a dangerous argument which implies a moral equivalence between the two sides. In a television interview in 1988, he said: 'The IRA isn't a thing upon which war can be declared. If we make it a nation state and say we are going to treat you as a nation state and recognize you as a nation and declare war upon you, then you would in fact have installed the IRA in the very position which it seeks to attain by means of terror.'

# 21

# Disaster at Newry

Just a few days after the Strabane incident the IRA succeeded in launching a spectacular attack on the RUC – a blow characterized by some as the RUC's equivalent to the Army's loss at Warrenpoint in 1979. The mortar attack on Newry police station demonstrated several things. It showed the IRA's willingness to develop weapons to suit its own particular needs and its patience in persevering with such technology despite many years of failure.

In November 1983 the IRA had attacked Carrickmore police station with home-made mortars. They killed one police officer and injured several others, but, prior to Newry, this was the only real success which they had had with such weapons. The Provisionals' willingness to carry on attempting such attacks seems something of a mystery in retrospect. Between 1973 and early 1978 they attempted a total of seventy-one attacks using such weapons without killing a single member of the security forces. The firing tubes and shells, usually made in workshops in the Republic, could not be made to sufficiently high tolerances to produce an accurate weapon. Many shells failed to explode, others scattered wildly off target – raising the prospect that an attack could go disastrously wrong and kill civilians.

Nevertheless, mortars continued to offer an important advantage to other means of attacking security forces bases. They allowed the Provisionals to remain some distance away from their targets, which meant it was a safer means of attack. Their continued use, despite so many failures, was partly a product of an attitude summed up by Sinn Fein publicity director Danny Morrison, when after the Brighton bombing he said, 'Remember, we have to get lucky once.'

The ASU which attacked Newry police station used a heavy mortar, the design of which had evolved from much trial and error. Army explosives experts dubbed it the 'Mark 10' mortar. The mortar tubes were bolted on to the back of a Ford lorry which had been hijacked in Crossmaglen. Each tube was made from an oxy-acetylene cylinder with the top cut off. The tubes, each containing a bomb full of high explosive, were sloped at different angles to provide a scatter of shot around the target, increasing the odds of a hit.

Early in the evening of 28 February 1985 the lorry was driven through Newry. The driver got out, starting a timing device which was connected to a battery which would send the impulse to launch the shells. As it began to fire, some of the rounds overshot the target falling into the street in front of the police station. A group of police officers in the flimsily built canteen did not have time to take cover. The IRA had only to hit with one shell: each of them contained 40 lb of high explosive. When one crashed through the roof of the canteen nine police officers were killed.

The Newry attack was followed, like many other IRA 'spectaculars', by calls from politicians, mainly Unionists, for the government to 'do something', to 'increase security'. Officers at Lisburn and Knock are philosophical about such demands. In this case they knew perfectly well that the loss of nine officers had followed years of almost complete failure with mortar attacks. But telling people that the IRA had simply been lucky was hard when questions are being asked about why so many soldiers and police officers were accommodated in temporary wooden buildings which offered no protection against mortar shells.

After Newry a major programme of construction, costing millions of pounds, was started to protect bases from mortar attack. This usually involved building blast-deflecting walls around the base of a building and a reinforced roof over the top.

Another aspect of the post-Newry 'security review' was the stepping-up of Army patrols around bases. This operation, code-named COUNTERPOINT, had several functions. There was a chance that the soldiers might encounter people preparing an attack, although all previous experience had shown this to be a remote possibility. Rather, COUNTERPOINT was intended to deter the IRA from planning such attacks. The generals at Lisburn well understood the value of visible Army patrols for frightening off would-be attackers. It was felt that if a side-street near a base was patrolled every few hours or even days the 'dickers' sent to scout out targets would report back that it was too dangerous.

RUC morale in Newry remained fragile in the months after the attack. Under directions from Knock, the police assumed responsibility for patrolling one of the most dangerous towns in Ulster. Many officers thought this a highly dangerous assignment which had been ordered without proper consideration by their chief constable, says an RUC man.

Matters came to a head after an attack on 26 July 1986. A sergeant and two constables were observing Newry's Market Square from their stationary police car. Although armour plated, the vehicle's doors were open. Three Provisionals approached the vehicle and opened fire. All three police officers were killed. As they turned to leave, one of the terrorists lobbed a grenade into the vehicle. It failed to explode.

After the attack an IRA member telephoned the Newry RUC station to taunt them. He said one of the police officers had been 'squealing like a pig' before they shot him. This was entered into the station log book and, according to a police officer, had an understandably damaging effect on morale. Although it is well known for police in certain rural areas sometimes to refuse to enter a particular area until the Army have swept it, what followed was highly unusual. The town's constables and sergeants gathered and held an angry meeting. According to an RUC man who was party to the discussions which followed, they refused to go out on the streets unless the Army was brought back into the town. They said they would limit themselves to guarding the police station and courthouse.

Chief Constable Hermon agreed to seek the Army's help once more and the situation calmed. The incident is cited by some police to show how out of touch their Chief Constable had become by not anticipating the near mutiny.

Mortars were among a variety of weapons which the IRA manufactured itself. There were practical and financial reasons for doing so. Although properly manufactured mortars could be bought on the arms market, the Provisionals appeared to prefer the home-grown alternative. The anti-armour grenades carried by the men at Strabane were also a product of the IRA's workshops.

During the 1970s the organization had acquired some RPG-7 anti-tank rocket launchers but had found them difficult to use. One projectile had missed a security forces vehicle and ended up landing in a school. The IRA designed its own anti-armour weapons. Grenades were designed on the shaped charge principle – a technique which involves packing explosive around a cone-shaped cavity to enhance its penetrative effect. The anti-armour weapons were designed either to fly a short distance to their target or as 'drogue bombs'. The latter were grenades thrown underarm which deployed a small parachute so that the shaped charge would detonate at the right angle relative to the armour.

These improvized weapons sometimes proved dangerous to the firer. Charles English, a Derry Brigade volunteer, was killed in August 1985 while attempting to use one of the anti-armour weapons. English had been one of the masked men who had fired shots over the coffins at the funeral of the men killed at the Gransha hospital. Though unreliable like the mortars, an anti-armour bomb was used to lethal effect during a later attack in Belfast's Divis flats.

During the mid 1980s the Provisionals succeeded in obtaining virtually any modern firearm they wanted. Terrorists carried Belgian FNC 5.56 mm assault rifles and the more modern, compact, version of the Armalite. They even obtained the FNC rifles before many of the countries whose regular armies had ordered them. The Provisionals also obtained G3 rifles made by the German firm Heckler and Koch. From 1986 these firearms were supplemented by a large number of Kalashnikov firearms provided by the Libyan government. The Libyan shipments also included SA-7 shoulder-launched missiles and heavy machine-guns, both of which could be used against helicopters.

During the summer of 1985 negotiations were carried on in the United States between Noel Murphy, a resident of Boston, and Provisional sympathizer, and an arms dealer. They discussed a purchase of 500 Armalite rifles, Heckler and Koch MP5 sub-machine-guns like those favoured by the SAS and belt-fed M-60 machine-guns. After consulting with senior IRA figures in Ireland in January 1986, Murphy returned and told the arms dealer that he was also interested in buying Redeye portable anti-aircraft missiles. Murphy was joined by Kieran Hughes, reportedly representing the Provisional leadership. In May, with the weapons about to be shipped, the dealer was revealed as an FBI agent and Murphy, Hughes and several accomplices were arrested.

As with mortars and drogue bombs, the preoccupation with shooting down helicopters eventually paid off. In May 1985 south Armagh Provisionals staged a complicated ambush near Crossmaglen. They had fitted a heavy machine-gun to a vehicle and covered it with a tarpaulin. They opened fire on an RAF Wessex helicopter which was using the Crossmaglen helipad. They hit the aircraft, but it did not crash.

In June 1988 they ambushed another helicopter with a heavy machine-gun near Crossmaglen. The Army Lynx was hit several times. While Lisburn determinedly used the phrase 'forced to land', anxious to deny the

Provisionals the propaganda coup of admitting it had been 'shot down' it is clear that, in lay language, that is what happened. The aircraft landed heavily, injuring a crewman. IRA members were said to be closing in to finish off the crew with small arms when Army patrols arrived and saved them. Many Army pilots took to flying with an MP5 machine-gun for self-defence strapped to their seat after this. The damaged Lynx had to be carried off under a Chinook helicopter. Republican mural painters portrayed the aircraft as having had its tail shot off.

With its home-made mortars and anti-armour grenades and with its attempts to shoot down helicopters, the IRA demonstrated both its patience in waiting years, if necessary, to achieve its aim and its ability to improvise new weapons. The use of these mortars and anti-armour bombs had as much to do with the propaganda effects of using them and with letting the movement's better technical intellects have their experiments, as it did with the weapons' real effectiveness.

# 22

# Acceptable Levels

The period from December 1983 to February 1985 had seen aggressive use of Army special forces. From then on, however, the pace of operations seemed to slow slightly, although there was another spate of special forces operations in 1990 and 1991. The reasons for this slight reduction are unclear. It may have been simply that the Int and Sy Group was unlucky and that planned operations produced no results, but it may also have been the case that officers had deliberately cut down ambush-type operations because they perceived a small reduction in the levels of IRA activity and because of pressure from external political developments.

Douglas Hurd, who took over as the Secretary of State for Northern Ireland in September 1984, was a shrewd enough politician to understand the potential damage to relations with the Republic that fatal operations involving undercover soldiers could cause. It is worth recalling the comment by a senior officer at Lisburn following the wave of lethal SAS operations in 1978 that the Army is not in the business of 'embarrassing politicians'. Mrs Thatcher's major initiative on Ireland, the Anglo-Irish Agreement with the Dublin government, was by this stage at an advanced point in negotiations. Signed in November 1985, the Agreement was welcomed by the non-violent section of Northern nationalism (in the form of the Social Democratic and Labour Party), but its provisions allowing the Dublin government regular consultations with Britain over affairs in Ulster smacked to the loyalist community of a sell-out. They launched a campaign of protest under the slogan 'Ulster Says No!'.

In the wake of the Agreement the RUC had to confront loyalist demonstrators. Many police officers were firebombed out of their homes. In the eyes of many of those around him, John Hermon's handling of this difficult period marked his finest hour as Chief Constable. A senior officer at Lisburn who watched with alarm as many loyalists turned on the RUC says, 'Jack Hermon personally kept the RUC on the rails. That man saved

Ulster from a terrible bloodbath by forcing the RUC to face up to its responsibilities.' Many nationalists confessed that their faith in the force had been boosted, for example by the Chief's refusal to allow a loyalist march into a Catholic area of Portadown – a move which brought his officers into violent conflict with the crowd.

In 1985 a new CLF arrived at Lisburn, Major General Tony Jeapes. He had the unique distinction among CLFs of being a former CO of 22 SAS Regiment. He had run the unit during the 1970s and had published a book about his experiences in the Dhofar campaign in Oman. There was also a new GOC, Lieutenant General Robert Pascoe who, some years before, had worked on Maurice Oldfield's Planning Staff at Stormont. Both men were open to the idea of using special forces for ambushes, but both were also aware that there were circumstances when such operations were not desirable and that other courses of action were available.

During the previous few years the covert operators had tried various approaches to the use of the foreknowledge which their penetration of republican groups gave them. 'It is all a matter of acceptable levels', says an intelligence officer borrowing a phrase used by politicians a decade before in a reference to terrorist rather than security forces violence – 'We could ambush a lot more, but people realize that would stir things up too much.' If the covert operators still had foreknowledge, but attempted to ambush on only a few occasions, what did their revised strategy consist of?

Some of those who have worked in the world of undercover operations in Ulster are frank about the alternatives to ambushing which the SB can choose. SB officers tend to be concerned first and foremost with protecting the life of their source. An action which causes the IRA to stop and think about where the security forces obtained their information must be avoided because it may lead them to the source. It is worth emphasizing that it is on this basis that some SB officers object to ambushing on principle, since operations like those at Tamnamore or Gransha in 1984 are bound to trigger witch-hunts within the organization. On the other hand, the SB is often reluctant to arrest Provisionals on lesser charges, for example picking them up at an arms cache and charging them with possession of firearms because many covert operators feel that sentencing someone to seven or eight years in prison, 'which means three or four with remission' as one officer puts it, does not justify the risks to the source and surveillance operators of a long-term covert operation.

Instead, the undercover experts have evolved various types of operation which can be used to prevent an attack happening while protecting the identity of a source. The technique of doctoring of firearms and bomb-making materials was used many times in the 1980s, says an intelligence officer. The IRA emerges from such an operation uncertain as to whether its cache was compromised, whether the Army simply managed to defuse the bomb in time or whether its detonator failed.

Another important tactic is to use uniformed patrols. For example, an IRA team sent to assassinate a UDR reservist will not press home its attack if there are several uniformed police, perhaps stopping vehicles to check their tax discs, outside his or her house. The police or soldiers involved will almost always be ignorant of the covert reason for their presence. Such patrolling is usually requested from battalion commanding officers or RUC divisional commanders by the TCG.

The vagueness of much informer intelligence means that the security forces may have to show great ingenuity in their attempts to frustrate the terrorist. Police cannot check tax discs in the same place every day, to follow our example, since this would arouse suspicion and make *them* the target for terrorist attack. If the terrorists are under surveillance the intelligence specialists will wait for an 'indicator' of a forthcoming attack, for example the meeting of three individuals associated with previous incidents, before triggering their thwarting operation.

It may be that the target of their attack is not known. In this case it may be necessary to step up checkpoints on the road around the ASU's village. Such duties are normally carried out by Army, UDR or police DMSU uniformed patrols. To the terrorists and to most of the security forces personnel taking part there is nothing to distinguish this activity from their normal work.

An intelligence officer relates one incident where it was known that an IRA team was to travel along a particular route on its way to an attack. They arranged for a car 'accident' to take place on the road. 'There wasn't a uniform in sight,' he recalls, 'but it was assumed that they would get unnerved sitting in the tailback, thinking the police were about to arrive.' The ploy succeeded.

Such operations can also be used to channel terrorists in a particular direction. One intelligence officer believes, 'You can say, "Let's persuade the operation to go this way by putting a heavy presence in an area" – it comes down to the rules of war and deception.'

IRA members are acutely aware of surveillance and informers. Many attacks are called off after what communiqués refer to as 'suspicious security forces activity'. In some cases they are duped by the TCG. In others they may simply have imagined innocent patterns of traffic to be connected with undercover operations. Sometimes, rarely, the compromise of a covert observation post or car may alert them to the presence of real danger. These contests of nerve increased during the mid 1980s and contributed to the slow decline in IRA operations. Republicans admit in private that most of their operations are cancelled but stress in public the increasing amount of preparation which has to go into an attack if it is to be successful in current conditions. The fact that surveillance and thwarting operations are more easily carried out in the bustle of urban life contributed in particular to the continuing decline in IRA activity in the cities.

Despite all these methods for avoiding and pre-empting confrontations with terrorists, there were still some instances where security forces did select the option of an aggressive operation. In February 1986 security chiefs authorized an Army undercover operation in the village of Toomebridge, County Londonderry. An IRA arms cache at the rear of a house, among some outbuildings, was placed under observation. It contained an Armalite rifle, which subsequent tests were to show had been used in several killings, and an FNC rifle. On the evening of 18 February two unmarked cars drove into the village. Five SAS soldiers were dropped by the two cars and made their way to positions behind the buildings. Soldier A, a thirty-eight-year-old senior NCO, said later that there were reports of terrorists in the vicinity of the buildings and 'We had been instructed to take up the most suitable positions to apprehend them.'

A car arrived and shortly afterwards two men appeared at a gap between two of the outbuildings which is a few feet wide, the soldiers said. Francis Bradley, a twenty-year-old local man, went into the yard and the soldiers opened fire. Soldier A said he had called 'Halt!' but, 'Before I could say any more the gunman turned sharply as if to confront me.' Bradley had picked up the rifle and turned it towards the soldiers, the Army said. He was hit by eight bullets and died a few minutes later.

The soldiers arrested Colm Walls, forty-six, owner of the house and Barney McLarnon, fifty-three, who had been driving the car. The logic of the soldiers' evidence was that McLarnon had accompanied Bradley into the back yard, something which he denied.

None of the three men belonged to the IRA or INLA. Bradley had been questioned by the police and, it was subsequently claimed, threatened by them, but had never been charged with any offence. There can be little doubt that the Provisionals would have said Bradley was a volunteer if he had been: the importance of martyrs being greater in the republican move-ment than the chance to make propaganda capital out of the death of a non-member. But if Bradley was not a Provisional, what was he doing recovering a weapon?

Local people suggest that the IRA pressurized Bradley into moving the weapons on its behalf. After the shooting, a man in Toomebridge told the *Irish News*, 'It is common knowledge that soldiers have been lying in the fields around the house for the last two weeks.' The locals felt that the soldiers had mounted a stake-out and were intent on shooting whoever came into the yard.

The possibility that the SAS soldiers might have been unknowingly compromised in an ambush position opens many lines of speculation. It is, for example, possible that the local IRA knew there was a chance their cache was under observation and therefore chose to risk somebody else's life rather than one of their own member's when the time came to move the weapons. The possibility that the cache had been under surveillance for several days also prompts the question why the Army did not send in Weapons Intelligence Unit experts to render the weapons safe in the event of a confrontation with those who came to collect them.

During the inquest one year later forensic evidence was used to challenge the soldiers' version of events. One bullet had hit Bradley in the buttock – its impact was consistent with having been fired as he knelt to recover a weapon, rather than standing up. The post-mortem examination showed he had been killed by a burst of three bullets fired from about 3 metres away as he lay on his back. It appeared from the analysis of his wounds that Bradley had been hit by four bursts of fire. The first had hit his buttock, he had then been hit in the arms. The third burst had caught him down the left side, injuring his arm, leg and one bullet entering his armpit. The fourth, fatal, burst had been fired by the soldiers after they had moved forward from their positions with Bradley lying on his back and presumably incapacitated after already being hit by five rounds.

The inquest also led to further questions about the way soldiers are interviewed and their statements prepared after such incidents. The shoot-ing had happened at about 9.50 p.m. All of the soldiers had made a note in their depositions saying that it had been a bright night: Soldier A had said there was, 'a good moon'; Soldier B that there was 'good visibility'; Soldier C, 'a moon and visibility was good'; Soldier D, 'a good moon' and Soldier E, 'a good moon'. However, a witness from the local weather centre said under oath at the inquest that the moon had not appeared in the sky until 11.08 p.m. that night. The significance of this episode, the Bradley family solicitor felt, was that it suggested the Army was writing the same script for each soldier and that if they had got wrong the time when the moon appeared, how much credence could be placed in the soldiers' assertions that Bradley had picked up the gun and turned it towards them?

Toomebridge was an unsatisfactory episode for the Army. Neither Walls nor McLarnon was subsequently convicted of any offence for their part in the evening's drama. A man had died who was, if not entirely innocent of connections with terrorists, at least not a member of the IRA. The possibility that the soldiers had been compromised in their position for days without knowing it must also have been a worrying one. The only comfort that could be taken was in the recovery of the firearms.

For the security forces, possession of informer intelligence posed real dilemmas. While most attention centres on operations to counter actions by republican groups it is apparent that penetration of loyalist terrorist organizations must also sometimes offer the chance to pre-empt their actions. Yet, in the many years of special forces operations only one loyalist has ever been shot dead by Army special forces, following the killing of a Catholic late in 1989.

From 1987 members of the Field Research Unit, the Army's élite agent running team, had an agent high in the Ulster Defence Association. Brian Nelson, a former member of the Black Watch regiment, returned to Ulster at the behest of the FRU after working in Germany. Nelson had been both a loyalist terrorist and an Army agent before, but on his return became the UDA's senior intelligence officer, with a key role in targeting Catholics. Nelson's work put him in an ideal position to give the security forces the chance to pre-empt such killings. In January 1990 detectives of the Stevens inquiry, investigating how loyalists had obtained security forces intelligence documents, arrested Nelson. At his trial in January 1992, Nelson pleaded guilty to five charges of conspiracy to murder and fifteen other offences. Crown lawyers dropped two murder counts at the last minute, leading to claims of a deal whereby Nelson pleaded guilty to lesser charges to prevent details of his secret work becoming public.

It emerged that Nelson had told his handlers in advance of UDA plans to kill two loyalists believed to be republican terrorists. Gerald Slane and Terence McDaid were gunned down in 1988 despite these warnings. An unnamed colonel, in fact a former Commanding Officer of the FRU, appeared in court to plead mitigation for Nelson, saying the agent had warned of 217 individuals targeted by the UDA. Nelson's information was said to have saved Gerry Adams from a UDA bomb in 1987.

Despite evidence of Nelson's success as an agent, the case raised uncomfortable questions about the difference between the security forces' response to foreknowledge of republican and loyalist attacks. Clearly Nelson's intelligence and that of other loyalist informers has been used to thwart attacks, in the same way as information from republican groups. But it is clear that attempts to exploit this intelligence to ambush loyalists have rarely if ever been made.

During the 1980s the TCGs and Int and Sy Group had exploited informer intelligence to intercept republican terrorists on a number of occasions. As their practice in such techniques improved, their ability to tell good information – 'hard int' – from vague informer hearsay allowed them to place surveillance teams and SAS men in the right place at the right time more often. However, a by-product of this process was that regular infantry battalions in Ulster on four-month and two-year tours very rarely had the chance to take any kind of initiative against the IRA or INLA. Uniformed Army or police patrols remained the target for terrorist attack but were rarely used when the security forces had the intelligence to pre-empt it.

The character of Northern Ireland tours had changed considerably since the early 1970s, when battalions fired hundreds of rounds in running street-battles during their four-month tours. During the period from December 1983 to February 1985 when the Group had been involved in the deaths of nine IRA men, the other 10,000 members of the Army in Ulster had not been involved in a single killing of an IRA member. When such incidents did happen, for example in the case of Tony Gough, a Derry Brigade member killed in February 1986, they resulted largely from chance encounters between uniformed patrols and IRA members who were preparing or had just carried out an attack on them.

For the vast majority of soldiers Northern Ireland tours mean an often frustrating combination of avoiding IRA ambushes and trying to keep your temper in the face of insults and provocation from an alienated nationalist population. Squaddies often invoke the imagery of the rifle range. 'We're just Figure 11s out on the streets', a young commando says – the 'Figure 11' is the graphic representation of a charging enemy soldier which the Army uses for target practice. Better trained battalions are normally able to contain these frustrations, but where discipline is not so good they sometimes result in assaults on local people, death threats to terrorist suspects and vandalism during house searches.

Officers tend to be philosophical about the position in which the centralization of intelligence and covert operations places normal units. 'Attrition,' the commanding officer of an infantry battalion says, 'is most effectively carried out by the many specialist agencies who are specifically trained to do it.' But very occasionally ordinary soldiers can play a key role in a covert operation.

During a patrol of the south Fermanagh countryside in April 1986, a young soldier noticed something unusual – a wire which he felt might be a command wire for a bomb. It was near a road which runs along a field outside Rosslea, only about one mile from the border with the Republic. When the soldiers returned to their base, he kept his discovery to himself during the routine de-briefing which follows all such patrols. Afterwards he told his commander about what he had seen and the SB was notified. What followed was, an Army intelligence officer says, 'about the only recent example I can think of of an SAS operation which did not result from informer intelligence'.

Int and Sy Group carried out a covert investigation of the area and discovered that it was indeed a command wire: there was an 800lb bomb on the end of it. The explosive had been placed, in classic IRA fashion, under the road in the hope of blowing up a security forces vehicle. The SAS and SB detectives discussed what to do next. They agreed that the soldier's discretion had been exemplary. Had he spoken up at the de-brief, everybody in the battalion would have known about the discovery within hours – with the danger that the news might leak out via a civilian employee or UDR member.

On 25 April, SAS men took up positions around the firing point end of the command wire. In the early hours of 26 April two men appeared in the field, one armed with a Ruger rifle, the other an FNC assault rifle. As they went to the firing point the SAS opened fire. One man, Sean Lynch from Lisnaskea a few miles away, was injured; the other was dead. Seamus McElwaine, Maze escaper and scourge of the security forces in Fermanagh for years, had been killed.

Lynch staggered into the darkness, hit several times. The SAS soldiers fired illuminating flares into the sky and Lynch rolled into a hedgerow for cover. He lay there first as a special forces QRF helped to search the area and then as other police and soldiers came to cordon and search the area.

In evidence at Lynch's trial, the Army said there had been four soldiers in two OPs overlooking the firing point when the shooting happened.

Police from the DMSU, who had been waiting in a nearby RUC station, continued their search into the following morning. Lynch said later he was found by a soldier who said, 'Have you been shot, mate?' Lynch replied, 'I'm riddled.' The IRA man said that DMSU officers then discussed killing him, but were stopped from mistreating him by an Army doctor.

Lynch attained the distinction, exceedingly rare among IRA members in the 1980s, of surviving SAS gunfire. He was later to claim that McElwaine had been injured in the first burst of shots and that the soldiers had questioned him for half an hour before finishing him off. Such allegations cannot be corroborated independently and, as of mid 1991, no inquest had taken place at which pathological evidence on the nature of McElwaine's gunshot wounds could be presented.

The loss of McElwaine, only twenty-six but active in terrorism for ten years of his life, was a grave blow to the Provisionals in Fermanagh. There is little doubt that he had planned many killings and been personally responsible for several. His funeral across the border in Monaghan was attended by an estimated 3000 people, including Gerry Adams and Martin McGuinness.

Some years later, when I visited an Army unit in the area, an officer expressed the opinion that the IRA in south Fermanagh had become largely inactive since McElwaine's death. In his funeral oration, McGuinness said McElwaine 'was a brave intelligent soldier, a young man who gave up his youth to fight for the freedom of his country'. The epitaph given him by an Army intelligence officer reveals both respect and loathing for the man: 'He was an extraordinary bloke who would have been in the SAS if he was in the Army. It is just as well he is dead.'

# 23

# Tyrone Brigade

During the mid 1980s Tyrone was one of the key arenas in the battle between the Provisionals and undercover forces. The IRA cells in the area did not match south Armagh in terms of the number of security forces members killed, but they were able to carry out more operations than those in Londonderry or Belfast. IRA enforcers, however, appeared unable to stop widespread informing among the Tyrone republican community – something which allowed the security forces to stage many more covert operations in this area than in south Armagh.

Tyrone, the largest of the six counties, is a heterogeneous area. It stretches from Strabane, on the Republic's border in the west, across desolate moors to undulating farmland where the county touches the Republic again at Monaghan. Some villages are exclusively Protestant, others Catholic, and towns such as Cookstown and Dungannon contain roughly equal numbers.

The IRA infrastructure has clusters of ASUs grouped in particular parts of the county. Around Dungannon, in villages like Cappagh, Pomeroy and Coalisland there are several ASUs, with close connections with groups across the border in Monaghan and in north Armagh. There is also a cluster of them in the central part of the county in moorland villages such as Carrickmore, Gortin, Greencastle and Eakra. Around Strabane there are groups with close connections with the IRA in Londonderry and Donegal in the Republic. These groups of ASUs sometimes referred to themselves, respectively, as 'East Tyrone', 'Mid Tyrone' or 'West Tyrone Brigade'. In reality there were individuals who held sway over groups of ASUs, each sometimes only three or four members strong. The total number of active Provisionals across the county was perhaps fifty or sixty, with another 100 or 200 Sinn Fein activists and other highly motivated supporters.

In his 1978 report, *Future Terrorist Trends*, James Glover had noted the weakness of the Provisionals' middle level of command. Those who ran groups of ASUs were in a difficult position. The Northern Command leadership expected to exert control over the direction of policy and the types of targets attacked and ASU commanders expected to have considerable operational freedom. Matters were made more difficult by problems of co-ordination and communication. Telephones were assumed to be tapped and known activists frequently followed.

But in the mid 1980s the Tyrone leadership overcame many of these difficulties, bringing together groups of ASUs to mount complex attacks. Their primary targets were off-duty members of the security forces and remote police stations. The IRA had realized that the RUC's network of small stations in rural areas was vulnerable. There were about twenty-four police stations in rural Tyrone, many of them run by four or five officers, during the day-time only. These buildings were often at risk since they could not all be protected by Army patrols. Mortar and bomb attacks on police stations were backed by intimidation against contractors called in to repair the damage.

The campaign against police stations in Tyrone peaked late in 1985. The most spectacular operation was an attack on Ballygawley police station. It was a complex operation, involving teams of dickers, a group of armed members and bomb-making experts. The IRA attacked the station with gunfire. Reserve Constable William Clements and Constable George Gilliland were shot dead at the entrance to the station. The IRA members then went into the wrecked building taking guns and documents and planting a bomb in the entrance to the building. It went off: three other police officers who had been inside escaped through the back door.

The Ballygawley attack delighted the terrorist leaders. An IRA man referring to it in a later magazine interview said, 'That is the type of operation that we would like to have all of the time. Unfortunately most times it doesn't present itself to be as easily worked as that.' Episodes like Ballygawley appealed to the terrorists' self-image as guerrilla fighters. They also offered the chance to humiliate the authorities. The IRA made much of the claim that three police officers had fled the station during the assault.

Provisional members used an RUC standard issue Ruger revolver, taken from the body of Reserve Constable Clements, in a way which must have caused a further blow to morale for members of the force. When it was recovered nearly two years later it was established that the dead policeman's gun had been used to kill a UDR man in March 1986, as well as a building contractor in Greencastle who did work for the security forces, a Magherafelt businessman and in two other attempted killings.

The December assault on RUC outposts in Tyrone was continued ten days after Ballygawley by a mortar attack on Castlederg station. Two days later, on 22 December, there was a further mortar attack. Carrickmore station and several nearby buildings were damaged. Nobody was injured in the Castlederg or Carrickmore attacks, but they underlined the vulnerability of the outposts and the vitality of the IRA command in the county.

The IRA's offensive against police stations in rural areas and the disturbances from loyalists opposed to the Anglo-Irish Agreement led in 1986 to the Army reversing the pattern of the previous decade, and increasing its troop strength. Two more battalions were sent to Ulster, taking the number of regular soldiers from 9000 to about 10,200. These units were referred to as 'incremental reinforcement battalions', the idea being that their presence was only temporary. However, the Army's later attempts to remove them were thwarted by IRA activity in the border area and cries of alarm from Protestants who objected to any diminution in the Army presence.

One of the architects of the IRA's strategy in Tyrone was Patrick Kelly, a thirty-year-old Dungannon man believed by security chiefs to have effective control of the group of ASUs around the town. Late in 1986, Kelly is thought to have devised a plan to attack another RUC station. Although nobody was killed at The Birches, it was an operation which demonstrated a tactical approach still more sophisticated than at Ballygawley.

The Birches, like many other stations, had been surrounded by a high wire fence. This was intended to give protection against attack with anti-tank weapons, hand-thrown bombs and stones. The IRA decided to hijack a mechanical excavator and put a bomb in its front bucket. The digger would then be driven through the fence and the bomb detonated.

Early in 1987 I was given a briefing by a member of the security forces which contained a detailed account of how the attack on The Birches had been carried out. There had been several teams with different tasks. One group had staged a diversionary incident in Pomeroy, more than 20 kilometres north-west of Dungannon, which was designed to draw security forces away from the target. Another group had hijacked the digger and other vehicles needed for the job in Washing Bay, several kilometres to the east of Dungannon. A further team had mounted the attack itself. The attackers evaded security forces roadblocks after the raid by escaping by boat across Lough Neagh. When hijackers, 'dickers', gun-carrying members and bombers were included, the attack had involved thirty-five people, the person giving the briefing said. The Birches RUC station was destroyed by the bomb, creating problems for the authorities about how to re-build it.

The Tyrone IRA was able to combine practical skills such as bomb-making and the welding needed to make mortars with considerable resources and know-how. Its members went on operations carrying the latest assault rifles and often wore body-armour similar to that used by the security forces, giving them protection against pistol or sub-machine-gun fire. By 1987 they had also succeeded in obtaining night-sights, allowing them to aim weapons or observe their enemy in darkness.

In April 1986 Jim Lynagh, a veteran IRA member, had been released from the Republic's Portlaoise prison. Lynagh had a lengthy record of involvement with the Provisionals and had been imprisoned several times as a result. He came from Tully, in Monaghan, one of fourteen children. In 1973, in Moy, county Tyrone, he had narrowly escaped death when a bomb he was carrying blew up prematurely. He spent the next five years in Long Kesh. He was then elected on to the Monaghan Council as a Sinn Fein member. In 1980 he appeared in a court in the Republic charged with IRA membership but was released a few months later. In 1982 the Gardai arrested Lynagh with twelve rounds of ammunition and he was sentenced to five years in Portlaoise.

The IRA later described Lynagh as 'commander of a unit'. He held sway over a group of IRA members in Monaghan, north Armagh and east Tyrone. Some later reports were to describe him as overall commander of the IRA in the border region, although it seems more probable that he led groups of members on specific missions in the area he knew well. 'Lynagh saw himself as the leader of a guerrilla band, not a member of a terrorist cell', says an Army intelligence officer.

His *modus operandi* bore little resemblance to that of many other IRA leaders. Whereas other commanders might arm only one or two volunteers, Lynagh would lead ten or twelve with assault rifles to carry out a mission. This tactic had the advantage that it made them very difficult to arrest. In January 1981 Lynagh was believed to have led twelve members in an attack on the house of Sir Norman Strange, the eighty-six-year-old former speaker of the Stormont assembly and long-serving MP for Mid Armagh. His son James, who had succeeded him as Official Unionist member for the constituency, was also home. Both men were killed. The local police sent several officers in an armour plated car in an attempt to head off the terrorists. As the IRA gang left the gates of Tynan Abbey, the Stronge residence, they riddled the car with automatic fire. The police survived but were pinned down and unable to prevent the gang's escape.

The disadvantage of operating in such a large group is that it makes it more vulnerable to informers. But Lynagh was not greatly concerned by this possibility, as the men around him were tied by close bonds of loyalty. Many were part of the same committed republican community in Monaghan. Lynagh had been a close friend of Seamus McElwaine, the south Fermanagh commander killed in April 1986 who also lived in the border county.

After Lynagh's release in 1986 he was kept under close surveillance by the Gardai, an Army intelligence officer says. The flow of information from the South had improved greatly following the Anglo–Irish Agreement.

Lynagh and Paddy Kelly were keen to join forces for a 'spectacular' along the lines of Ballygawley and The Birches, devising a plan to repeat their technique used at The Birches to attack a small police station in the north Armagh village of Loughgall. Throughout late 1986 and early 1987, however, intelligence officers in the North frustrated them from doing so, says someone serving in a key position at the time. What Lynagh and Kelly did not know was that they were under intense surveillance and that there was an informer in their midst. On several occasions the coming together of various ASU members presented an 'indicator' of a forthcoming attack, says the intelligence expert. These attacks were deterred by stepping up patrols by local UDR units and by other measures.

On 25 April, at about 8.30 a.m., the IRA blew up Lord Justice Maurice Gibson and his wife Cecily. Northern Ireland's second most senior judge, and the man who had spoken of bringing terrorists to the 'final court of justice', had been driving back from holiday having taken the ferry to a Southern Irish port. The Gardai had accompanied them to the border but the RUC was not there to meet them. The RUC had stopped escorting VIPs on the border road because they had had several constables killed on such duties. In May 1985 four RUC officers had been blown up at Killeen in south Armagh while on escort duties. The incident produced a chill in relations between Jack Hermon and his opposite number in the Republic.

As Lord Justice Gibson's car crossed into the North a 500 lb bomb was detonated at the side of the road. The affair caused profound embarrassment to the British government. There were claims that details of the Gibsons' route might have leaked out of Gardai headquarters, and also the usual Unionist calls for more security on the border.

On the evening of the same day as the Gibsons died there was another terrorist attack. William Graham, a forty-four-year-old Ulster Defence Regiment full-timer from Pomeroy in east Tyrone, was working in the yard of his farm when two masked men carrying assault rifles walked up behind him. Graham's wife, seeing what was about to happen, shóuted to him to run. For some reason he did not hear her and the two IRA men opened fire. A post-mortem examination was to show that Graham was shot in the back and fell forward. The two IRA men stood almost over him and continued shooting him as he lay on the ground. At least nineteen rounds were fired. The east Tyrone IRA said that they had carried out the killing.

Superficially, there seemed little to distinguish Graham's death from those of the scores of other reservists killed in their homes by the IRA. In fact, it was closely connected to the events which were about to unfold at Loughgall. Ballistic tests were to show that assault rifles recovered at Loughgall were the same ones used to kill Graham. But there are other connections between the incidents.

A member of the security forces in a position to know alleged to me during the preparation of this book that Graham's killers had been under surveillance when they carried out the attack. The attack on Graham may have been allowed to proceed because the intelligence officers handling the case did not want to jeopardize their plans to mount a major ambush, and Graham's death may have been part of a plan to let the east Tyrone ASUs get so cocky that they would mount the Loughgall operation.

I have not found people prepared to corroborate the allegation that the IRA was allowed to kill Graham. I have included it because the person making it was, I believe, saying what he believed to be the truth. That some of the people who would carry out the Loughgall attack were involved in Graham's killing seems highly probable. The person who made the allegation against the intelligence officers in charge of the operation says that a footprint from a training shoe found in the mud of Graham's farmyard matched one of the shoes on one of the men who would carry out the Loughgall operation.

What several other interviewees have confirmed is that the ASUs who were preparing to attack Loughgall police station had indeed been under surveillance for weeks before the attack. Several sources have also told me that there was at least one informer in the east Tyrone IRA. Graham's killing appears therefore, at the very least, to have represented a major error on the part of those conducting the intelligence operation against Lynagh and Kelly's units. The Graham incident may be comparable to John Stalker's discovery that the death of three police officers at the Kinnego embankment in 1982 was highly embarrassing to the RUC because the explosive used to kill them had been removed from a hayshed which was under surveillance at the time.

The evidence of the footprint, the guns, the east Tyrone IRA's own claiming of the attack and the fact that nobody else was ever to be charged with Graham's killing all suggest that his assailants were among those involved in the forthcoming Loughgall operation. It may be that the Provisionals simply gave their watchers the slip on the evening of 25 April 1987 or that not all of them were under surveillance at the time. If this was not the case, it may suggest that the desire to protect an informer or to allow an ambush to proceed on the best possible terms might lead the intelligence officers to sacrifice the lives of members of the security forces.

Although Graham's killing appears in all probability to have been carried out by Lynagh and Kelly's units, there is no evidence to tie them to the Gibson killings. But it was following the events of 25 April, an intelligence expert says, that security chiefs decided to allow the terrorists' plan to attack Loughgall police station to run. An ambush would be prepared in Loughgall as 'an act of revenge', he says – adding that the military plan had been cleared at a very senior level. The operation would draw together informer intelligence, expert surveillance and the firearms skills of the SAS – all of the elements practised during the previous decade.

The ASUs involved once more began preparations for the co-ordinated series of actions which would need to be carried out to stage the attack. Early in May, a few days before the plan was due to go into effect, Lynagh and another man were stopped by the Gardai while out walking. Local people say they were hoping to find a weapon on him, so that he might be charged again for possession. They found nothing, but the incident showed 'how closely he was being watched', according to a local. Lynagh slipped across the border and the Loughgall plan moved into effect.

# 24

# Loughgall, 8 May 1987:
# Prayers and Tapdancing

Loughgall is a small, overwhelmingly Protestant village in north Armagh. It is in what the locals call 'orchard country', where the slopes of the rolling countryside are dotted with apple trees. It is 13 kilometres from Armagh city, which can be reached in about fifteen minutes by car, and somewhat further from Dungannon, which is twenty or twenty-five minutes away.

The RUC station in Loughgall is a small affair, opening limited hours in the morning and afternoon. It is normally run by a sergeant and three or four other officers. As you approach the village from Armagh, the road slopes gently downhill and there is a walled copse on the right. This is Balleygasey Road; the RUC station is on the left, between a row of small bungalows which are occupied mainly by retired people and a former UDR barrack building, the local football team's clubhouse, and a small, operator-less telephone exchange. The road then curves slightly to the left and goes uphill into the main part of the village. A church stands at the top of this slope, in the centre of Loughgall. Along the right side of Balleygasey Road is a football field.

In 1987 Jim Lynagh and Paddy Kelly planned to destroy Loughgall police station after it had closed at 7 p.m. Because the RUC officers would normally have left by this time, it would appear that their aim was not to kill but to destroy police stations, as they had done at The Birches. As with the previous attack, they intended to use a digger with a bomb in its excavating bucket to crash through the gates in the wire fence which surrounded the station.

The operation to intercept the IRA team had been taking shape for some days before the attack. Intelligence authorities at the TCG and special forces experts of the Int and Sy Group knew that Lynagh would lead a large, heavily armed group against the station. They also knew from The Birches attack that the preparation for the operation could involve dozens of people across long distances. They decided to bring in enough of their own people to deal with the situation. It was to be, in the words of an officer briefed on the operation, 'a massive ambush'.

Commanders decided that the twenty-four SAS soldiers resident in Ulster were insufficient for this task, so 22 SAS headquarters in Hereford was alerted. A troop of about fifteen soldiers belonging to G Squadron was flown over from Britain to boost the forces in Ulster. At that time G Squadron was doing a six month spell as the Regiment's special projects team, which stands by at Hereford ready for an anti-terrorist emergency anywhere in the world.

In addition the Provisionals would be shadowed by Army surveillance experts and those of the Special Branch's E4A. It is also believed that members of the RUC's highly trained HMSU were deployed in the area. At least fifty of the Army's and the RUC's troops most highly trained in surveillance techniques and the use of firearms were committed to the immediate operation, and several companies of UDR and regular Army soldiers as well as mobile police squads were to be available to cordon off the Armagh/Dungannon area after the operation. Loughgall was to be an operation involving hundreds of soldiers and police.

Lynagh's group had hidden their explosives in a farmyard some kilometres to the north of Loughgall, close to the Armagh/Tyrone border and the republican strongholds of Coalisland and Washing Bay. It is clear from interviews and press reports at the time of the incident that this cache was under close surveillance for days or even weeks before the attack. It is thought that E4A were given this task.

A few days before the IRA operation had begun, the members of the SAS and other elements taking part in Operation JUDY – the code-name apparently used for the security forces plan to defeat the terrorists – attended a briefing. It set out the kind of attack which Lynagh and Kelly were believed to have planned. Most of the details were to be proven correct, although the briefing officers did get some things wrong. They said that it was believed likely that the IRA group would approach the police station across the football field across the Balleygasey Road, rather than by road. They also told the soldiers that they believed the IRA bomb would be set off by a timer or a remote control device (in fact it would be a simple fuse lit by one of the terrorists).

The SAS soldiers went into position many hours before the planned attack. Some of them were spotted by one of the elderly residents of the Balleygasey Road out walking his dog. Despite this 'compromise', it was decided that it would be safe for the troops to remain in place.

During the afternoon of Friday 8 May, IRA terrorists wearing masks hijacked a blue Toyota Hiace van from a business in Mountjoy Road, Dungannon. Some time after 5 p.m. they hijacked a digger from a farmyard, also near Dungannon. The digger was driven to the farmyard to be fitted with a powerful bomb.

Lynagh and Kelly had been joined for the attack by six other men: Patrick McKearney, thirty-two, who had escaped from the Maze and who came from the village of Moy halfway between Dungannon and Armagh; Gerard O'Callaghan, twenty-nine, from Benburb in Tyrone; Seamus Donnelly, twenty-one, from Galbally near Dungannon; Declan Arthurs, the same age and from the same village; Eugene Kelly, twenty-five, from Cappagh; and Tony Gormley, twenty-four also from Galbally. The complexity of the plan, and its similarity to the one used nine months before, would indicate that there were many other people involved as well, but these eight men were chosen to ride into the village. Gormley and O'Callaghan rode on the digger itself. The others went in the blue van which was driven by Donnelly. Lynagh was in the back of the van and Kelly probably rode beside the driver.

The men drew their weapons. They had three Heckler and Koch G3 7.62 mm assault rifles – a standard weapon of the German army – two 5.56 mm FNC rifles, an assault shotgun and the Ruger revolver taken from Reserve Constable Clements at Ballygawley. Subsequent tests were to show that the G3s and FNCs had been used in three killings of UDR men. They clad themselves in boiler suits, balaclavas and gloves and set off.

The digger made its way down small country lanes, rather than taking the main road from Dungannon to Armagh. The van went ahead to make sure the coast was clear. Given that the point where the explosive was collected was under observation, it is possible that there was also surveillance along the route, perhaps from unmarked cars or OPs. The undercover operators, after all, needed some assurance that the IRA really was going to attack the target.

The SAS troops in Loughgall were commanded by the most senior NCO in the Ulster troop – a Hereford veteran with the rank of staff sergeant. Their officers were not on the ground. The briefing had stated that the mission was an OP/React – an Observation Post able to react. As we have already seen, this was a coded term for an ambush, and the soldiers' weaponry and deployment had more in common with what the regiment practises in the jungles of Brunei than is considered normal in Ulster. According to members of the SAS, there were two or more 7.62 mm belt-fed General Purpose Machine Guns in the ambush party, operated by members of the resident troop. Its other members carried newly issued

7.62 mm Heckler and Koch G3-A4K assault rifles, which had replaced the Armalite and HK53 assault rifles used by SAS troops in Northern Ireland prior to 1987. Most of the reinforcement troop from G Squadron carried 5.56 mm M-16 Armalites.

The main body – what would in Army manuals be termed the 'assault' or 'killer' group – was deployed in two main groups. The larger, including the belt-fed General Purpose Machine Guns, was positioned in the copse overlooking the RUC station close to the Armagh road in order to be able to concentrate fire on the football field in front of the station, reflecting the SAS commander's belief that the IRA group was likely to approach across this ground. The other main group was in and around the police station itself. These men were at considerable risk from the bomb: the SAS commander had probably gambled that, because there was a low wall running along most of the front of the station which could not be crossed by a digger, the excavator would be driven into the gate – directing the blast at one end of the building. The SAS soldiers inside the station would have been at the rear and at the other end of the building. One or two may have been crouched behind a blast-proof wall built to protect the station entrance.

The SAS commander's decision to put men inside the police station may have owed something to the philosophy of the 'clean kill'. Many of those involved in the operation regarded it as a simple ambush, part of a terrorist war. But it was vitally important that a judicious use of force appeared to be maintained and that the soldiers be seen to have acted within the terms of the Army Yellow Card. The IRA assumption that the police station would be unoccupied at the time of the attack might make it hard to justify killing the terrorists, as they were not presenting an immediate danger to life.

An SAS man explained to me the commander's decision to put men inside the police station in the following terms: 'The Yellow Card rules are officially seen to cover Loughgall, but of course they don't. You put your men in the station. That way they [the IRA] are threatening you without even knowing it. That's how you get around the Yellow Card.'

There were also at least two 'cut off groups' in the village. These were where you would expect them to be in a 'Type A' ambush (an attack where the enemy comes along a known route), at points on Balleygasey Road on either side of the RUC station. As well as the group in the copse by the Armagh road, there was another SAS group close to the church, probably sheltering behind the stone wall which runs alongside the road. It is likely that there were other groups of SAS men in the village, acting as look-outs and covering other possible routes of escape. There may also have been an Airborne Reaction Force waiting with helicopters at a nearby security forces base in case the IRA men had to be blocked from getting away across the countryside.

The Toyota van entered the village at about 7.15 p.m. It went past the church where the SAS men were hiding behind the wall and went down the hill towards the station. People living nearby had noticed nothing unusual. They had not been told that RUC intelligence had good reason to believe that terrorists were going to try and bomb their police station. The risks of informing civilians, or evacuating them, are considered too great by the covert operators, even in a largely loyalist village. A woman living near the RUC station remembers the blue Toyota appearing: 'I saw the van go up and down. I thought it was from the corporation.' The men inside the vehicle were in fact checking the coast was clear.

After a few moments the van came back down the road, past the church, followed by the digger. The excavator trundled down the Balleygasey Road, the bomb in its front bucket concealed under rubble. The van went slightly past the police station and stopped.

Patrick Kelly and a couple of the others climbed out of the van, levelled their assault rifles and opened fire on the police station. It would appear that, unlike Balleygawley where RUC officers were shot, this fusillade was an act of bravado, as the IRA were not expecting Loughgall station to be occupied. At this point the main body of the SAS ambush party opened fire. As at least a dozen SAS men fired automatic weapons. 'All hell broke lose on the radio net,' says someone who was part of the operation. The IRA men around the van were caught in a withering deluge of rounds coming from two directions: SAS troops around the police station were firing into the rear and side of the Toyota. Those in the copse opened up with their GMPGs and other weapons, sending bullets into the front of the van.

Patrick Kelly was hit several times and fell to the ground close to the driver's door of the van. A heavy bloodstain from a head wound was still visible when press photographers visited the area the following morning. Lynagh and McKearney – two of the most experienced men – appear to have realized what was happening and to have thrown themselves back into the van. However the Toyota was under a hail of bullets and Seamus Donnelly, the driver, was mortally wounded before he could move off. Lynagh and McKearney died in the back. The fact that they were wearing flak jackets 'didn't do them much good', remarks an SAS soldier. Eugene Kelly and Declan Arthurs died trying to take cover behind the vehicle.

The SAS men failed initially to shoot Michael Gormley and Gerard O'Callaghan, who had set the fuse on the 200 lb bomb alight with a zippo lighter. The two men took cover as the fuse burnt down. The soldiers had not been expecting such a simple device and were perhaps distracted by the gunfire.

The digger blew up, flattening the end of the police station closest to the gate and the telephone exchange building next door. A shower of masonry came down on the football club house. One of the digger's large rear wheels was blown 30 or 40 metres through a slatted wooden fence backed by small conifers opposite the station, landing on the football pitch. Keeping the ambush force in the station had held risks, and it seems some police and SAS men were injured by the blast.

The woman living nearby heard the blast: 'It was very frightening – I went into the hall and just stood there praying until it was all over.'

After the bomb had gone off Gormley and O'Callaghan tried to run away. Gormley, carrying the zippo lighter but no weapon, was shot dead after emerging from behind a wall where he had taken cover. O'Callaghan, carrying an assault rifle, was killed as he ran across the road from the station.

There were later claims that the SAS fired more than 1200 rounds at the IRA men. It is hard to know the exact figure but it was certainly some hundreds. Many of the holes in the wooden fence opposite could still be seen when I visited the area in 1989. The bullet numbers, chalked by CID Scene of Crime Officers after the incident, from 184 to 192, were still visible.

An SAS man later joked to colleagues that he had tap-danced as he used the General Purpose Machine Gun. The angle of the bullet marks in the fence and those in the side of the van suggests that most of the bullets fired in this area came from an area around the entrance to the RUC station.

Concentrating relatively heavy firepower in the village carried risks for the SAS. They were using powerful weapons across open ground and four cars being driven by people uninvolved with terrorism were caught in the ambush area. The group in the copse fired many rounds across the lower ground, where the RUC station and football field are, into the main part of the village. The IRA men had also opened fire. An SAS man recalls, 'the bad guys were shooting all around, panicking like hell.' Bullets smacked into the wall of the church hall, where children were playing. Three cars were in the area between the RUC station and the church.

Oliver and Anthony Hughes, brothers from another village, were driving their white Citroën past the church and down the hill towards the RUC station. Oliver Hughes said later, 'We heard the bang and Anthony stopped the car, not wanting to drive into the troubled area. We decided to reverse away from the scene.' Soldiers hiding nearby probably thought that the reversing vehicle also belonged to the terrorists and they opened fire.

'The car hadn't moved far before the firing started,' Oliver Hughes continued. 'The shots were deafening, blazing away behind us and lots of them hitting the road. The back of the car must have been hit. There were terrible fumes so I began to wind down the window for air. Then there was a crash of glass and I heard Anthony let a bit of a shout out of him. I didn't even have time to turn round to see him when I was hit myself.'

Anthony Hughes, a thirty-six-year-old father of three, was killed. His brother survived, despite having been hit at least four times – three rounds went into his back and one into his head. It appeared that the SAS men had poured fire into the car without issuing any challenge or knowing who was in it. The soldiers' explanation was that the brothers had been wearing overalls, as were the IRA terrorists, and appeared to be about to open fire.

Another vehicle, containing a woman and her young daughter, was going the other way, up the hill towards the church. As bullets began hitting the car, the commander of one of the SAS stop groups rushed over to the vehicle to rescue her. The soldier was awarded the Military Medal for this act of valour.

An elderly couple were in the third vehicle caught in this area. Herbert Buckley and his wife jumped out of their car and threw themselves in a ditch.

On the other side of the RUC station, between the IRA men's Toyota and the copse where the SAS assault group had opened fire, another motorist had stopped his car. The man, a salesman for a brewery, apparently watched transfixed as hundreds of SAS bullets hit the van just ahead of him. As the firing stopped he jumped out of the car and ran towards the bungalows beside the road. He was rugby tackled by an SAS man and held until his identity could be established.

As the shooting subsided the area was sealed off by armed police. Helicopters flew over as troops scoured the countryside in case other terrorists were in the area. Within half an hour the first SAS troops were on their way out of the area by helicopter. The IRA had lost eight men, its worst single setback in sixty years. Tom King, the Secretary of State for Northern Ireland, told an RUC passing out parade, 'If people do launch terrorist acts, they must recognize they have to face the consequences.'

The funerals of the Loughgall eight became the platform for threats of revenge. Sinn Fein's Gerry Adams said, 'Loughgall will become a tombstone for British policy in Ireland and a bloody milestone in the struggle for freedom, justice and peace.' Ten months after the Loughgall incident an IRA team was sent to attack a British military band in Gibraltar, but this unit too was intercepted and killed by SAS soldiers.

In allowing the heavily armed IRA unit to enter the village and set the bomb off, the covert operators had achieved, in their terms, the ultimate 'clean kill'. One of Gerry Adams' first reactions was, 'I believe that the IRA volunteers would understand the risk they were taking,' which implied that the operation would be regarded as 'fair', even by many in the republican community.

The IRA later said that some members of its team had survived. It claimed furthermore that they had witnessed the SAS men summarily executing the eight men. It is quite possible that there were others in the general area who survived – both the numbers involved in The Birches attack and the fact that the SAS group opened fire on the Hughes' car suggest that the soldiers' briefing indicated there were others around – but any surviving member of the IRA team would presumably have got away as fast as they could rather than wait to see what had happened to their comrades. None of the civilian bystanders involved in the incident have made any claim to substantiate the IRA allegation, which is vigorously denied by those who took part in the operation.

Did the intelligence officers and SAS have another option or was the Loughgall operation inevitable? The intelligence expert who regards the ambush as 'an act of revenge' says there were several choices open to them. First, if E4A did have the explosives under observation for days or weeks, then Weapons Intelligence Unit specialists might have been able to make the bomb components inert. This would have meant the people inside the RUC station would not have been at risk, even if the operation had been allowed to proceed. That they did not render the explosives safe may be seen in terms of their desire for a 'clean kill' – had the men been shot at the site without the digger blowing up, it would have been harder to justify the need for an ambush.

Second, the covert operators had the chance to step up UDR patrols, as they had done, according to the intelligence expert, with the same IRA group on several previous occasions. Third, they could have arrested the men as they came to fit the explosives in the digger. They could also have arrested Lynagh or Kelly, if they knew where they were, shortly before the attack. Finally it is also possible that the security forces could have allowed the attack to go ahead, keeping the group under surveillance, and then attempted to arrest them as they returned to their homes. However this last option involved unacceptable risks for the people of Loughgall, as there was no guarantee that nobody would be killed by the bomb.

In November 1989 a court in Armagh awarded £2652 damages to the Buckleys, the couple who had taken cover in a ditch during the firing, for the nervous distress they had suffered. In April 1991 the Ministry of Defence paid Anthony Hughes' widow 'substantial' compensation in an out of court settlement. The Crown lawyers insisted that the payment did not constitute an admission of liability.

The lawyers' stance may have reflected the belief of the three SAS soldiers who shot the Hughes that the brothers were in fact part of the IRA operation. They told colleagues that they had seen Oliver Hughes climb into the Citroën after soldiers opened fire on the Toyota van. Although SAS men administered first aid to Oliver Hughes, some believe he would have died but for an RUC HMSU officer insisting that an ambulance be brought for him immediately.

The SAS soldiers' belief notwithstanding, all other evidence points to the Hughes brothers being law-abiding citizens who inadvertently wandered into the ambush. Although they wore boiler suits, neither had gloves, balaclavas or weapons. Since this shooting was the only blemish on the security forces 'clean kill', security chiefs would clearly have preferred to have announced publicly, if it were true, that the brothers were IRA men and one had been arrested. Local nationalists, people deeply critical of the IRA, deny that the brothers were members of that organization.

The *Sunday Times* journalists, in their book *Ambush*, say that after the incident speculation was rife, 'newspaper reports quoting the usually unnamed intelligence sources "revealed" that a high ranking "sleeper", a mole in the IRA's ranks, had been activated to divulge forthcoming IRA plans that would allow the security forces to set up an ambush and score a quick victory to counter the swell of republican pride that had greeted the news of Judge Gibson's assassination.' The journalists despatched such speculation saying, 'In fact the ambush was handed to the SAS on a plate. The east Tyrone Brigade had devised a plan so ambitious, yet so cumbersome, that routine surveillance and good detective work had given the RUC plenty of warning.'

IRA statements also discounted the possibility of an informer. It was not the right time for them to sling allegations that the men had been betrayed from within their own community. Later suggestions emerged from within the republican community that the police had known about the forthcoming raid because two Provisionals on a reconnaissance mission had been recognized after their car broke down in Loughgall. As in other incidents, both the security forces and the IRA wanted to deflect attention from treachery within the nationalist community.

The intelligence expert who was familiar with the operation says there was indeed an informer. The confidence of the *Sunday Times* journalists in ruling out the likelihood of a mole must be questioned in the light of events which took place in 1989, a year after their book appeared.

On 21 May RUC officers stopped a car outside Ardboe in Tyrone. In the back, hidden under a coat and nearly hysterical, was a woman in her late thirties, Collette O'Neill. Also in the car was John Corr, later claimed by Crown lawyers to be the commander of the IRA in Coalisland, and Brian Arthurs, brother of one of the men killed at Loughgall. The odds of a police patrol making such a discovery by chance were slim.

There was speculation that Mrs O'Neill was the Loughgall informer and that she had activated her 'panic button' transmitter shortly before her abduction. The *Irish News* suggested that the IRA had discovered her identity by taking documents from the car of two senior RUC officers killed in south Armagh in March 1989.

Following the incident O'Neill and her two children were taken into protective custody and housed at HQNI, Lisburn. Three weeks later she was taken to Nottingham to a safe house where she was protected by RUC officers. Meanwhile the Crown prepared a case of kidnapping against Corr and Arthurs.

Such is the power of community ties that O'Neill soon became unhappy in her exile. It appears that her husband and others in her village disowned her. She left the safe house and telephoned her mother from a phonebox. In October she made contact again telling her mother that she would make a deal with the IRA if they would allow her to come home. A bargain was reached whereby the Provisionals would guarantee her safety in return for her withdrawing evidence against Corr and Arthurs.

O'Neill went back and in December the Crown case against her alleged abductors collapsed. In an interview with the *Sunday Tribune* newspaper she denied that she had been the Loughgall informer. But there can be no doubt that O'Neill was closely involved with the group of people who planned the bombing. She admitted in the interview that the phonecall on the morning of Friday 8 May 1987, giving the go ahead for the Loughgall attack, had been made from her home. The Crown lawyer had noted during a hearing of the kidnapping charges against Corr and Arthurs that O'Neill was the 'alleged' Loughgall informer.

A senior security forces officer who played a key role in the operation told me, 'Loughgall was a plum – it was an exceptionally heavy team of good operators. The temptation was there to remove them in one go. The terrorists played into our hands and everything went our way. Was it a decision to kill those people? I don't think it would have been phrased like that. Somebody would have said, "How far do we go to remove this group of terrorists?" and the answer would have been, "As far as necessary." '

Loughgall was the apotheosis of the 'clean kill', a cleverly planned exploitation of intelligence resulting in the humiliation of the IRA. Whether supplying the republican movement with eight new martyrs furthered or hindered the cause of peace is another matter.

# Conclusion

The advent of Police Primacy in 1976 – which granted the RUC the authority to direct all security operations, including those of the Army – coincided with a pronounced shift towards the improvement of intelligence-gathering and the establishment of more effective methods for its exploitation. Throughout the ten years which followed, the importance of the 'Green Army' – groups of uniformed regular soldiers – in confronting terrorism fell as the role of the undercover forces grew. This is illustrated most graphically by the statistics of IRA men killed. During the period from the commitment in 1976 of an SAS squadron to south Armagh to late 1987, conventional units of the Army killed nine IRA men and two members of the INLA. During the same period, the SAS and 14 Intelligence Company killed thirty IRA members and two INLA. This is despite the numerical superiority of the regular Army: whereas the combined strength of the SAS and 14 Company in Ulster has never normally exceeded 150 soldiers, the regular Army fluctuated between about 9000 and 14,000 during this period.

It is harder to be specific about the figures for arrests and convictions. I believe that covert work has increased in importance in the building of cases against suspects, but that the bulk of such work is still carried out by uniformed police and soldiers. From December 1978 to December 1983 the Army's special forces themselves carried out many arrests. The 'supergrass' convictions, which, despite the success of many later appeals, had a pronounced impact on the terrorist infrastructure, also developed as a result of the most important covert activity – agent-running.

It is important to note that from 1976 to 1987 the RUC and Army only ever killed *republican* terrorists with their undercover units. Loyalists, although responsible for many scores of killings during the same period, have never been subjected to an ambush at one of their arms dumps, for example. On the other hand, many loyalist terrorists have been convicted of serious crimes. In 1990, for example, there were about 260 republican and 130 loyalist prisoners in the Maze. This shows some correlation between convictions and the respective levels of violence perpetrated by the two wings of terrorism in Ulster. Unlike in the mid-1970s, when the two sides produced similar levels of violence, throughout the 1980s, the republicans killed considerably more people than the loyalists.

The special forces did not carry out action based on intelligence which was likely to result in the death of loyalist terrorists. Security forces officers tend to argue that this is because the loyalists are not a threat to the security forces themselves. But the fact that loyalist paramilitaries were not killed by Army and police undercover squads raises two key points: first, it further discredits the idea – so frequently voiced in the authorities' dealings with the courts and media – of chance meetings between undercover forces and armed republican terrorists, since the odds of stumbling on and shooting a loyalist would appear to be almost as high. Second, it heightens the sense of injustice felt by many nationalists.

The ambushing of republican terrorists by the security forces has generally been followed by public expressions of approval from loyalist politicians. Clearly, such SAS operations are popular in the Orange ghettos where intense frustration is felt at the frequent inability of the security forces to prevent the killing of off-duty police officers and UDR soldiers. Even if the Westminster politicians in charge of security are not guilty of deliberately applying the ambush weapon in a sectarian way, they are at the very least culpable of acquiesing in this state of affairs. It would be surprising if they did not appreciate the value of such operations in soothing militant loyalists and bolstering the morale of the security forces – particularly those recruited locally.

Several phases are discernible in the development of the forces designed to act on intelligence. Although the SAS arrived in south Armagh in early 1976, it only really began to operate as the cutting edge of the intelligence effort in late 1977 and early 1978. During this period the SAS squadron began operating throughout Northern Ireland, and the first centre for fusing intelligence and covert operations, the Tasking and Co-ordination Group at Castlereagh, was opened. Between 1976 and 1978 the SAS carried out large numbers of operations, killing seven IRA men. Ironically, south Armagh – the area where the SAS was first committed – was to prove the least suitable for operations by the Regiment because the republican community there has always been more successful than other communities in preventing informing.

As the tactics and procedures for handling human source intelligence developed, so the operations of the SAS changed, and became more ambitious. Several of the early incidents involved encounters at arms dumps: these were places where the soldiers had reasonable confidence that somebody might turn up if they waited long enough. During the 1980s such operations became rarer; instead the SAS aimed to catch republican terrorists in the act of attacking security forces members or installations.

Ambushes were discontinued after December 1978. There followed five years in which the SAS did not kill anybody. This period is interesting, not least because it disproves the idea that lethal confrontations between IRA members and special forces are inevitable. It resulted to some extent from the RUC's desire to take on the more adventurous side of covert operations itself.

There are several reasons for supposing that the killing of six people in late 1982 by members of one of the RUC's Headquarters Mobile Support Units may have been an aberration rather than a return, sanctioned at the highest level, to an ambush policy using RUC rather than Army special forces. Most importantly, the RUC's special units had conducted a good many operations in the two years prior to those incidents, and these had brought them face to face with terrorists without resulting in shootings. The arrest of the team which planned to bomb the RUC band in Belfast in July 1982 is one example.

The conduct of the HMSU incidents gave rise to direct political pressure for the RUC to abandon any aggressive special forces operations. But they also resulted in a series of conspiracies at various levels of the force, designed to protect its members from prosecution and from criticism by the Stalker inquiry. The legacy of distrust which these events left between Stormont and Knock meant that the declining role of the SAS in Ulster was checked. The Armagh shootings were a disaster for those senior figures in Stormont and the security forces who believed that the police could supplant the SAS.

From December 1983 there were more SAS ambushes and a pattern of occasional 'executive action' based on informer intelligence emerged. These operations were considerably more sophisticated than those carried out by the SAS during its earlier period. The art of the 'clean kill', according to people interviewed, was to eliminate members of the opposition so cleverly – ideally catching them armed and on the way to carry out an attack – that even committed republicans would feel there was little they could complain about.

I do not believe that special forces operations were resumed as a result of an explicit order from politicians. Rather, my research suggests that the key role in advocating ambushes is played by middle-ranking police and Army officers, such as a Regional Head of Special Branch or the commanding officer of the Intelligence and Security Group. The attitude of those at the top of the RUC and Army in Northern Ireland is obviously important, but in the cases described to me that attitude has been more one of acceptance than of initiating a wave of ambushes. Officers like Lieutenant General Richard Lawson, GOC from 1979 to 1982, or Major General James Glover, CLF from 1979 to 1980, were explicitly opposed to the aggressive use of Army special forces. Some of their successors have simply chosen not to veto the proposals for such operations made by more junior officers.

Some of the incidents involving special forces during the years 1983 to 1987 were not initiated by the Army. The Dunloy shooting in 1984 was started by the IRA. The killing of three IRA men in Strabane in 1985, an incident which aroused considerable media interest, probably started as an observation mission rather than an ambush, even though that is what it turned into.

In other cases – Coalisland in 1983, Tamnamore and the Gransha hospital in 1984, the shooting of Seamus McElwaine in 1986 and, most famously, the 1987 Loughgall incident – the evidence indicates that it was the soldiers' intention to ambush from the outset. Interviewees have told me explicitly that this was the case.

When I began this study, I was open to the idea that ambushing the IRA might help to lower the level of terrorist violence. All of my research, however, convinces me that it does not and that, on the contrary, such operations carry significant human and moral costs.

What then did these killings achieve? At the simplest level they made a good many members of the security forces feel better. Most soldiers who have served in Northern Ireland or police officers who live there are prepared to admit to satisfaction at seeing terrorists get their 'comeuppance'.

Advocates of ambushes argue that they are one of the few ways of deterring terrorists. The IRA itself admits that the level of covert surveillance deters them from carrying out many more attacks. They are less comfortable about admitting that the presence of so many informers in their ranks has a similar effect. However, it is entirely different to suppose that the fear of death, rather than the fear of imprisonment, has reduced the level of terrorism.

Clearly neither side in the argument can prove conclusively whether the level of terrorism would have been higher at certain times without the use of ambushes. What we can be certain of is that during the early 1980s – the period of no SAS killing – terrorist violence was at its lowest level since 1969. There were many reasons for this, notably the republican movement's decision to divert resources from fighting to Sinn Fein's grassroots political activity. Claims that times were more peaceful because such operations had stopped cannot be proved, but the experience of the years 1979 to 1980, when no IRA members were killed by the SAS and only two by the security forces in general, proves that ambushes can be stopped without any noticeable deterioration in the security situation.

There is a feeling among some in the security forces that occasional ambushes are necessary because the many members of the IRA will not be deterred by prison sentences. They dispute Northern Ireland Office statistics which indicate that the rate of reconvictions for terrorist offences is much lower than that for common crime. The majority of those killed by the SAS during recent years were not men who had failed to be deterred by a spell in prison. Of the twenty IRA men killed by the SAS and 14 Company between 1983 and 1987, only six had previously been convicted for terrorist offences. In 1978 Brigadier Glover, in his report on terrorist trends, said that members of IRA units usually had ten years' experience of terrorism. The success of the security forces in putting them away meant that by the 1980s the Provisionals were dependent on less experienced volunteers. The average age of those killed between 1983 and 1987 by the SAS was twenty-three years old, while five were in their teens.

Some soldiers claim that ambushes have restored tranquillity to an area for a measurable period. Undoubtedly the level of sectarian killing in south Armagh did diminish in the months after the arrival of the SAS in 1976. But after a few months of wait-and-see the activities of the IRA against the security forces in the area returned to their previous high levels.

Successive ambushes in Tyrone during the 1980s appear to have had no noticeable effect on the level of terrorist activity there. The IRA killed seven people in east Tyrone and north Armagh in the two years before the 1987 Loughgall ambush, and eleven in the two years following. Security did not improve: the IRA carried on killing and the SAS mounted further ambushes. Two IRA men were shot dead by the SAS near Loughgall in 1990 and three Provisionals belonging to an east Tyrone unit were killed in the village of Coagh in 1991. In 1990 the IRA succeeded in destroying the half of Loughgall police station that was still standing after the 1987 incident.

If the impact of ambush operations on the level of terrorist violence is debatable, what of its cost? The SAS has killed six people by mistake since it was committed to Ulster. Is the death of six bystanders too high a price to pay for the deaths of twenty-five terrorists? Even some members of the SAS confess they believe it is. And does the death of terrorists create a desire for revenge and so contribute to the level of violence?

A friend of the Loughgall IRA group returned to terrorism and was arrested in West Germany. A brother of one of those killed there was subsequently accused of kidnapping a woman alleged to have been the informer who made the ambush possible. I have also been told of the cousin of someone killed by accident by the SAS who became involved in terrorism out of a desire for revenge. It is, of course, impossible to prove that these people would not have become involved in terrorism anyway.

If the security benefits of ambushing terrorists are questionable, and such operations may lead to the deception of courts and the killing of bystanders, why do ministers allow it? In part this can be explained by the politicians' lack of real power over these forces. But it is also due to the fact that public opinion in Britain, desensitized by years of terrorism, tends to care little for the lives of its perpetrators.

The activities of 14 Intelligence Company, the special Army surveillance unit, have shown that it is possible to conduct large numbers of covert operations without ambushing, but also that a small number of accidental confrontations are inevitable in this work. Four members of the unit were killed by the IRA between 1974 and 1984. In cases where IRA or INLA terrorists have been killed by 14 Company operators the threat has generally been very apparent. The most imporant exceptions to this have been the killing in January 1990 of three robbers carrying replica firearms at a bookmaker's shop in west Belfast and the shooting of Brian Robinson, a UVF terrorist, in 1989.

Although I have not been able to investigate these incidents fully, I believe the evidence points to both of them being the result of decisions taken by the surveillance operators on the spur of the moment rather than being pre-planned ambushes. The actions of the 14 Company operators in these two incidents appear all the more unusual given the fact that ambush work is very clearly reserved for the SAS, and during the period 1976 to 1987 the Company's members appeared to act only in self-defence.

The intelligence contest in Ulster has been pursued at a moral cost to many of those involved. Sources have been deceived and lost their lives due to the incompetence of their handlers. Detectives have had to allow attacks to go ahead to deflect suspicion from their sources. But there seems little doubt that the gradual improvement in the security of Ulster would have been impossible had the police and Army not immersed themselves so completely in the world of agent-running and treachery. Improved intelligence increases the amount of arms seized, reduces the level of inconvenience to the nationalist community at large and results in more convictions. Nobody who believes that terrorism should be checked can really argue that informer intelligence should not play a key part in such a campaign.

About twenty-five people active in the IRA were named as informers between 1976 and 1987. This includes those killed by the organization itself and supergrasses. Many others have declared their treachery to the Provisionals and have been pardoned, have been taken into protective custody, or have ceased to provide intelligence but remained within their community. It is possible to estimate that around fifty active Provisionals had been informers during this period. This represents a very significant level of penetration – perhaps one in thirty or one in forty of the organization's frontline membership during these years. Loyalist organizations also contain many informers, although the material they produce, as I have already noted, is often used differently.

The widespread recruitment of informers has not prevented a great many acts of violence. Clearly many IRA ASUs remain free of informers. Nevertheless, the security forces have on occasion known so much about IRA operations that they have rendered them a farce. Those operations which have been allowed to proceed so as to keep suspicion from the informer have been rendered harmless – for example, by the substitution of dud bomb components or the emptying of police stations prior to their bombing. With few informers prepared to enter the witness box it is hard to see what alternative the security forces have but to let a great many of these penetrated IRA units carry on their compromised operations.

Although the culture of the republican estates is generally merciless towards those who become 'touts', it is probable that the IRA's attempts to flush out informers slowly erode its cadre of determined supporters. Young volunteers joining the IRA in the 1980s were almost as likely to die at the hands of their own comrades through accusations of informing as they were to be killed by SAS. Doubtless the IRA has committed 'miscarriages of justice'. One intelligence officer told me that he had read a republican account of the killing of somebody described as a self-confessed informer, a person whom 'we had never heard of'. Even the killing of real informers is likely to damage the organization's standing in the eyes of the informer's immediate relatives; in an organization where family involvement is so important, such consequences cannot be overlooked.

The effects of the informer war are profound: the level of violence is reduced; the republican community is rendered increasingly paranoid and must eliminate a proportion of its own membership in an attempt to retain its integrity. Those in the intelligence organizations who run agents are aware that their efforts are the key to the containment of terrorist violence. But there are also some risks inherent in this vital work.

It is evident that many principles of informer handling considered standard by the British police forces are not accepted in Northern Ireland. Allowing attacks to go ahead to keep suspicion from a source, and dealing with people who are themselves continuously involved in terrorist crime, are two important areas of difference. Where the lives of sources are at stake, intelligence work will inevitably require tight security and this makes effective scrutiny of such operations problematic. But when intelligence officers abuse their position – most famously the Special Branch and MI5 officers found by the Stalker and Sampson inquiries to have conspired to pervert the course of justice over the 1982 Armagh shootings – security considerations have in practice made it impossible to convict them. Inevitably, this freedom from sanction also heightens the sense of injustice felt by nationalists.

It is apparent, and none of those involved in covert operations whom I interviewed ever denied it, that attempts to protect intelligence sources and techniques have frequently resulted in the deception of the courts in Northern Ireland. It is also apparent that deception has been used to allow soldiers or police officers who have acted mistakenly to escape criminal charges. The powers of courts, in particular those dealing with inquests, have been modified in such a way as to make it extremely unlikely that they will ever uncover dishonesty on the part of the security forces.

John Stalker suggested in his book that the best means of protecting intelligence sources was to say very little about them rather than to lie. This eminently sensible view is not shared by many of those at the heart of covert operations, who would argue that such niceties are an expensive luxury in a 'war'. Yet so long as the government uses criminal law against terrorists, rather than calling them prisoners of war, this argument must be resisted.

As undercover operations developed in Northern Ireland, so the government's sense of what kind of force would be considered reasonable and necessary by the majority of the public altered. Statements by Army or police officers that the three IRA men killed at Ballysillan in 1978 were armed, or that the gun picked up by John Boyle in the Dunloy graveyard in the same year was loaded, were quickly proved to be false. In both cases I am confident that lies were knowingly disseminated by these agencies in an attempt to make shooting of unarmed men at Ballysillan and of a teenager uninvolved in terrorism at Dunloy appear more reasonable. As one incident has followed another, and the ability of lawyers to examine them in the courts has been drastically reduced, the authorities have felt progressively less need to justify their actions by deliberate disinformation.

In the Loughgall ambush of 1987, the Strabane shootings of 1985, the Drumnakilly incident (in which three IRA men were killed by the SAS) in 1988, and the Coagh shootings in 1991, there has been no official suggestion that the SAS ever challenged the terrorists – inviting them to give themselves up – before opening fire. Whether or not challenges were in fact issued in previous incidents (for example, at Coalisland in 1983 or at Gransha hospital in 1984), as the authorities claimed, is a matter for speculation. The significant point is that either the Army no longer feels it necessary to issue a challenge as often as it used to, or it no longer feels it has to pretend that its soldiers have done so. It is easy to conclude that the reduction of scrutiny has changed the organization's attitude to the use of lethal force by special forces units.

As ordinary soldiers or police officers have been moved further and further away from covert operations, a gulf has opened up between the standards of behaviour acceptable in the 'Green Army' and police and in undercover work. Patience and discipline have been fostered as professional virtues among soldiers going to Northern Ireland for uniformed tours of duty. The statement that a small cadre of SAS and surveillance operators has been responsible for the great majority of IRA deaths in recent years does, after all, also show that the 10,000 or so soldiers walking the streets of Northern Ireland have generally behaved with restraint when they have met people known to them as IRA members. During my research, one of the strongest testimonials to the improvement in the behaviour of the British Army in Northern Ireland during the 1980s was given to me by a republican in the Bogside area of Londonderry. Republicans have also admitted to me in private that the treatment of suspects by the RUC has improved since the inquiries into security forces brutality of the 1970s which prompted the introduction of safeguards against the abuse of detainees.

The cultures of the uniformed and covert security forces in Ulster have become so different that knowledge and supervision of the undercover units' actions has lessened even within the Army and police. The SAS contingent in Ulster has become an élite within an élite. Reduced in strength during the early 1980s to little more than twenty men, SAS men wishing to join this troop must submit themselves to further scrutiny. The selection of these men is carried out by long-serving SAS NCOs who, increasingly during the 1980s, were drawn from the ranks of the Parachute Regiment – an organization with a reputation for action rather than for skills in tasks where tact or political sensitivity were required.

The 1980s saw the emergence of a pattern of aggressive special forces operations with the acquiescence of politicians and senior officers, who knew little of the operational detail, and who in any case were more easily convinced than their predecessors had been of the political benefits. This did not involve the killing of any and every IRA volunteer who could be found, as republican propagandists try to imply. Rather, it meant that those in possession of unusually specific intelligence about a forthcoming terrorist attack provided that knowledge, via a special co-ordinated system, to the SAS. With the honing-down of the SAS contingent in Ulster to an even tougher élite, it was understood that these soldiers would then take the opportunity to play big boys' games by big boys' rules.

# Appendix I

## Republican Terrorists: Cause of Death,
## April 1976–November 1987

### PROVISIONAL IRA

| Date | Name | Place | Organization Responsible |
|------|------|-------|--------------------------|
| **1976** | | | |
| April | Peter Cleary | S. Armagh | SAS |
| June | Brian Coyle | Londonderry | IRA/accident |
| July | Peter McElcar | Tyrone | IRA/accident |
| July | Patrick Cannon | Tyrone | IRA/accident |
| August | Danny Lennon | Belfast | Army |
| October | Paul Marlowe | Belfast | IRA/accident |
| October | Frank Fitzsimmons | Belfast | IRA/accident |
| October | Joseph Surgenor | Belfast | IRA/accident |
| | | | |
| **1977** | | | |
| January | Seamus Harvey | S. Armagh | SAS |
| April | Trevor McKibbin | Belfast | Army |
| April | Brendan O'Callaghan | Belfast | Army |
| July | Thomas Tolan | Belfast | IRA |
| August | Paul McWilliams | Belfast | Army |
| | | | |
| **1978** | | | |
| February | Paul Duffy | Tyrone | SAS |

## Appendix I

| Date | Name | Place | Organization Responsible |
|------|------|-------|--------------------------|
| June | Dan Jos McErlean | Belfast | IRA/informer[1] |
| June | Denis Heaney | Londonderry | 14 Company |
| June | Denis Brown | Belfast | SAS |
| June | William Mailey | Belfast | SAS |
| June | John Mulvenna | Belfast | SAS |
| November | Patrick Duffy | Londonderry | SAS |
| **1979** | | | |
| January | Frank Donnelly | Belfast | IRA/accident |
| January | Lawrence Montgomery | Belfast | IRA/accident |
| April | William Carson | Belfast | Loyalists |
| June | Peadar McElvenna | S. Armagh | Army |
| July | Michael Kearney | Fermanagh | IRA/informer |
| **1980** | | | |
| January | Kevin Delaney | Belfast | IRA/accident |
| April | Robert Carr | Down | IRA/accident |
| June | Terence O'Neill | Belfast | RUC |
| **1981** | | | |
| February | Patrick Trainor | Belfast | IRA/informer |
| February | James Burns | Belfast | Loyalists(?) |
| May | Charles Maguire | Londonderry | 14 Company |
| May | George McBrearty | Londonderry | 14 Company |
| July | John Dempsey | Belfast | Army |
| **1982** | | | |
| January | John Torbitt | Belfast | IRA/informer |
| March | Seamus Morgan | S. Armagh | IRA/informer |
| April | Patrick Scott | Belfast | IRA/informer |
| August | Eamonn Bradley | Londonderry | Army |
| November | Eugene Toman | Armagh | RUC/HMSU |
| November | Gervaise McKerr | Armagh | RUC/HMSU |
| November | Sean Burns | Armagh | RUC/HMSU |

1 The classification 'IRA/informer' includes those killed by the organization itself for alleged informing. In some cases those killed may not in fact have been passing information to the security forces.

| Date | Name | Place | Organization Responsible |
|------|------|-------|--------------------------|
| **1983** | | | |
| December | Brian Campbell | Tyrone | SAS |
| December | Colm McGirr | Tyrone | SAS |
| | | | |
| **1984** | | | |
| February | Jas Young | S. Armagh | IRA/informer |
| February | Henry Hogan | Antrim | 14 Company |
| February | Declan Martin | Antrim | 14 Company |
| April | Richard Quigley | Londonderry | IRA/accident |
| July | William Price | Tyrone | SAS |
| August | Brendan Watters | Down | IRA/accident |
| December | Tony McBride | Fermanagh | SAS |
| December | Daniel Doherty | Londonderry | SAS[2] |
| December | William Fleming | Londonderry | SAS |
| December | Sean McIlvenna | Armagh | RUC |
| December | Kieran Fleming | Fermanagh | IRA/accident |
| | | | |
| **1985** | | | |
| February | Michael Devine | Tyrone | SAS[3] |
| February | Charles Breslin | Tyrone | SAS |
| February | Danny Devine | Tyrone | SAS |
| August | Charles English | Londonderry | IRA/accident |
| August | James McCann | Belfast | IRA/accident |
| October | Damien McCrory | Londonderry | IRA/informer |
| | | | |
| **1986** | | | |
| February | Tony Gough | Londonderry | Army |
| April | Seamus McElwaine | Fermanagh | SAS |
| August | Patrick Murray | Belfast | IRA/informer |
| September | David McVeigh | S. Armagh | IRA/informer |
| September | James McKernan | Belfast | Army |
| | | | |
| **1987** | | | |
| March | Gerard Logue | Londonderry | IRA/accident |
| April | Lawrence Marley | Belfast | UVF |
| April | Finbar McKenna | Belfast | IRA/accident |

2 Members of 14 Intelligence Company may also have opened fire during this incident.
3 Some sources suggest that soldiers from 14 Intelligence Company, not the SAS, were involved in this incident. I do not believe this is correct.

| Date | Name | Place | Organization Responsible |
|------|------|-------|--------------------------|
| May | Patrick Kelly | Armagh | SAS |
| May | James Lynagh | Armagh | SAS |
| May | Anthony Gormley | Armagh | SAS |
| May | Padraig McKearney | Armagh | SAS |
| May | Declan Arthurs | Armagh | SAS |
| May | Seamus Donnelly | Armagh | SAS |
| May | Eugene Kelly | Armagh | SAS |
| May | Gerard O'Callaghan | Armagh | SAS |
| August | Eamonn Maguire | S. Armagh | IRA/informer |
| October | Eddie McSheffrey | Londonderry | IRA/accident |
| October | Paddy Deery | Londonderry | IRA/accident |
| *Total* | 78 | | |

## HUNGER STRIKERS

| Date | Name | Place |
|------|------|-------|
| **1981** | | |
| May | Bobby Sands | Maze |
| May | Francis Hughes | Maze |
| May | Patsy O'Hara (INLA) | Maze |
| May | Raymond McCreesh | Maze |
| June | Joseph McDonnell | Maze |
| July | Martin Hurson | Maze |
| July | John Dempsey | Maze |
| August | Kieran Doherty | Maze |
| August | Tom McElwee | Maze |
| August | Kevin Lynch (INLA) | Maze |
| August | Michael Devine (INLA) | Maze |
| *Total* | 11 | |

## INLA

| Date | Name | Place | Organization Responsible |
|------|------|-------|--------------------------|
| **1977** | | | |
| December | Colm McNutt | Londonderry | 14 Company |

## Big Boys' Rules

| Date | Name | Place | Organization Responsible |
|------|------|-------|--------------------------|
| **1978** | | | |
| March | Thomas Trainor | Armagh | Loyalists |
| June | James McConnell | Londonderry | Army |
| **1980** | | | |
| October | Ronnie Bunting | Belfast | Loyalists |
| **1981** | | | |
| May | James Power | Maze | H/strike |
| May | Emmanuel McLarnon | Belfast | Army |
| **1982** | | | |
| December | Seamus Grew | Tyrone | RUC/HMSU |
| December | Roddy Carroll | Tyrone | RUC/HMSU |
| **1983** | | | |
| February | Liam McMonagle | Londonderry | 14 Company |
| August | Brendan Convery | Tyrone | RUC |
| August | James Mullan | Tyrone | RUC |
| **1984** | | | |
| June | Paul McCann | | |
| **1987** | | | |
| February | Tony McCloskey | Armagh | INLA/feud |
| February | Michael Kearney | Belfast | INLA/feud |
| March | Thomas Maguire | S. Armagh | INLA/feud |
| March | Gerard Steenson | Belfast | INLA/feud |
| March | Fergus Conlon | S. Armagh | INLA/feud |
| March | Emmanuel Gargan | Belfast | INLA/feud |
| March | Kevin Duffy | S. Armagh | INLA/feud |
| October | Jim McDaid | S. Armagh | INLA/feud |
| *Total* | 19 | | |

## Accidental Killings During SAS Operations

| Date | Name | Place |
| --- | --- | --- |
| **1978** | | |
| June | William Hanna | Belfast |
| July | John Boyle | Antrim |
| September | James Taylor | Tyrone |
| **1984** | | |
| October | Fred Jackson | Tyrone |
| **1987** | | |
| April | Oliver Hughes | Armagh |
| **1988** | | |
| July | Ken Stronge | Belfast |
| *Total* | 6 | |

## Members of 14 Intelligence Company Killed by Republican Terrorists[4]

| Date | Name | Place |
| --- | --- | --- |
| **1974** | | |
| April | Captain Anthony Pollen | Londonderry |
| **1977** | | |
| December | Corporal Paul Harman | Belfast |
| **1978** | | |
| August | Lance-Corporal Alan Swift | Londonderry |
| **1984** | | |
| February | Sergeant Paul Oram | Antrim |
| *Total* | 4 | |

4 I have listed only those who I am confident belonged to this unit. However, there have been a number of army casualties who may have been members of 14 Company, but the evidence is uncertain. It is therefore safest to say simply that the unit had lost at least four soldiers in action by 1987.

# Members of the SAS Killed by Republican Terrorists[5]

| Date | Name | Place |
|------|------|-------|
| **1980** | | |
| May | Captain Richard Westmacott | Belfast |
| **1984** | | |
| December | Lance-Corporal Alastair Slater | Fermanagh |
| *Total* | 2 | |

## Republican Terrorists Killed by Security Forces in Total

| Organization Responsible | Number killed |
|--------------------------|---------------|
| 14 Company of IRA/INLA | 7 |
| SAS of IRA | 25 (1983–87: 18) |
| Other Army of IRA | 9 (1983–87: 2) |

---

5  Two members of the SAS died in car accidents while serving in Northern Ireland: Staff Sergeant David Naden was killed in 1978 and Corporal Tommy Palmer in 1983.

# Appendix II  Development of Covert Operations Units

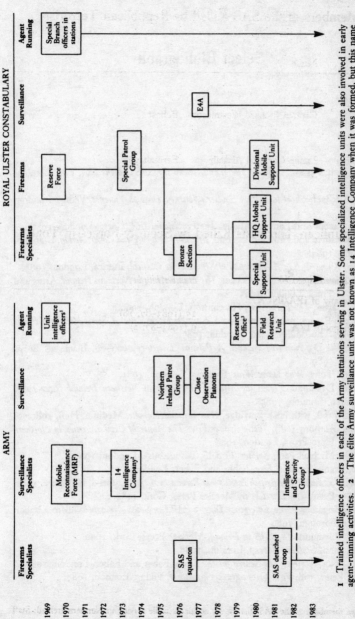

ARMY

| | Firearms Specialists | Surveillance Specialists | Surveillance | Agent Running | Firearms Specialists | Firearms | Surveillance | Agent Running |
|---|---|---|---|---|---|---|---|---|

ROYAL ULSTER CONSTABULARY

1  Trained intelligence officers in each of the Army battalions serving in Ulster. Some specialized intelligence units were also involved in early agent-running activities.  2  The élite Army surveillance unit was not known as 14 Intelligence Company when it was formed, but this name has become almost universal in the Army. It has also been called the Reconnaissance Force, NITAT (NI) and Int and Sy Group.  3  Research Offices were agent-running units in each of the Army's three brigade HQs in Northern Ireland.  4  Intelligence and Security Group had also been used as a cover name for the élite surveillance unit alone. From 1982 onwards the difference was that the SAS troop and 14 Company's three surveillance detachments were under the overall command of a single officer.

# Select Bibliography

Adams, James et al., *Ambush: The War Between the SAS and the IRA*, Pan, London, 1988.

Asher, Michael, *Shoot to Kill: A Soldier's Journey Through Violence*, Viking, London, 1990.

Bishop, Patrick and Eamonn Mallie, *The Provisional IRA*, Corgi, London, 1988.

Bloch, Jonathan and Patrick Fitzgerald, *British Intelligence and Covert Action*, Brandon, Dublin, 1984.

Deacon, Richard, *'C': A Biography of Sir Maurice Oldfield*, Futura, London, 1985.

Dewar, Lieutenant Colonel Michael, *The British Army in Northern Ireland*, Arms and Armour Press, London, 1985.

Dillon, Martin, *The Dirty War*, Hutchinson, London, 1990.

Fitzgerald, Patrick and Mark Leopold, *Stranger on the Line: A Secret History of Phone Tapping*, The Bodley Head, London, 1987.

Flackes, W. D., *Northern Ireland: A Political Directory 1968–88*, Blackstaff Press, Belfast, 1989.

Geraghty, Tony, *Who Dares Wins*, Fontana, London, 1983.

Hammill, Desmond, *Pig in the Middle: The Army in Northern Ireland 1969–1984*, Methuen, London, 1985.

Holroyd, Fred, with Nick Burridge, *War Without Honour*, Medium, Hull, 1989.

Jennings, Anthony (ed.), *Justice Under Fire: The Abuse of Civil Liberties in Northern Ireland*, Pluto Press, London, 1988.

Kennedy, Michael Paul, *Soldier 'I': SAS*, Bloomsbury, London, 1990.

Kitson, Frank, *Bunch of Five*, Faber and Faber, London, 1977.

Lindsay, Kennedy, *The British Intelligence Service in Action*, Dunrod, Ballyclare, 1981.

McArdle, Patsy, *The Secret War*, Mercier Press, Cork, 1984.

Morton, Brigadier Peter, *Emergency Tour: 3 PARA in South Armagh*, William Kimber, Wellingborough, 1989.

Murray, Raymond, *The SAS in Ireland*, Mercier Press, Cork, 1990.

Stalker, John, *Stalker*, Harrap, London, 1988.

Taylor, Peter, *Stalker: The Search for the Truth*, Faber and Faber, London, 1987.

Wright, Peter, with Paul Greengrass, *Spycatcher*, Viking, London, 1987.

# Index

# Index

Bourn, John, 17
Bourn Committee, 89
Boyle, Con, 63, 65
Boyle, Harry, 63
Boyle, John, 63–6, 68, 70, 73, 74, 83, 177, 201, 246
Boyle, Mrs, 64
Boyne, battle of the, 133
Bradley, Francis, 214–15, 216
Bramley, Patrick, 191, 193
Bramshill, Surrey, 89
Brandywell, Londonderry, 42, 44
Brecon Beacons, 6
Breslin, Charles, 197, 199
Brighton bombing (1984), 166, 206
BRINTON project, 114–15
Britain, bombing campaign, in, 123–4
British Army: and SAS, 4, 7, 8, 9, 81, committed to NI (1969), 4, 7, 14; and Special Branch, 8, 23, 24, 53, increased undercover operations, 11, 12; overt presence on streets resented, 12; relationship with RUC, 13, 18–19, 23, 24, 64, 83–4, 85, 87, 91; numbers peak (1972), 15; army casualties peak, 15; distrust of UDR, 16; specialist units, 20–21; sets up new élite surveillance unit, 22, 35; and IRA use of military terminology, 28; Gardai refuses to deal with, 29; estimate of Provisionals' strength, 31–2; experience with MRF, 36, 37–8, 46; 14 Intelligence Company recruits from, 38; and surveillance duties, 44, 45, 47, 48–9; and Special Patrol Group, 47; UVF/UDA street confrontations with, 51; nationalists' stereotype of, 69; and the courts, 73, 74, 75; and new coroners' rules, 75; and lying to press, 77; and TCGs, 95, 96, 160; and DCI, 97, 98; and informers, 104, 105, 106, 108–11, 112, 144; jamming signals, 112; communications, 114; computerized records, 116–17; and WIU, 119; decrease in strength, 125; as IRA target, 188; increases troop strength (1986), 222; and IRA death statistics, 238; improved behaviour (1980s), 246
British Army Information Policy Unit, 77
British Army Legal Service, 38, 75, 203
British Army of the Rhine, 125
British Army Press Office, 44, 61, 64, 182
British embassy, Dublin, 22
British Security Services Organization (BSSO), 125–8, 159
Broderick Report, 75
Bronze Section, 46, 47, 48, 60, 145, 146

Brown, Bobby, 143–4
Brown, Denis, 60
Brunei, 162, 229
Buckley, Herbert, 233, 235
*Bundesamt für Verfassungsschutz (BfV)*, 126, 127
*Bundesnachrichten Dienst (BND)*, 126
Bunting, Ronnie, 27, 58
Burns, Sean, 151, 154

C Branch (MI5), 100
Calcutt, David, 77
Campbell, Brian, 174, 175
Campbell, Duncan, 21
Cappagh, 220, 229
Capper and Lambe, 189
Carrickmore, 220
Carrickmore police station, 206, 222
Carroll, Roddy, 152–5
Carroll, Owen, 132
Carson, Sir Edward, 50–51
Carver, Lord, 22, 35, 39, 51
Castlederg station, 222
Castlereagh, near Belfast, 29, 92–3, 95, 131, 133, 239
Chiswell, Major General Peter, 168
CIA (Central Intelligence Agency), 126
CID (Criminal Investigations Department), 88, 203; takes over interrogation of suspects, 20, 29, 92–3; and Special Branch, 20, 29, 48, 92, 93, 94; improved results, 29; and TCGs, 95; and Armagh killings (1982), 155; Whiteside in charge of, 158; and McMonagle/Duffy incident, 181; and Gransha shootings, 200–201; and Loughgall incident, 232
Clark, James, 191, 193
'clean kill', 164, 169, 175, 191, 200, 230, 234, 235, 237, 240
Cleary, Peter, 9, 75, 164
Clements, Reserve Constable William, 221, 229
Close Observation Platoons (COPs), 45, 46, 48, 61, 72, 72, 188
Coagh shootings (1991), 242, 246
Coalisland, 173, 174, 189, 204, 220, 228, 236, 241, 246
Coldstream Guards, 42
Conservative Party, 27, 83
Cookstown, 220
Cooper, Frank, 87
Cornamucklagh, 9
coroners, amended rules for (NI), 74–5
Coroners' Courts, 73
Corr, John, 236, 237
Costello, Seamus, 26

# Index

# Index

General Purpose Machine Gun (GPMG), 229–32

Gibraltar incident (1988), xx–xxi, 32, 72, 75–6, 143, 144, 145, 162, 199, 216, 234

Gibson, Cecily, 224, 226

Gibson, Lord Justice Maurice, 153, 224, 226, 235

Gilliland, Constable George, 221

Gilmour, Patrick, 136

Gilmour, Raymond, 135, 136

Gilvary, Maurice, 102–3

Glenshane Pass, County Londonderry, 71

Glover, Brigadier James, 24, 28, 31, 42, 49, 82, 83, 108, 109, 138–9, 220, 241, 242

Glover Report, 114

Goodman, Jackie, 136, 165

Gorbachev, Mikhail, 100

Gormley, Tony, 229, 232

Gortin, 220

Gough, Tony, 217

Gough Barracks, Armagh, 87, 92, 95, 151, 153

Graham, William, 224–6

Grand Hotel, Brighton, 166

Gransha psychiatric hospital, 194, 197, 200–201, 204, 209, 212, 241, 246

Gray, Colin, 182

Green, John Francis, 53–6, 58

'Green Army', 11, 69, 238, 246

'green slime', 62, 63, 109

Greencastle, 220, 221

Gregg, John, 182

Grew, Seamus, 151–5

Guildford Four, 124

H-blocks, 28, 71, 102, 131, 132, 133, 165

Hailsham, Lord, 74

Hamill, Thomas, 140, 143

Hamilton, Archie, 77

Hanna, William, 61, 62, 63, 75, 76, 204, 235

Harman, Corporal Paul, 43, 44, 55, 141

Harvey, Seamus, 9, 10–11

Hatton, Corporal William, 41

Headquarters Mobile Support Units (HMSUs), 146, 151, 159, 240

Heaney, Denis, 44, 55

Heckler and Koch gun/rifle, 41, 120, 173, 194, 195, 209, 229–30

Hegarty, Frank, 107–8

Hereford, 4, 5, 6, 40, 72, 146, 171, 172, 228

Hermon, John (Jack), 12–13, 62, 89–91, 132, 133, 145, 152, 153, 154, 156, 157–8, 160, 168–9, 208, 211–12, 224

*Hibernia* (newspaper), 37

Hogan, Henry, 177, 178, 179

Holroyd, Captain Fred, 21, 40, 53–7, 121

Holywood, 104

Home Office, 107

House of Lords, 70

HQNI (British Army Headquarters, Northern Ireland), 4, 16, 23, 39, 62, 97, 109, 152, 236

Hughes, Anthony, 233, 234, 235

Hughes, Brendan, 131

Hughes, Francis, 71

Hughes, Kieran, 209

Hughes, Oliver, 233, 234

hunger strikes, 131–3, 180

Hunt Report (1970), 15, 18, 90

Hurd, Douglas, 195, 211

Huxtable, Major General, 139, 168

*Independent*, xix, 55–6, 216

Ingram machine-pistol, 67

Ingram sub-machine gun, 41

INLA *see* Irish National Liberation Army

Intelligence and Security Group (NI) (Int and Sy Group), 39, 96, 139, 140–41, 143–5, 165, 170, 171, 177, 180, 188, 189, 196, 197, 200, 211, 217, 218, 227

Intelligence Corps, 20, 39, 43, 52, 62, 109, 125, 139

internment, 14, 19, 51, 73, 90

interrogation, 20, 29–30, 93

IRA (Irish Republican Army): and informers, xvii, 59, 101–8, 205, 244–5; changes in, 11, 25–8, 30–34, 35, 102; and internment, 14; McGuinness becomes head of, 26; and 'long war', 27, 31, 113, 131; and Sinn Fein propaganda, 30; organization, 31, 102; bomb-making, 32–3, 85, 112, 113, 223; weapons, 33, 34, 119, 123, 208–9; attacks on rural areas, 33–4, 85; and MRF operations, 36, car-hijacking, 41; assassination of UDR members, 51, 187–9, 194, 213; and the courts, 74; and martyrdom, 82–3, 118–19, 164, 169; and bombing campaigns in Britain, 96; sets up own Security Department (1980), 102; communications, 113–14; and jarking, 119–22; contacts abroad, 123–9; need for political mobilization, 131; hunger strikes, 131, 132; and supergrasses, 133–7; successful Int and Sy Group operations against (1980–81), 139–41; selection of soft targets, 187–8; and uniformed patrols, 213; loss of McElwaine, 218–19; in Tyrone (mid 1980s), 220–26; statistics of men killed, 238

IRA Army Council, 25, 26, 32, 102, 124, 131

# Index

MacBride, Tony, 191, 192, 193, 195, 200, 205
McCann, Danny, 76
McCartney, Raymond, 133
McCauley, Martin, 151, 154
McConnel, Robert, 58
McCormick, Charles, 106
McCourt, Edward, 142
McCrory, Damien, 199
McDonnell, Gerard, 166
McElhone, Patrick, 69, 70
McElwaine, Seamus, 140, 141, 143, 163, 166, 218, 219, 241
McFarlane, Brendan, 166
McGirr, Colm, 174, 175, 204
McGlinchey, Dominic, 155
McGrady, Kevin, 135, 137
McGuinness, Martin, 25, 26, 108, 131, 219
McGurk, Patrick, 165
McIntyre, John, 129
McKearney, Patrick, 229, 231
McKenna, Sean, 9, 10
McKeown, Clifford, 135, 136
McKerr, Eleanor, 152
McKerr, Gervaise, 151, 152
McKiernan, Thomas, 143, 144
McKittrick, David, 56, 57, 216, 217
McLarnon, Barney, 214, 216
McMonagle, Liam, 181
McNutt, Colm 'Rooster', 43, 55
McQuillan, Thomas, 183, 184
Magherafelt, 18, 221
Magheramulkenny, near Coalisland, 173
Maguire, Charles, 142, 180, 181
Maguire, Peter, 128, 129
Mahon, Catherine, 121–2, 199
Mahon, Gerard, 121–2, 199
Mailey, William, 60
Mallie, Eamonn, 31
Mallon, Sean, 136, 165
Manchester, 156
Mangold, Tom, 166
*Marita Ann* (Irish trawler), 129
Martin, Declan, 178, 179
martyrdom, 82–3, 118–19, 132, 164, 169, 237
Mason, Roy, 11, 12–13, 62, 83
Maze prison, 26, 28, 30, 32, 130, 131, 133, 165–6, 191, 193, 229, 238–9
Metropolitan Police Special Branch, 100, 124
MI5 (Security Service), 21, 22, 24, 47, 57, 77, 78, 95–100, 105, 107, 109, 110, 124–8, 154, 155, 158, 159, 170, 245
MI6 *see* SIS
Miami Showband, 53–6

mid Tyrone, 31
Mobile Reconnaissance Force (MRF), 35–8, 39, 46
Monaghan, 31, 140, 219, 220, 223, 224
Morrison, Danny, 131, 206
Morton, Peter, 23, 164
Mountbatten, Louis, 1st Earl Mountbatten of Burma, 86, 112
Moy, County Tyrone, 223, 229
Mulgrew, Kevin, 134
Mullaghmore, 86, 112
Mullin, Chris, 124
Mulvenna, James, 60
Murphy, Noel, 209

Nairac, Lieutenant Robert, 40, 53–7
Narrow Water, near Warrenpoint, 85
National Council for Civil Liberties, 100
Neagh, Lough, 3, 66, 222
Neave, Airey, 58, 87
Nelson, Brian, 216, 217
Netherlands, 124, 166
New Lodge, west Belfast, 104
*New Statesman*, 21
Newman, Kenneth: appointed RUC Chief Constable, 12, 18; and SAS, 12–13, 83; and SPG, 18; internal reorganization of Special Branch and CID, 20; intelligence-gathering, 24; and basic standard of police work, 29; sets up Regional Crime and Intelligence Units, 29, 48, 94; and expansion of surveillance units, 46–9; on RUC's members, 52; expansion of RUC, 87; respected by RUC men, 88–9; and Hermon, 90; and Bennett Report, 93; orders cut in house searches, 108
Newry, 31, 85, 206–8
9/12th Royal Lancers, 177
No Go Areas, 15, 27
north Antrim, 31
north Armagh, 31, 220, 223, 242
north Belfast, 137
north Down, 31
*Northern Ireland: Future Terrorist Trends* (Glover), 28, 31, 220
Northern Ireland Director of Public Prosecutions, 70
Northern Ireland Office (NIO), 17, 152, 158, 164, 167
Northern Ireland Patrol Group, 45
Northern Ireland Police Authority, 158
Northern Ireland Security Police Committee, 12, 17
Northern Ireland Training Advisory Team (NITAT), 39

# Index

# Index

MRF, 38; and 14 Intelligence Company, 39; and observation duties, 44, 45; loyalties, 50, 51, 159; payment of members, 51–2; recruitment, 52; and UDA, 54; and McKittrick articles, 56; and 'shoot to kill' policy, 70; and new coroners' rules, 75; and lying to the press, 77; and Oldfield, 88; and Hermon's style, 89–90; protection of suspects' rights, 91; and DCI, 97, 98; and HAWK operation, 114; computerized records, 116; and WIU, 119; and supergrasses, 134, 135, 136; and SSU, 146; acts as back up to SAS, 160; as IRA target, 188, 236; in wake of Anglo-Irish Agreement, 211–12; improved treatment of suspects, 246

Ryder, Chris, 110, 111

SA-7 missile, 209
Sampson, Colin, 157, 158, 245
Sands, Bobby, 132
SAS (22nd Special Air Service Regiment), and killing of IRA members, xvii, 9, 10–11, 38–9, 72, 75–6, 81, 161, 164, 165, 174–5, 182–4, 187, 218–19, 239, 246; committed to NI (from 1976), xviii, 3–4, 7, 11, 238, 239, 242; and Parachute Regiment, 5, 171–2; training, 5–7; regional centres, 8; and McKenna 'abduction', 9, 10; border incident (1976), 9–10, 66; and Newman, 12; and 14 Intelligence Company, 38, 180, 181; and propagandists, 43, 44; and COPs, 45; and informers, 62–3; and ambushes, 81, 118, 138, 143, 161–5, 240; and TCGLOs, 95; and FRU, 109; and jarking, 120; reasonable use of force, 141; trains SSU, 146, 160; evolution of an operation, 169–70; organizational and tactical changes (1980s), 171, 240; strength, 238, 247; mistaken killings, 243
SAS squadrons, 6–11, 41, 228, 230
SAS Training Wing, 5, 6
Savage, Sean, 76
SDLP (Social Democratic and Labour Party), 62, 132, 211
Secret Intelligence Service see SIS
Security Co-ordinator, 87, 88, 109, 110, 111
Security Liaison Offices (MI5), 97, 125
Security Policy Committee, 84
Security Services see MI5
Security Service Act (1989), 97, 98
Shamrock club, Ardoyne, west Belfast, 60
Shankhill, 26
Shankhill Company (Official IRA), 26–7
*Shoot to Kill* (Asher), 46, 93

'shoot to kill', 70, 152, 153, 164, 183–4, 195, 201, 204, 205
Simmons, Eugene, 103, 107
Sinn Fein, 204; casts doubt on legality of SAS operations, 10; and prisoners issue, 27–8; propaganda, 30, 37, 44; 'Roll of Honour' of fallen volunteers, 81; Irish flag incident, 89; political work boosted, 102, 130, 242; and informers, 105, 108; and attacks on British targets overseas, 123; wins Fermanagh and south Tyrone seat, 132–3; and supergrasses, 135; and Adams assassination attempt, 182; in Tyrone, 220; Lynagh elected to Monaghan Council, 223
SIS (Secret Intelligence Service; MI6), 21, 22, 57, 87, 96, 97, 105, 111, 123, 125, 126, 127, 129, 166
Sittingbourne, Kent, 107
16/5th The Queen's Royal Lancers, 43
Slater, Lance-Corporal Alistair, 192, 193
Slevin, Mick, 93–4, 108, 156
Social Democratic and Labour Party (SDLP), 62, 132, 211
soft targets, 187–95
south Armagh, 3, 4, 7, 8, 9, 11, 31, 34, 42, 45, 47, 54, 82, 103, 121, 138, 220, 236, 238, 239
'South Armagh Republican Action Force', 4
South Fermanagh, 140, 166, 218, 219
Southern Command (IRA), 28
Soviet Army, 39
Special Air Service Regiment see SAS
Special Boat Service, 35
Special Branch (SB) (E Department): and the Army, 8, 23, 24, 53; role of, 20, 90; and CID, 20, 29, 48; and SMIU NI, 21; Lord Carver on, 22, 35; on Adams, 26; and E4A, 46, 47; initiates most surveillance operations, 48; RUC applicants vetted by, 52; and informers, 92, 96, 102, 106–10, 134, 204; split into five divisions, 94; and TCGs, 95, 96, 196; and MI5, 96–7; and jarking, 121–2; and Metropolitan Police SB, 124; and HMSUs, 146; officers pushed out of force, 158–9; Whiteside in charge of, 158; Forbes becomes Head of, 169; attitude to ambushing, 212; and death of McElwaine, 218
Special Category status, 14, 28, 130
Special Investigation Branch, Royal Military Police, 9
Special Military Intelligence Unit (Northern Ireland) (SMIU NI), 20–21, 55, 94

# Index

# Index